TWIN PEAKS
Behind-The-Scenes

An Unofficial Visitors Guide to TWIN PEAKS

Designed and Edited by Hal Schuster

MARK A. ALTMAN is a prominent film and television journalist whose work has appeared in such magazines as the PANACHE, STARLOG, COMICS SCENE, SCIENCE-FICTION VIDEO MAGAZINE and CINEFANTASTIQUE which featured his acclaimed cover stories on LICENCE TO KILL and STAR TREK: THE NEXT GENERATION.

Mr. Altman's articles have also been featured in the BOSTON GLOBE and THE JUSTICE. Altman served as editor-in-chief and co-publisher of GALACTIC JOURNAL MAGAZINE for nearly ten years.

Among his other credits are the screenplays for the independent films MOVING TARGETS and, its sequel, MOVING TARGETS II. He is currently finishing work on a new script in Manhattan where he lives with an Epson 286 computer and a Winnie The Pooh clock.

As a 1988 graduate of Brandeis University the author never knew or met Diane Shapiro.

TWIN PEAKS
Behind-The-Scenes

An Unofficial Visitors Guide to TWIN PEAKS

By Mark A. Altman

Books for the entertainment buyer

PIONEER

Library of Congress Cataloging-in-Publication Data

   1.   Twin Peaks: Behind the Scenes (television)

I. Title

Dedicated in memory of Seymour Isserson

I would like to graciously acknowledge the many individuals who have helped make this book possible (and conveniently ignore the publicists who were no help whatsoever).

For everyone who consented to interviews, thank you. I think your loyal fans will appreciate it...or hope they will, at least. I still laugh when Miguel Ferrer called me late on a Saturday night and said,"It's Miguel Ferrer, I heard you want to do an interview." I didn't believe him.

To all the cast, directors, producers, writers and particularly the unsung heroes of Lynch/Frost Productions like Lori Mitchell, Bob Engels and Harley Peyton's assistant, thank you. Also at Lynch/Frost I'd like to thank Gaye Pope who was quite helpful. At ABC, Peter Murray's office and, of course, Bob Bright and his assistant Randy.

For their help in getting this monster of a book off the ground: my good friend Steven Simak who encouraged me to write about something other than STAR TREK, Diane Eisenberg who forced herself to sit through endless hours of TWIN PEAKS even though she despises the show and Ed Gross whoseWISEGUY book I kept referring to for inspiration. Also many thanks to Hal Schuster, my publisher, and my mother for continuing to nag me to get off the phone and work on the book. She was right.

TWIN PEAKS: BEHIND THE SCENES

BACKGROUND

David Lynch

The Wild-at-Art Genius Behind *Twin Peaks*

INTRODUCTION:

"I'd Rather Be Here Than Philadelphia"

Five miles south of the Canadian border and twelve miles west of the Washington state line lies the mythical town of Twin Peaks, a place which has captivated the hearts and minds of millions of television viewers. The investigation led by FBI agent Dale Cooper, brought to town by the murder of the town's homecoming queen, Laura Palmer, and rape and attack of her friend Ronette Pulaski, who had staggered across state lines, has ushered in a new age in television drama. Not since Philip Gerard's quest for the One-Armed Man has television so successfully captured the ongoing search for truth. Captivated viewers were introduced to the bizarre inhabitants of the town ranging from the stolid Sheriff Harry S. Truman to the absolutely downright bizarre Log Lady who carries a log around which gives her a special wisdom that eludes the enormous ensemble of characters who populate the town.

It soon became apparent that the murder of Laura Palmer which had lent impetus to the investigation was only the "mcguffin" for introducing viewers into the bizarre world of Twin Peaks. As the series evolved, the murder case's ultimate resolution became less and less important.

At the same time, audience members uncomfortable with the show's mix of style, surrealism and self-reflexive humor deserted the show in droves so that by the time the killer was finally revealed mid-second season, many of the original viewers who had initially been intrigued by the mystery had deserted. Only the die-hard "Peaks Freaks", as they've come to be called, who realized that TWIN PEAKS had far more to offer than just Laura Palmer, remained.

"I think the audience is a very core audience who are really into the TWIN PEAKS phenemona," says director Todd Holland, a UCLA film school graduate who has helmed two of the second season's shows. "The hard-core mystery people dropped out a while ago. The people who really get into the weird mystery of TWIN PEAKS; the jokes about cherry pie and the whole supernatural, Tibetan FBI extravaganza are the people who watch every week now."

It is people such as Holland who comprise one of TWIN PEAKS biggest trump cards; the impressive roster of talent that not only work in front of the camera but behind it — the wide array of talented writers, producers and directors who have allowed the show to evolve and break the mold of contemporary television.

"Shows break molds over a period time because of the uniqueness the creators bring," says Warren Frost who portrays Dr. Will Hayward on the show, Donna's dad, and in real-life, father to TWIN PEAKS co-creator Mark Frost. "I think probably the reason why television gets in trouble anyway is that once the mold's been broken they're seven other shows trying to copy it. You can't copy it and have it be very successful. You have to go and make your own mold which is what TWIN PEAKS has done. It's so hard to be original today...it's all been done so many times."

"I always thought the murder was a great way to get to know the town," says creator Mark Frost. "To introduce all the characters and involve everybody in a complicated mystery. And also to give us a chance to have a life beyond the resolution of that mystery so it kind of amazed me the way people responded to Laura Palmer. I can't remember a dead character ever getting that kind of response before over this long a period of time."

"It's kind of amazing," says PEAKS producer Harley Peyton who scripted two of first season's best episodes and has produced and written the show in its second. "Certain shows manage to tap into the zeitgeist, but it still does surprise me. I do know that if I had nothing to do with this show I'd be watching it every week and be a huge fan. At it's best, television is truly kind of magical. A friend of mine called me after a show one week and I said I can't believe I get to see this every week and get to watch it for free. That's the great thing about television, not only enjoying it, but entering a community after a while because on a weekly basis you get to enter these people's lives." Despite the attention it had garnered, and the millions of people for whom the murderer of Laura Palmer had become the number one conversation piece at cocktail parties and, ironically, coffee breaks at work, the writers and producers soon felt the murder had become an albatross. It was the catalyst for involving the

audience in the TWIN PEAKS universe, but at the same time the heightened anticipation over the storyline's ultimate resolution was diverting.

"Laura Palmer was obviously a blessing and a curse," says Peyton. "Everyone was watching to find out who killed Laura Palmer, but for us it certainly became an albatross after a while. When we started thinking about the episodes after that storyline was finished, we did so with a certain amount of relief just because it allows you to concentrate on other things, new mysteries and maybe new murderers. Who knows? In a way, we had to wait as long as we did but it was a relief to finally be able to move on from that."

"What we wanted people to start to realize is that there is more to the show than Laura Palmer," adds Mark Frost. "The purpose of much of the plot development in second season was to get viewers more involved with the other characters. The predominant feeling we were looking for was to get people to like to go up to TWIN PEAKS and see what they see.

Part of my strategy," continues Frost, "was I felt we had a better chance of getting renewed if the mystery wasn't solved at the end of the first season. We wrote all the scripts before any of them had aired so we had no idea what kind of reception we were going to get. I felt it was a stronger card for us to play to not solve the murder in the first seven and hope that might stimulate the network to give us a pickup."

Frost hardly needed a hook for ABC to renew the show after its first season. Greeted by nearly unanimous critical acclaim and respectable ratings in its competitive timeslot on Thursday evenings, the network renewed the show for a second season repeatedly eluding the question of the when the Laura Palmer murder case would be resolved, and often, erroneously reporting that it would be solved in a number of episodes in which the burning question was never answered.

"We always had one killer in mind," says Frost. "We knew who it was from the very beginning and we always planned to reveal it at a certain time. People wanted to know the solution to a mystery. But, we weren't trying to tease anyone."

After the initial seven episodes aired and the season finale ended with more questions than an swers leading into a long summer hiatus, some viewers became incensed.

"We weren't trying to tease anybody," says Frost. "Some of it I thought was genuine anger that probably wouldn't have been so bad if we hadn't had a five month hiatus between that episode and the next one, but it wasn't the kind of anger that was going to prevent people from coming back and sampling the show again once we were on the air again."

Yet when the show began second season, there was a discernible difference. The novelty had worn off, replaced by something equally intriguing. TWIN PEAKS realized it couldn't sustain itself off donut and coffee jokes forever and just as the Laura Palmer murder became a smaller part of a larger tapestry intricately weaved by its creative team, the show evolved. The characters who had proved so endearing first season were more fully realized in the second second, and a whole new host of characters joined the fray. TWIN PEAKS cast, already enormous by television standards with over 21 featured characters in its ensemble and numerous other recurring roles, continued to grow. The myriad murders, suicides and shootings which closed out the series first successful season failed to truncate the already overflowing roster of PEAKS citizens as most returned in body, if not in mind, second season.

So now, get out your Micromac pocket taperecorder, put in your hearing aid and take a thermos full of good steaming coffee because we're on our way into TWIN PEAKS. If you're lucky, maybe we'll stop at the Lamplighter Inn on the way. I hear they serve a damn good cherry pie.

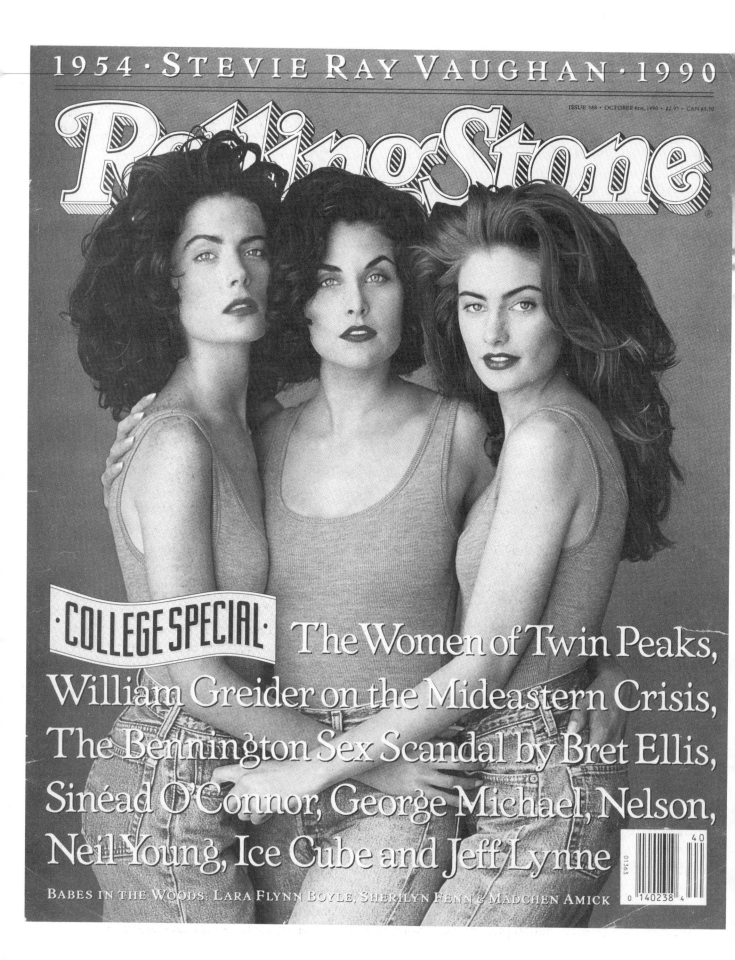

1954 · STEVIE RAY VAUGHAN · 1990

RollingStone

ISSUE 588 · OCTOBER 4TH, 1990 · $2.95 · CAN $3.50

·COLLEGE SPECIAL· The Women of Twin Peaks, William Greider on the Mideastern Crisis, The Bennington Sex Scandal by Bret Ellis, Sinéad O'Connor, George Michael, Nelson, Neil Young, Ice Cube and Jeff Lynne

BABES IN THE WOODS: LARA FLYNN BOYLE, SHERILYN FENN & MÄDCHEN AMICK

CHAPTER ONE:

The Genesis Of Twin Peaks— "Wrapped In Plastic"

David Lynch was still reeling from the disaster that was DUNE, his ill-fated adaptation of the sprawling science-fiction classic, when he availed himself of the opportunity to make BLUE VELVET. Dino De Laurentiis, the Italian producer with a propensity for making big-budget films that often bombed at the box-office (such as TAI-PAN and HURRICANE), had offered Lynch, the promising auteur of such films as ERASERHEAD and THE ELEPHANT MAN, that in return for directing DUNE he would allow Lynch to make one smaller-budgeted film of his choice for his studio, the now defunct DEG Entertainment Group.

Lynch had made a deal with the devil. He allowed DeLaurentiis and Universal Pictures, who distributed the film final cut, the right to edit the final version of the movie in return for the chance to direct BLUE VELVET. Now he was paying the price. DUNE, whose rough cut ran over several hours, was pared down by the studio to a little over two hours and destroyed, according to Lynch. Critics seemed to agree. What had been promoted as a classic, a science-fiction "Gone With The Wind", bombed, and the critics who had extolled Lynch, now just as quickly excoriated him.

"I sold out on DUNE," the director told TIME Magazine recently. "I was making it for the producers, not for myself. That's why the right of final cut is crucial. One person has to be the filter for everything. I believe this is a lesson world; we're supposed to learn stuff. But 3 1/2 years to learn that lesson is too long."

In striking contrast to Lynch's introspective assessment today, he was quoted at the time as saying, "I'd never heard of DUNE. I thought Dino said JUNE. But I read the book, loved it, and began the screenplay. There's something of ERASERHEAD, THE ELEPHANT MAN and some of both in DUNE. There's some sort of thread that connects the three of them in my mind. They're all strange worlds that you can't go into unless you build them and film them. I just like going into strange worlds."

Despite Lynch's protestations to the contrary, DUNE very much bears the stamp of a Lynch production. Filled with bizarre, unsettling images and a number of dream and prophecy sequences, DUNE almost seems to be a science-fiction precursor to TWIN PEAKS. Lynch presented a dark and depressing futureworld rather than an easily digestible science fiction setting such as those of the popular myth-maker of the time, Steven Spielberg. While Spielberg's films presented a warm and comforting view of suburbia, Lynch showed us the flip side, first in space with DUNE and later on earth in BLUE VELVET.

Viewed now, in the aftermath of the show, the viewer will not only see PEAKS Everett McGill and Jack Nance donning full sci-fi regalia long before McGill picked up a gas line at Big Ed's gas farm and Pete Martell ever left a fish in a peculator, but be struck by a strange sense of deja vu in the prophecy images of Paul Atredies (Kyle MacLachlan).

"I saw a half hour of that on cable recently,"says TWIN PEAKS Producer Harley Peyton, "and you immediately see certain things which are right out of Lynch's work. You see a great deal of him in that. Disown it or not, there's still a lot of him on the screen."

MacLachlan described Lynch as a visionary while working on DUNE, an opinion he has echoed working on PEAKS. "His ideas are so different from mine," MacLachlan says. "Things I hadn't thought of, motivations, which is very exciting to work with. At the same time, if any of us, the actors, bring something good, he's willing to go with it. David puts me at ease. I don't feel I have to put *him* at ease, which is the biggest burden to take off an actor."

LYNCH AND MacLACHLAN

The association between Lynch and MacLachlan has proved long and fruitful. After the two were castigated in the aftermath of DUNE, they once again worked together on Lynch's next project, BLUE VELVET. In much the way that Jimmy Stewart served as an on-screen persona for Alfred Hitchcock and DeNiro for Scorcese, MacLachlan has become Lynch's celluloid alter-ego. The persona is that of an inquisitive and quirky hero fascinated by the world around him which not only includes all its scars, but shares a particular fascination for the dark underbelly of society.

BLUE VELVET, the story of Jeffrey Beaumont, a college student who returns to town to visit a father who has had an adverse allergic reaction to a bee bite, discovers a severed ear in a field. Once he brings his discovery to the police, he is denied further knowledge of the case and driven by insatiable curiosity to begin his own personal investigation with the assistance of the police chief's daughter played by Laura Dern. His investigation leads him to discover murder, mutilation and madness. He finds the dark side of life in which Frank (Dennis Hopper), a crazed character, takes him prisoner and turns his rose-colored world upside down.

Lynch's vision is disturbing and powerful. He vividly captures the darkness of a malevolent world which underlies seeming normalcy. The innocence of suburban reality is shattered when Jeffrey's father is attacked by a bee while watering the lawn. The camera withdraws into an ominous hive of innocuous creatures turned into terrifying marauders.

Teenagers looking for a fight when they find Jeffrey has apparently stolen their pal's girlfriend, drive up to her house to discover a naked, battered and bruised body on the doorstep and are thrust into turmoil. A lulling '50s melody, "Blue Velvet", transforms into a chilling and morose wail and Roy Orbinson's classic "In Dreams" becomes the marching song to hell. And choosing the right beer has never been more important....

Strangely Lynch creates this iconography without being certain himself what they mean. At the film's premiere at the Boston Film Festival all Lynch could say was "The film changed my sex life forever." By the film's completion, nearly half of the audience had walked out; the other half extolled it as a classic.

Paul Sammon, a publicist for DEG charged with promoting the seemingly unpromotable film, terms the movie, "a perverse HARDY BOYS adventure and a satire on LEAVE IT TO BEAVER."

MacLachlan's character in BLUE VELVET is fascinated by the flame, but unlike Laura in TWIN PEAKS fears getting burned. He is a voyeur, not like Laura who thrust herself into the decadent world that Jeffrey could only watch. In a scene cut from the film, Sammon reveals, Lynch reinforces this aspect of the character's persona.

"He is coming out of football practice at college," says Sammon. "He goes down into the basement of the fraternity house and sees an attempted rape of a sorority girl. He watches for a while and doesn't interfere until the penultimate moment, so to speak. Then he says, 'Hey, cut that out' and the guy panics and runs away. That added a very interesting dimension to Kyle's character."

FROM DUNES TO PEAKS

Audiences weren't quite sure what to make of the strange film and despite massive critical acclaim, it fared poorly at the box-office. Many of the pieces which led to TWIN PEAKS were in place, including the bucolic setting in a town whose major industry is lumber.

Lynch, now hailed by the critics as as master of his craft, embarked on his next project — the ill-fated RONNIE ROCKET. Despite several aborted attempts to mount his film, it ultimately became embroiled in the graveyard of lost film projects resulting from the DeLaurentiis film studio collapsing into Chapter 11. Not daunted, Lynch collaborated with his new partner Mark Frost, who he had met in 1986 while working on GODDESS, a film about the last months of Marilyn Monroe. Together they worked on a screenplay called ONE SALIVA BUBBLE, a science-fiction comedy. Despite securing the interest of Steve Martin and Martin Short in the project, the producers could not arrange for financing.

Frost had served for three years as writer, story editor and executive story editor on HILL STREET BLUES winning a Writers Guild Award and an Emmy nomination. He also wrote the John Schlesinger helmed occult thriller for Orion, THE BELIEVERS.

Together, they embarked on a new project. After a false start on a science fiction series, their newest idea would be a twisted, offbeat and quirky serial called NORTHWEST PASSAGE. It would soon become TWIN PEAKS.

"The germ of TWIN PEAKS came out of David and I just talking about a town, a city in the Northwest full of mysteries and secret relationships," Mark Frost told SEATTLE WEEKLY. He continued, "This sort of film noire under-

tone that led to the idea of starting with the discovery of a body, a mysterious crime that would get the show off the ground and serve as a spinal column for the series.

"Obviously this is a town that comes from the hearts and minds of David and Mark, but I grew up in the Northwest so I certainly feel a certain kinship to it and a lot of the characters seem familiar to me in a way," says Producer Harley Peyton. "After a while, you basically just join the family and your own experiences can certainly be poured into it. It's not so much as drawing upon your past but taking your experiences and putting them through that filter that somehow they end up in TWIN PEAKS."

"We used to sit in coffee shops and David would throw back five or six cups of coffee at a sitting," says Frost. "I don't drink coffee, but he drinks it to calm him down and we would just noodle things around. Maybe there's a doctor in the town and my dad could play him and gradually the town took shape one little piece at a time. Originally it was going to be set in North Dakota, but I said to David that I spent a weekend there once, there's not a lot going on in North Dakota...and there aren't a whole lot of trees. It's a flat barren place that's very cold and I didn't want to shoot there. We moved it to the Northwest where David spent his time growing up and he felt very connected to the landscape. The big primeval forests are very important to the tone of the show."

The story behind the story of TWIN PEAKS really began in 1946 when David Lynch was born in Missoula, Montana. He moved to Sandpointe, Idaho two years later. Soon afterwards, his family moved again, this time to Spokane, Washington and then onto Boise, Idaho and Alexandria, Virginia.

"My father was a scientist for the Forest Service," Lynch told TIME Magazine. "He would drive me through the woods in his green Forest service truck, over dirt roads, through the most beautiful forests where the trees are very tall and shafts of sunlight come down. In the mountain streams, the rainbow trout leap out and their little trout sides catch glimpses of light. Then my father would drop me in the woods and go off. It was a weird, comforting feeling being in the woods. There were odd mysterious things. That's the kind of world I grew up in."

While Lynch's partner, Mark Frost, was more of a city boy, his father's profession as an actor occasionally required the family to uproot themselves. The reflections of his father offered fertile ground for TWIN PEAKS to grow from.

"Small towns are funny because they're like ingrown toenails and sometimes just as painful,"says Warren Frost. "Small town people are marvelously supportive of each other; they're supportive because they know so much about each other. It isn't that anything different goes on in a small town — it's just that everybody knows about it."

Warren Frost, cast by his son as the warm and dedicated Dr. Will Hayward, recalls the impact the country doctor had on the population of the town he was brought up in.

"I grew up in a little small town and I knew what the doctor meant to the people," says Frost. "You try and do your own thing, but when the police and the politicians can't solve anything, you go to the doctor. He's the last bastion. Being in the theater we moved around and Mark spent summers in a small town and he saw that."

Together, Lynch and Frost intended to introduce a new element to the television medium...reality, or rather, their own peculiar view of reality. The world would be presented where people behaved in a way true to life and not simply a product of television.

"Television is always getting hammered because everything tends to happen a certain way," Frost says. "We try to play with time and space and dimension. Why can't films and television be more like real life? Real life is really wild. There's death, mayhem and murder everywhere and it's just that we now apply this veneer of happy talk over it so we don't have to feel it. What we're trying to talk about in TWIN PEAKS is that violence is real and has real consequences and is awful and is pervasive and true about our lives and it is something we don't look at very often."

SELLING PEAKS

Having assembled the critical pieces of the

PEAKS puzzle, Lynch and Frost met with the head of drama at ABC, Chad Hoffman. They presented their concept of a small town rocked by the murder of a good girl with sordid secrets. The meeting lasted about ten minutes.

"We talked about the show for an awfully long time," says co-creator Mark Frost. "We went in and met with this adventurous ABC executive who had approved CHINA BEACH and THIRTYSOMETHING. We said we had this idea for a show and there's this wind and there's a lot of people and something bad happens, we didn't know what yet. They looked at us like we were animals in a zoo and they nodded and were very cautious but they kept inviting us back because something we had said intrigued them. Chad gave us the go-ahead to write the two hour pilot."

Hoffman's boss, Brandon Stoddard, he head of ABC Entertainment, wasn't overwhelmed. Soon afterwards, Stoddard stepped down to assume the reigns of ABC's in-house television production company and Robert Iger assumed the reigns of power at the network. Iger, a former weatherman and graduate of Ithaca College, was more intrigued. Assuming the position with only six weeks left in which to choose fall programming, Iger green-lighted production and championed it despite opposition from many at ABC who deemed the pilot too strange and uncommercial.

ABC's own in-house research department seemed to bear the naysayers right. 25% of viewers gave up on the show during its test runs. Despite the statistics, Iger remained committed, granting Lynch and Frost the freedom from network interference usually reserved for veteran television producers such as Steven Bochco (L.A. LAW, COP ROCK).

"We didn't really want to do television," says Frost. "It's backbreaking and we said we were not going to do it unless they let us do what we wanted to do. For some weird reason, they said okay and they haven't interfered at any stage except that in the original script the population of Twin Peaks was 5,201 and ABC said the town should be bigger. I went back and put 51,201 on the sign and they felt better. Of course now we should have something to keep count of the changes so we can keep lowering the number."

"We've been left alone in a way which is tremendous," Producer Harley Peyton says. "They leave us alone. There's no feedback criticism or praise even though they have a vested interest in the development of the show. We are pretty much allowed to do whatever we want, which is one of the reasons the show is so good. It makes the experience a lot more enjoyable. They're willing to trust us."

The challenge, according to Peyton, is getting the show picked up initially. Once you're on the air, the pressure to conform to the networks precise vision of what a show should be becomes less confining.

"Once it's on the air, you've developed your own little fiefdom as long as the ratings remain at a certain level," Peyton explains. "In television, writers are allowed to chart their own course to a greater extent then in film. Television is a medium for the writer/producer. In features, you're always the sort of uninvited guest in the room. While I was working on LESS THAN ZERO I was getting script notes back with different executives writing in different colored ink in either margin and frequently their notes would conflict with each other. That gets to be a little crazy."

A series as daring and ambitious as TWIN PEAKS getting a seven episode commitment seems surprising in light of the conservative climate which abounds among the three television networks. "We were in exactly the right place at the right network at the right time," Mark Frost remarked to TIME. "The end of the Reagan era, a new decade — there were a lot of pointers.

"The television business is strictly bottom line. The only reason we're still on the air is because enough people are watching it to make the show profitable to the network. They're not a public service organization and their job is to make money for their stockholders. 10,000 episodes of WHO'S THE BOSS makes them a lot of money although it doesn't do much for the collective soul of our culture."

The seven initial episodes budgeted at a little less than $1 million each were a risky gamble. Not only were they expensive, but continuing serials rarely, if ever, do well in repeats. Even the die-hard fans usually pass on watching soaps a second time around. If TWIN PEAKS wasn't a success from the beginning, it was unlikely to ever

be.

So NORTHWEST PASSAGE was born. Frost and Lynch collaborated on the screenplay for the initial two hour opener. Budgeted at about $4 million, they wrote the pilot in nine days and Lynch shot it in 23. The seven episodes, once approved, would not be filmed until months later.

BUILDING PEAKS

Several familiar names were recruited for the pilot: Lynch's regular editor Duwayne Dunham (who would direct the second episode), BLUE VELVET casting director Johanna Ray, and composer Angelo Badalamenti, whom Lynch had developed a rapport with since BLUE VELVET. The two soon became linked in much the way that John Williams & Steven Spielberg, Alfred Hitchcock & Bernard Herrmann, Robert Zemeckis & Alan Silvestri, and Jerry Goldsmith & Joe Dante have collaborated.

"At the time we began work on TWIN PEAKS, it was still called NORTHWEST PASSAGE and nothing had been shot," Badalamenti told MOVIES USA. "David would tell me what he was seeing and what he wanted. For example, for the show's theme he asked for something in a minor mode, dark, ominous and beautiful with a melody that would change to signal anticipation, build to a climax that would tear your heart out and then segue back into an ominous, beautiful feeling. That became the 'Love Theme' or 'Laura Palmer' theme of TWIN PEAKS. He'd say these things and I'd just start improvising on the piano. After 20 minutes of improvising and him saying 'play it slower — no slower', he said, 'that's it, don't change a note, you've captured 75% of TWIN PEAKS.'"

"On that first season we came up with sixteen cuts right on the spot," Badalamenti continues, "ranging from cool jazz to the slightly surreal melody of 'Audrey's Dance'. David is very easy to work with not only because he knows what he wants, but because he's able to recognize it when he hears it. Whether it was cool jazz, rock and roll, or something symphonic, it was as if he could hear it in his head. And so could I."

Joining the large cast were a number of staples of the permanent Lynch ensemble; Kyle MacLachlan as the quirky Agent Dale Cooper, Jack Nance, a mainstay of Lynch's films, as Pete Martell, Everett McGill, another DUNE veteran, as Ed Hurley, and Catherine Coulson as the strange Log Lady. Coulson had last worked with Lynch in front of the camera on ERASERHEAD.

"I was working on ERASERHEAD and had been hired to act and one day I put on my glasses and David said someday you're going to play this girl with a log," recalls Catherine Coulson. "I'm going to do this television show which will be called I'LL TEST MY LOG WITH EVERY BRANCH OF KNOWLEDGE and you'll be wearing little plaid skirts and your glasses and you're going to take your log to various doctors and get their opinions and it's going to be Ponderosa Pine. Now I didn't really believe David would ever do a television series, but I thought somehow, in some incarnation I would play this woman with a log so when it came time to do the pilot David called me and asked if I was ready and I said for what and he said to do the Log Lady."

Also in contention for one of the leads was actress Isabella Rossellini, linked to Lynch romantically since BLUE VELVET. She is the daughter of Ingrid Bergman and had been mentioned for the leading role of Giovanna Packard, the owner of the Packard sawmill and widow of Andrew Packard. When Rossellini decided not to accept the part, Joan Chen was hired to portray Josie Packard, no longer of Italian descent, but Oriental.

"The part was originally written for an Italian woman," Joan Chen told SOAP OPERA WEEKLY. "But when we met, he said 'Why not a Chinese?' That's also part of the reason I wanted to do it. I like people who are open-minded, to acknowledge that people are people, and obviously he is."

Chen, whose most memorable role to date was that of the Wan Jung in Bertolucci's THE LAST EMPEROR, is entangled romantically with the Sheriff of TWIN PEAKS, then called Dan Steadman. Another snag arose when David Strathairn, the outstanding actor who had starred in EIGHT MEN OUT and DOMINICK & EUGENE, also turned down the chance to star in the show so that he could continue to pursue his career in fea-

ture films. Ironically, Strathairn soon afterwards appeared in an arc of WISEGUY as Sheriff Stemm, a quirky and offbeat law enforcement officer in the TWIN PEAKS-like town of Lynchboro.

Brought in to play the character now called Harry S. Truman was veteran actor Michael Ontkean. "Michael always says he's the designated driver for TWIN PEAKS," jokes Executive Story Editor Robert Engels. He says the actor is one of the few earthbound characters on the show. Truman is straitlaced and realistic, a quality which the casting of Ontkean clearly reinforces.

"Good people are harder to write than bad people," says Producer Harley Peyton. "Normal people are harder to write than eccentric people. I suppose by definition that makes Harry Truman a somewhat more difficult character to write and to some extent he's going to be Watson to Cooper's Holmes, but you don't want to leave it only at that and certainly that makes Harry's character a little more challenging. He can project this kind of solidity that makes him a real anchor on the show in a lot of ways because we have characters that are going off in so many different directions and there are so many weird things that occur."

Lynch directed the two hour opener in which the body of the homecoming queen is found dead; naked and wrapped in plastic. Unlike conventional television drama, the murder is not the object of the show's fascination. When another of Laura's schoolmates is found staggering across the state lines after being brutally attacked, the FBI is recruited. Agent Dale Cooper enters the scene and the real fun begins.

COOPER (speaking into tape recorder): Diane, 2:15 in the afternoon, November 14th. Entering town of Twin Peaks. Five miles south of Canadian border, twelve miles west of the state line. Never seen so many trees in my life. As W.C. Fields would say, I'd rather be here than Philadelphia. It's 54 degrees and overcast. Weatherman said rain. How can you get paid that kind of money for being wrong 60% of the time and be working? Mileage is 79,345, gauge is on reserve. I'm riding on fumes, have to tank up when I get into town, remind me to tell you how much that is. Lunch was $6.31 and I left her a dollar tip, at the...Lamplighter Inn, that's on Highway 2 near

Lewis Fork. If you ever get up this way, Diane, that cherry pie is worth a stop. Okay. I'll be looking for a Sheriff Harry S. Truman, he's going to be at the Calhoun Memorial Hospital with that girl they pulled off the mountain. I'll be checking into a motel after we're through there. Sure the Sheriff'll be able to recommend a clean place. Reasonably priced.

Turns off the microphone. Turns it back on again.

COOPER (CONTINUED): Forgot to mention. I stopped for coffee and a pit stop about 10:30, little diner near Bitteroot Lake. Excellent coffee. Forgot to get the receipt, can you believe it? That was seventy five cents and I left a quarter on the counter. Got to find out what kind of trees these are. They're really something.

MacLachlan, is once again portraying a variation on the Lynch-ian persona, fascinated by everything within the realm of his senses. He remarks on the extraordinary quality of a cherry pie consumed during a pit stop on the road to TWIN PEAKS, the magnificent trees that fill the forests around the town and a box of chocolate bunnies. Cooper informs the Sheriff that the murder of Laura Palmer bears a striking resemblance to a murder that took place a year ago, that of Teresa Banks, and begins an investigation which will last for the next sixteen episodes of the series.

SHOOTING THE PILOT

The pilot was shot on location in Snoqulamie, Washington, a logging town 25 miles east of Seattle. The exteriors, which have since reappeared in the voluminous stock footage the series makes use of, were shot at the Salish Lodge, a huge resort overlooking a 268 foot waterfall which was transformed into the Great Northern, the hotel owned by Ben Horne. The Kiana Lodge, located on a Bainbridge Island in Puget Sound, doubled for the Blue Lake Lodge where Peter and Catherine Martell live with Josie Packard. The Weyerhauser Administration Building was redressed to magically become the TWIN PEAKS Sheriff's Office.

At the junction of Highways 202 and 203 in Falls City is the Colonial Inn, better known to "Peaks Freaks" as the Roadhouse. The shows interiors

are shot on sound stages in Van Nuys and all location footage since the pilot has been shot in and around the studio except for some second unit work done in Snoqulamie.

"I didn't hear from too many people that they thought the show looked like we were shooting in Van Nuys all of the sudden," says Mark Frost. "It's a question of economics, it's much more expensive to take a whole crew and cast on location. All our sets are built down in Van Nuys. We have them all on a stage and the locations we found locally seemed to work and sell the area."

The sets are located in City Studios on Balboa Boulevard in Van Nuys. There are numerous richly detailed standing sets which were designed meticulously to duplicate the locations that had been shot in Washington for the pilot. The Roadhouse was painstakingly realized as was the Great Northern and the Twin Peaks' police station. The halls of the hotel wind through the studio linking myriad sets from the Double R Diner to the prison cell in the Sheriff's station.

Each set is filled with the smallest of details, virtually indistinguishable on screen, but which lend to the reality of the show. In the Blue Pine Inn where Catherine and Pete Martell live there is a library stocked to the ceilings with books and filled with seemingly antique furniture. On its shelves are tomes of literature ranging from THE HISTORY OF THE JEWS to SHOGUN. On the kitchen table of the Johnson home lays the appropriately titled self-help book, "FACTS ABOUT LOVE, SEX & MARRIAGE" and empty cans of motor oil lay strewn in the corner. Giant matte paintings roll out for the background of shots and even the sink and toilet in the holding cell are suitably grungy.

In Norma's Double R Diner the special for the day is changed every episode. In the Sheriff's office hangs a picture of Harry S. Truman and the hallways of the station display a bevy of public service announcements and 'Wanted' posters.

Even the production offices were utilized during filming. By changing the door to read 'Warden's Office', the mundane space of the staff was transformed into another nook of TWIN PEAKS. The scenes of Hank and Norma visiting his parole hearing in prison actually took place in the main production offices adjoining the sound stages.

Outside in the parking lot, one of the fire exits was used in Episode Six, as the entrance to Doctor Jacoby's office where James had parked his motorcycle as Bobby plants cocaine in its gas tank. As the storylines change, some sets are struck and new ones are built to facilitate shooting the continuing plots.

LAUNCHING PEAKS

To boost interest in the premiere, ABC initially contemplated airing the pilot without commercials as a publicity gimmick. After assessing the cost of losing that much revenue, they chose to present the show with only limited commercial interruptions.

When it aired on Sunday, April 8 the show was greeted by nearly unanimous critical acclaim. The spate of cover stories, interviews and positive notices the premiere received were unprecedented and took both the cast and crew by surprise.

"The press was just incredible," says Warren Frost. "Almost to the point where you had to think, 'come on, it's only a television series...it's not the new messiah.'

"It's very exciting to be involved in something like that, particularly something your son has been one of the godfathers of. Overall television is not very good. It can't be; you can't put out that many hours of television and have it be very good. There are not that many writers; there are probably only 100 great plays in the history of the theater."

Television was once referred to by the head of the FCC as "a vast wasteland", a perception which has not dramatically altered with the passing years and a philosophy subscribed to by second season director Graeme Clifford — until the arrival of TWIN PEAKS. "Usual television fare for me means that I can stand it for about ten minutes at the most," he says. "TWIN PEAKS though had sinister undertones going and David's admittedly unique way of looking at things. It was interesting and I can't remember seeing anything as compelling since THE PRISONER, THE AVENGERS and THE FUGITIVE. Particularly at the time they were made in the '60s, they were really innovative television, but TV fare in the

'80s is not exactly scintillating. Most of the series they put on are not worth watching. You'd be hard pressed to watch without nodding off."

Warren Frost compares TWIN PEAKS to the so-called Golden Age of television.

"I think if you can live up to the expectations you set for yourself then you're all right," says Frost. "If you had expectations to begin with. I think most of television doesn't start out with expectations, but a funny idea. I go back to live television when it first started and it was so different back in the early days because no one was watching since no one had television sets. It was very easy to try and do things and be allowed to fail or succeed.

"In retrospect, there's a lot of early television that was praised to the skies as being great that's not so great today but it was great then because it was trying to do something," Frost says. "I don't mean all of it, because there was just as much junk, but there were great moments in early television. There was no pressure because no one knew what they were doing so even the broadcasters didn't have the great pressure on them. You may not be able to say all the words you can say on television today, but they had PLAY-HOUSE 90, PHILCO and OMNIBUS. They could try things because nobody knew. If you did the greatest television show in the world 20 million people would watch it and that would be 97 percent of the audience."

The early ratings on TWIN PEAKS seemed to indicate that ABC had a smash success on its hands. Yet in the following weeks, when the series was berthed on Thursday evenings, the weekly Nielsons indicated a continuing erosion as viewers jumped ship as the proceedings got weirder and Laura's killer remained at large. One source at Fox Television even said that ABC was planning not to renew the series when they got word that the fledgling, upstart Fox Network planned to place a bid to pick-up the show if ABC cancelled it. So instead the network gave the go-ahead for another year.

ABC continued to express satisfaction with the shows ratings, attributing its success to the series' ability to attract demographic groups most coveted by upscale advertisers. This has led to criticism of the network for emphasizing "narrow-casting", appealing to a small percentage of the viewing audience more attractive to advertisers with specialized programming than the largest possible group of viewers.

 "Any show that appeals to the entire spectrum of the television audience is going to be, by definition, bland," says Harley Peyton. "Brandon Tartikoff [the president of NBC], who was quoted in the trades as one of the people who gave TWIN PEAKS no chance of succeeding, said that the program is the way of the future for television. It's a show that's different enough that people are talking about it at the water cooler the next morning and one that can create a very specific audience that advertisers will want to sell their products to. Of course, typically, he was talking about the show in a businesslike way and not a creative way, but it is that creativity that makes our show special. It has set a standard that will be difficult to match."

 Recalling her experiences shooting the pilot, Sherilyn Fenn, who plays the mischievous Audrey Horne told ROLLING STONE, "on the set of the pilot, the makeup artist always called me Miss Twin Peaks. 'C'mere, Miss Twin Peaks!' But there's lots of twin peaks on the show...and there *were* those two beautiful mountains we shot."

 Indeed Frost did acknowledge in an interview with the NEW YORK TIMES that the title of the show is "a male joke about women's breasts. The Western landscape does, after all, prominently feature the Grand Tetons".

The question, which begs to be asked in the wake of the solution of the Laura Palmer imbroglio then, is whose TWIN PEAKS are they?

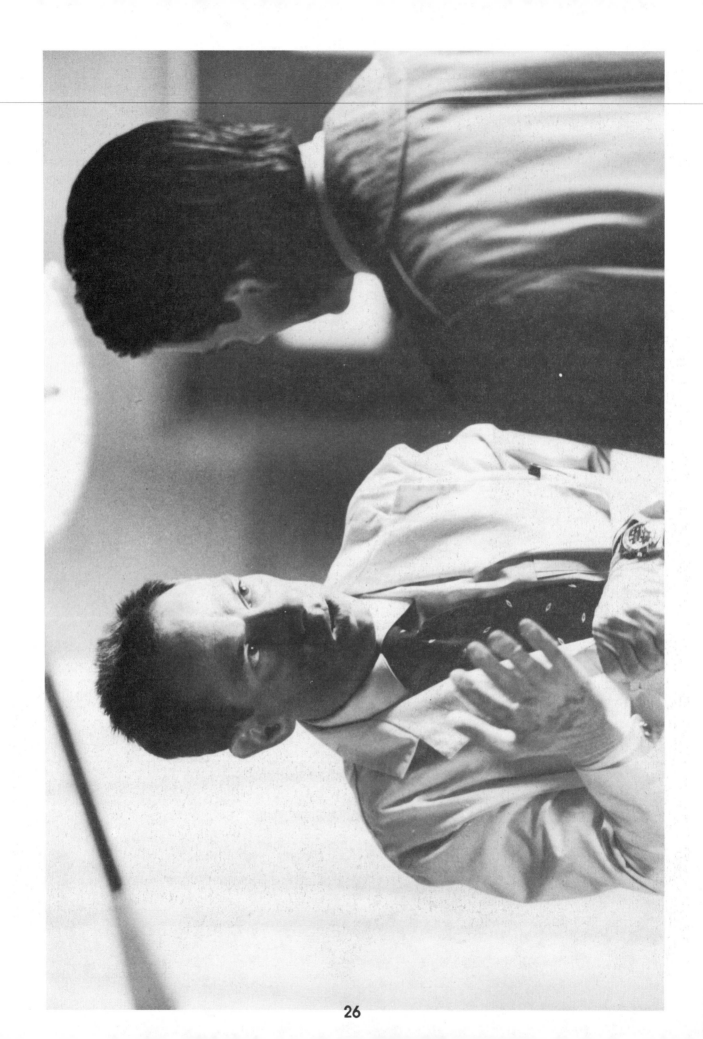

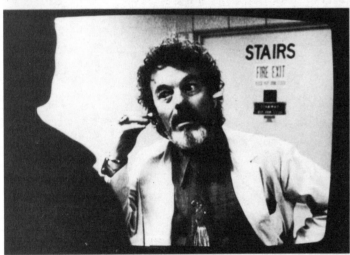

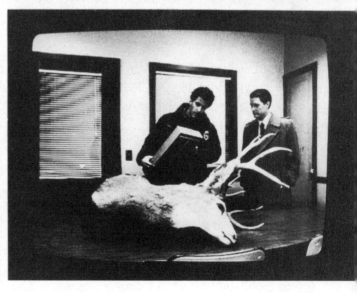

CHAPTER TWO:

First Season — "She's Full Of Secrets"

The TWIN PEAKS production team was full of secrets. The tight-lipped group of individuals not only to kept the identity of Laura's killer a secret until the unmasking in the second season (and for some, even past then as befuddled viewers failed to concur on who was actually the killer after the revelation aired), but almost every detail of the plot and future developments.

"It's sort of a gentlemen's agreement we have with all of them," says Mark Frost about the under-punishment-of-death atmosphere that surrounds the set. "I don't know if it's in their contract."

It wasn't in Miguel Ferrer's contract, but he's not about to spill the beans on what his lab-coated character may be up to next. "They're incredibly serious about that stuff," he says. "They sent out memorandum to everyone with a big heading, 'Loose Lips Sink Ships' and it went on to detail the proper way to dispose of old scripts or unwanted pages. 'Make sure to use the shredder in the office. Do not throw them in your garbage or the garbage of the studio because fans are going to go through it and we'd like to keep this completely confidential.'"

"Every one of our scripts says 'This is confidential, let's keep it this way'," Lara Flynn Boyle, who stars as the beautiful Donna Hayward, one of Laura's closest friends, told SOAP OPERA WEEKLY. "I had a script in my bag and when I opened it, my girlfriend said, 'What's that?' I said 'Nothing', and I zipped the bag shut. She asked if it was one of the scripts and if she could see it. I said, 'Please don't make me do this'."

Caleb Deschanel directed Episode Six first season and didn't necessarily find the gag order, which often left the cast and crew as mystified as its viewers, a drawback. "It's really not a problem," he says. "Sometimes you find that you add things to the show without knowing anything that contribute to the mystery and make it that much better. The scripts weren't generally done more than a week in advance so it's not like anyone is really keeping secrets from anybody because the directors who are on the show are all trusted and accepted by everyone."

RECRUITING PEAK DIRECTORS

Frost and Lynch recruited feature film directors (including Deschanel) with an impressive array of credits to helm the first seven episodes. Writers for the show included Harley Peyton, best known for penning the film adaptation of LESS THAN ZERO, and Robert Engels, formerly an actor with credits including starring in the soap opera EDGE OF NIGHT, and more recently as story editor on the third season of WISEGUY.

"My girlfriend at the time took me to a screening of the pilot," recalls Harley Peyton. "I knew Mark socially and I saw the show and it amazed me. Having little experience in television, I told him if you ever need someone to write an episode I'd like to do one just for fun. Suddenly I was writing one and based on that I was asked to write another one."

Peyton, a Harvard graduate, had gone to school with the intention of becoming a lawyer and soon thereafter discovered he wanted to pursue a career as a disc jockey and became captivated by film inevitably drifting into directing.

"I wanted to sort of become the Andrew Sarris of my generation," Peyton recalls. "I read Sarris and Agee a lot and I started reviewing films at Harvard. It sounded like a great way to make a living and just kind of go to the movies. When my mentor at school left to work on the production of a movie a light went on over my head. It was one of those things I couldn't imagine being an occupation you could have. It seemed too good to be true. Soon after, I entered the film program at Stamford and, like most people, just stumbled my way along and like most people who go to film school said I was going to become a director. Of course you're the 18th sound assistant on a small documentary about San Francisco and you realize that's not exactly the way it works so I kind of worked my way up to writing.

"I was working for producers as a reader and not very good at those jobs," he continues. "I was ac-

tually fired from one job and there was a Writer's Strike and I finally wrote a screenplay and got an agent and the work came and has never stopped and the writing of it still remains what I like to do best. The more I learn about directing, the more complicated it seems."

Lesli Linka Glatter can certainly attest to the sentiments expressed by Peyton. As director of several episodes during the first and second seasons of the show, Glatter has faced her fair share of challenges.

"I saw the pilot at a screening and loved it," Glatter remembers. "I'm also represented by CAA, as is David (Lynch), and I talked to one of the agents there and said I've never wanted to do episodic but if this particular thing goes into series I would love to have a shot at it. Tony Krantz, my agent, showed David my work and he called and so I was a happy girl."

Glatter has a background in modern dance choreography and has directed episodes of AMAZING STORIES and VIETNAM WAR STORY along with a made-for-cable film on the American neo-Nazi scripted by Anna Hamilton Phelan. She was thrilled when she answered the phone call from David Lynch and he offered her the opportunity to direct her first episode of the show.

"I got a call asking if I wanted to do one," says Glatter. "I had met with Mark and David came to my birthday party but it wasn't a terribly official meeting. He is truly one of the extraordinary people on the planet and we had a good mutual friend, Johanna Ray (TWIN PEAKS' casting director). I had worked with her several times before and she's done all of David's recent films and she always told me I should meet him. I really love his work. I think he is a visionary and so I figured he'd probably be a really interesting man."

"I love David," adds Miguel Ferrer who portrays the acerbic Albert Rosenfield introduced in Episode Two. "I've been a fan for years and years, ever since ERASERHEAD. He's just a great guy. I've been very fortunate to work for some incredible directors including Bill Friedkin, Paul Verhoeven and Tony Scott, and David Lynch must certainly be counted among the very highest. What David Lynch does, no one taught him to do. He's just hearing his own music on some separate level. He's absolutely unafraid to hang his ass out in the wind and get it shot off. He really just follows his own muse. That stuff isn't learned in film school."

Ferrer's sentiments are echoed by director Todd Holland. He came aboard during the show's second season.

"I was a huge fan of the pilot which was little different than the rest of his work," says Holland. "I loved it, it was so emotional. I watched the show out of the blue and was knocked off my feet. I enjoyed meeting David. He's incredibly friendly and very charming when you first meet him. If you don't get to talk to him very long, you have to look for the dark side. It's not very conspicuous, but you know it's there."

Lynch, whose oddball reputation gave the show its franchise and whose reputation for the eclectic was the show's hook initially, has played a very active role in continuing development.

"He approves the cast," says Holland. "He saw my cut and approves the final show and we make any changes necessary for him and he approves wardrobe and things I don't even deal with on a large level."

In speaking to EGG magazine about the outrageous auteur, Lara Flynn Boyle (Donna Hayward), said that "He finds things sexy that most people wouldn't and then they become sexy. I was shooting this scene where I'm coming onto this guy (James Hurley) any way I can think of and I start hanging on these bars. David decides that it's really sexy and I end up doing the whole thing hanging from these bars.

"He'll turn to a wardrobe lady and say, 'The wardrobe is all wrong. I want her to look like Sandra Dee on a ski trip. Or Lana Turner with more lipstick.' There's a scene where James Marshall and I come together because we're emotionally strung out, two people who've just lost their best friend. That scene was four pages long. We shot it 40 times. Two days, I read it and thought I might not be able to do it."

Peggy Lipton, best known for her work on the MOD SQUAD, told the same magazine her first reaction when she was called into read for the part of Norma Jennings, the owner of the Double R Diner.

"I knew something was up because it was David Lynch," said Lipton. "I think I read the script first. It was so great. I just went 'Oh my God, this can't be for television — it's wonderful.' It read like a book and then I went into Propaganda Films, which is in this far out building and I met David. Immediately, I felt the excitement. He didn't have me read right away so I never was on the spot. When I finally read after coming back several times, it was with his direction. It was pretty exciting and it was a good character. At first, I didn't want to be thrown into a series, but look what I fell into. When you are around him it's like every nerve cell in your body tunes up to your craft. One of the best things about David is his attention to detail. He can lose himself totally in detail. But I don't know what goes on in David Lynch's head."

After the premiere, seven episodes were produced for the first season of the show. Unlike most television shows where directors are just guns-for-hire moving from show to show without being allowed to complete post-production or create a distinctive style, TWIN PEAKS was different.

LYNCH DIRECTS PEAKS

Duwayne Dunham, who edited the pilot, directed the show's first episode, and Lynch returned to direct the second. Even moreso than the pilot, the second episode represented everything the series was about. If the pilot drew ripples of attention, the second episode caused a tidal wave. The episode ends with a spectacular dream sequence in which a dwarf dances to one of Angelo Badalamenti jazzy riffs after cluing Cooper into some very valuable information.

MIDGET: I've got good news, the gum you like is going to come back into style...she's my cousin...but doesn't she look just like Laura Palmer?

COOPER: But it is Laura Palmer. Are you Laura Palmer?

LAURA: I feel like I knew her but sometimes my arms bend back.

MIDGET: She's filled with secrets. Where we're from the birds sing a pretty song and there's always music in the air.

Cooper awakens from his dream and reaches for the phone on his hotel room nightstand. "Harry, it's Cooper," he says into the receiver. "Meet me for breakfast, 7 AM, the hotel lobby. I know who killed Laura Palmer....and no, it can wait till morning."

"David is the keeper of the flame," MacLachlan told TIME. "This is his world. The uniqueness is not necessarily transferable. It may madden the staff when David directs a segment because he throws the rules out. But to us actors, that freedom is an elixir, a magic potion. It's hard to have it watered down once you've tasted it."

Amick agrees that when David Lynch gets behind the camera, the experience of working on TWIN PEAKS is transformed. "With the other directors there's always a constant rush," she says. "Even when you're on time and schedule people are always rushing you through things and everyone seems uptight and working hard, but once David comes on the set, people give up. You can't rush him; he doesn't allow it. He takes his time and everyone feels very comfortable and there's a lot of joking and practical jokes.

"As an actor you normally memorize your lines the night before, but when you come to work with David, you don't memorize anything because everything goes out the door. He's going to rewrite lines. Everyone doesn't rush or push it because they know they can't and it just happens. Sometimes they think David is really behind because he's taking too long with something and then in the next scene he'll do it in one take and he's caught up. It's fun and everyone is happy and relaxed and it's definitely different."

TOUCH OF FROST

Despite the attention that's been lavished on David Lynch's contributions to the series, Mark Frost's input has been equally valuable in creating and maintaining the quality of the show. "He's very funny," Amick says of Frost. "When we were filming the pilot up in Seattle, we would have dinners on the weekend where all of the cast members would go up to the house that Mark Frost and David rented and we would play games and Mark would do impressions of people and it would be really fun. He's really a neat guy and I wish he would get more publicity because it definitely is split half and half. They both wrote it equally and he's the one who's actually there when we're filming and is on the set for any questions we have about the way things are going."

"We like to sit in a room and just sort of toss ideas back and forth," Frost says about his collaboration with Lynch. "Or one of us will come up with something and bring it in and the other one will give a response to it and then we'll alter it in some way. And before you know it, it starts to grow like topsy. It's a very hard thing to talk about, the creative process, because its mysterious. You don't know where ideas come from. And when you have a partner where the chemistry is such that ideas just pop up back and forth, you know, like daisies in April — that's a terrible thing."

The NEW YORK TIMES quoted Frost as attributing the success of his collaboration with the offbeat auteur to their shared perceptions about life in general.

"There is a design behind the world that we are living in which is veiled to most of us most of the time, but every once in a while you catch a glimpse of it. To David Lynch, any film or television show should be life casting a shadow."

Lara Flynn Boyle expounded on Frost's assessment of Lynch in an interview with ELLE. "People ask me if it was weird to work on TWIN PEAKS," she said. "To be honest, I was upset about how normal my character was. But David Lynch's characters are normal people, pushed to their extremes."

DIRECTING PEAKS

One would imagine with all the praise that has been lavished on Lynch by the cast and crew it would be difficult for anyone else to assume the reigns on an episode or risk the inevitable comparisons. Surprisingly most of the directors who have worked on the show have embraced the opportunity and not felt constrained. More than anyone else it is Lynch who has been the focus of the media attention that has been lavished on the series and the others who have worked on the show, with the exception of some of the actors, have done so in relative anonymity.

Caleb Deschanel, an accomplished director in his own right and a renown Academy Award winning cinematographer whose directorial work includes THE ESCAPE ARTIST and CRUSOE, appraises the situation this way.

"It's something you accept going in," Deschanel says. "Not only that but the reason I'm here is because I really like what he created. In any television there is a director who takes a back seat to so many people. Television is driven by the scripts and the actors moreso than features which are much more director driven. It was a really good chance to work with some really good actors and scripts and challenge myself to do that amount of work in a short period of time which is really good training no matter what you go on to direct. It is extraordinary to think if you have that kind of training and go on to a feature and get into trouble, you can do three days work in 15 minutes like you do in television. You go to the heart of the matter and you get it done."

Surprisingly, despite the various styles of the many directors who have been engaged to work on the series, all the episodes flow as a cohesive whole and none vary radically from the individual installments which have preceded them or followed them. Strangely, despite the diverse range of directorial styles, the series has proved incredibly consistent and faithful to the tone established by Lynch in the pilot.

"I think the consistency of the look of TWIN PEAKS is as much the schedule as anything else," remarks director Todd Holland. "No mention of style was ever discussed. It's the schedule that leads you to shoot a master with no coverage and therefore it begins to look like last week's. It's the schedule and the budget that gives them consistency because each director comes in with a very different eye."

In fact, Deschanel says the way in which he would shoot the show was never discussed with him by the producers or by Lynch. "Everybody assumed that you knew the tone of the show and had seen what was done before," he says. "Everyone's own style fits into the overall tone of the show. Everyone has been operating within the context of understanding the show up until now."

"When I was deciding if I was going to do the show or not," says actress Madchen Amick, who plays the battered wife of trucker Leo Johnson, "I was talking to them about how I wanted to do features and they said everyone involved is basically feature people. Once we started working with the different directors I was thinking that having a different director each episode could be really unsettling because once you got to know somebody, they're going to leave, but everyone had a lot of the same style as David. They kept a consistency while still bringing a new idea to your character that you didn't think of. In a way, it felt like a real long movie and directors would kind of come in and take turns and that's fun. When you watch television, you go from watching other shows until its time for TWIN PEAKS and all of the sudden you jump into this different world." "A series should look like it's all been directed by the same person and if you don't want it that way you shouldn't accept the job," says Graeme Clifford who shot Episode 5 second season. His prior directorial achievements include the Australian film BURKE & WILLS, GLEAMING THE CUBE and the movie FRANCES starring Jessica Lange.

"I have a great respect for David and I think my sensibilities aren't too far away from his. That little bizarreness is an undercurrent in my own films and although in certain of them you wouldn't notice it, I do feel very much in tune with it. I didn't have to work very hard to stay close to what he's doing. I think it's very important when you're coming into a series that you stick closely to what has been established or it's going to look like a series of unrelated episodes."

Lynch along with Frost approves every director hired for the series although he left the show after directing the pilot to shoot WILD AT HEART.

"David and Mark work as partners," says Harley Peyton. "I work primarily with Mark but David is certainly involved with the scripts and the way they're developed. It will depend on what's going on in David's life at the time. Last fall he was shooting WILD AT HEART and so he was gone for a good deal of it, but the second year there was a kind of ebb and flow. He's certainly involved with the larger storytelling decisions that are made. While it's not veto power, it's more like his eye looking at the way things are and the way they're going and that feedback will either send us in a new direction or the direction he's suggesting which is all kind of part of the process.

"It's like the old DICK VAN DYKE SHOW," Peyton continues. "Lynch is kind of Alan Brady and Mark Frost is Dick Van Dyke so I suppose there's that odd chain of command but they really do work as partners."

As a result of Lynch's commitment to shooting WILD AT HEART, his first feature film project since BLUE VELVET, Episode 3, directed by Tina Rathborne (who had actually directed David Lynch in ZELLY & ME), was shot before Lynch returned to shoot 2.

"I liked her very much," Ferrer says of Rathborne. "Her experience in television and feature film-making was rather limited and she didn't come in with a lot of preconceived notions. She was really sort of following her own inner voice, whatever the heck that was. She hadn't been spoiled by the machine yet and I do mean that as the highest compliment."

In Episode 3, Truman and Cooper are summoned to the morgue when Dr. Hayward and Albert get into a fight over releasing Laura's body for the upcoming funeral mediated by Ben Horne.

HAYWARD: You're the most cold-blooded man I've ever seen, I've never in my life met a man with so little regard for human frailty, have you no compassion?

ALBERT: I've got compassion running out of my nose, I'm the sultan of sentiment. Dr. Hayward, I have travelled thousands of miles, and apparently several centuries, to this forgotten sinkhole in order to perform a series of tests. Now I do not ask you to understand these tests, I am not a cruel man. I just ask you to get the hell out my way so that I can finish my works, is that clear?

HAYWARD: We need to conduct Laura Palmer's body to the cemetery. If you think we're going to leave here without her, you're out of your mind!

BENJAMIN HORNE: All right! Mr. Rosenfield, please. Leland Palmer couldn't be with us today, but I know I speak for everyone the Palmer family included when I say we appreciate and understand the value of your work, but as their representative I must insist that we consider the feelings of the Palmer family as well.

ALBERT: Mr. Horne, I understand that your position in this fair community pretty well guarantees banality, insincerity, and a rather irritating manner of expressing yourself but stupidity, however, is not necessarily an inherent trait, therefore please listen closely: you can have a funeral any old time, you dig a hole, you plant a coffin. I, however, cannot perform these tests next year, next month, next week or tomorrow. I must perform them now. I've got a lot of cutting and pasting to do gentleman so why don't you please return to your porch chairs and resume whittling.

PEAK PERFORMANCES

"We started shooting Episode 3 with the scene in the operating room where I was performing the autopsy," recalls Ferrer. "It was the hardest, most difficult day of dialogue I have ever had in 12 years of acting. It is probably the most difficult one I will ever have. It was just tongue twisters of unsayable dialogue and it was Shakespearean almost in that if you let one link of the chain drop, you couldn't ad lib this stuff so it really all had to come out letter-perfect. I sweated bullets to get through that day. It was very, very tough and Episode 2 which we shot weeks later with David was quite a bit easier. It was from the very first day a kind of test by fire.

"I'm not one of those method guys," Ferrer insists when asked about whether he researched the role before shooting. "I just try and look for something to play in the scene. I don't understand how some of these actors go in with all these backhistories. Which is not to say that some research in many cases can't be useful because I believe that's true, but actors who load themselves up with things that aren't really applicable in the scene really just tend to confuse themselves and that's not what my approach is."

As a visitor to Twin Peaks, Ferrer's FBI forensics specialist, Albert Rosenfield has a unique vantage point on the going-ons in the town. Never afraid to speak his mind, he's obnoxious, insolent and strangely endearing. In a world populated by dancing dwarfs, gregarious giants, and prescient logs, he serves as the voice of sanity...or at least reality as we know it outside of TWIN PEAKS.

"Everyone here loves to write Albert Rosenfield because you get to write the insults," says Peyton, whose work first season was nominated for an Emmy. "Albert was kind of introduced in my first episode so that's a character that I've always loved writing just because it's a kind of humorous one to write. There're a lot of people around here who can write him so he is always going to be well equipped. Mark came up with the character and he's pretty popular with the audience. Miguel nails those lines every time."

"I think Albert says the things the rest of us would like to say," says Ferrer. "The audience at some point wants to ask who are these crazy people and there's Albert to say it for them."

Rosenfield however is just one one of the large ensemble of characters that comprise the world of TWIN PEAKS. Despite the acclaim the show has received for its bold and innovative approach in redefining the very nature of network television programming, Peyton acknowledges that in many ways PEAKS is very traditional in its format.

"It's as old as the hills," he says. "Dickens books were serials. There's nothing new about the format, but the way we approach these characters and the way we tell these stories is certainly new."

Robert Engels, who began writing for the series with Episode 4, elaborates. "I think it is true that people who know soap operas take to this easily."

What makes TWIN PEAKS more than simply DYNASTY or DALLAS is not only the general weirdness that prevails in the town, but the hip, self-reflexive humor of the show which has served as a virtual bastion of pop culture history. The first season subtly offered an array of allusions including such obvious pairings as Ben (Horne) and Jerry (Horne) and the aliases of Barney and Fred taken by Cooper and Big Ed while undercover at One Eyed Jacks.

"Ben and Jerry's actually sent us ice cream," Frost laughs. "We would like them to actually in-

vent a TWIN PEAKS flavor that would benefit the fight to save the spotted owl with donut particles in there."

Other referential humor taken by some as keys to the resolution of the mystery were character names. Laura Palmer, whose identity was in doubt, had taken her name from the Gene Tierney movie of the same name, LAURA, and her virtually identical looking cousin (also played by Sheryl Lee) named Madeline Ferguson was derived from Kim Novak's name in VERTIGO and Ferguson was Jimmy Stewart's last name in the same film, a Hitchcockian psycho-thriller in which a murder perpetrated by a husband is covered up by a woman posing as his wife enticing Jimmy Stewart into being the perfect alibi. Later, after the woman's death, another woman appears who has a strange hold over him because of her striking resemblance to Madeline.

Even Cooper's supervisor, Gordon Cole (voiced by David Lynch first season and portrayed by him in the second), is taken from SUNSET BOULEVARD. ("Get Gordon Cole on the line," Cecil B. DeMille tells one of his production assistant's when Norma Desmond shows up on his sound stage at Paramount Studios.)

Most delectably, the over-zealous insurance agent in Episode 6 is Walter Neff, perhaps atoning for the sins of Fred McMurray who played that character in the film noire classic, DOUBLE INDEMNITY.

"We did layer it with a lot of different stuff," says Mark Frost, "and there were things that I thought people probably would never unearth. Some of the allusions to old pictures and things surfaced faster than I thought they would because the show was under more scrutiny than I ever thought it would be. It's fun for us to build the show in that way and I think it adds another layer of enjoyment."

"The four of us— David, Mark, Harley and myself— just kind of operate on that level," adds Story Editor Robert Engels. "We've all seen these kind of things and it just becomes a common ground but we don't really consciously try to play it out on different levels. We have a lot of leeway to tell our story. We have our own way of storytelling that makes it different and once again it's not as conscious at it seems."

TRUMAN: Anything we should be working on?

ALBERT: Yeah, you might practice walking without dragging your knuckles on the floor.

TRUMAN: Albert, let's talk about knuckles. The last time I knocked you down, I felt bad about it. The next time is going to be a real pleasure.

ALBERT: You listen to me while I will admit to a certain cynicism, the fact is I'm a naysayer and hatchetman in the fight against violence. I pride myself in taking a punch, and I'll gladly take another, because I chose to live my life in the company of Gahndi and King. My concerns are global. I reject absolutely: revenge, aggression, and retaliation. The foundation for such a method is love. I love you Sheriff Truman

Albert leaves.

COOPER: Albert's path is a strange and difficult one.

"You bust your butt to make sure the story works," says Engels. " If you don't have good stories, we can't have Albert tell Sheriff Truman he loves him and have it work." "They're incredibly well read and smart," says director Holland about the series producers. "They give all this stuff a great deal of thought. Everything is always referential or a homage right down to the name of the Mountie who is Preston King which comes from the radio show Sgt. Preston and his loyal dog King. They put a great deal of effort into weaving classic storylines throughout this and making it all payoff."

"When you're defining movies, REBEL WITHOUT A CAUSE and PALM BEACH STORY kind of define the range of our show," laughs Harley Peyton. "Bob (Engels) wrote a book about Preston Sturges and everyone around here is not only well versed in that stuff but loves it and I think that comes out in our work. The trick in writing a really great TWIN PEAKS scene is that it should have some very weird, tragic, odd dark twist in it that two beats later makes you laugh without going too far and dressing it up in something it doesn't deserve." The same philosophy that has allowed this hip, referential humor to predominate throughout the series and has given the show its "more than just a soap opera" reputation coupled with Lynch's already extolled position among the cinemaphile hierarchy has led

to equally intriguing casting in the past and some more provocative casting ideas in the future.

Richard Beymer and Russ Tamblyn, last seen together in WEST SIDE STORY, both are two of TWIN PEAKS most memorable residents. Peggy Lipton of MOD SQUAD fame enjoys newfound acclaim as the wise and respected proprietor of the Double R Diner and Piper Laurie has enjoyed even greater recognition in her Emmy Award nominated role as Catherine Martell, but some even more potentially interesting casting decisions await.

"You hear about people through the grapevine who really like the show and that enters into directing and casting, but for us the cameos are actors who don't really fit into the BATMAN mode," producer Peyton says alluding to the now infamous cameos offered by many '60s celebs anxious to share cowls with the Caped Crusader during the short lived Batman craze of nearly two decades ago.

"There was a chance that Clarence Williams would come in to read for something and I thought how great it would be to have Clarence and Peggy Lipton on the same show; kind of like having Russ and Richard Beymer on the same show. It's rarely a kind of obvious cameo and I think the closest we got to that was trying to get William S. Burroughs to be on the show."

The fact that the noted poet and scholar had wanted to work on the show attests of the power of PEAKS to cross over to a wide array of demographic groups.

"It was one of those grapevine things," Peyton says. "He loves the show and this and that and we were hoping he could play the mayor's brother but finally I don't think it was possible and that's one of the limitations of television. If we had the money to kind of fly down actors like you do with a feature we could get people like that but it's tough for us just to go out of town. It's a headache you can't afford."

Despite its popularity with the intelligentsia and general audiences alike, Peyton does not feel TWIN PEAKS is heir to the mantle of the show of the '90s. Rather he credits another popular television show with that distinction: THE SIMPSONS. Instead he feels TWIN PEAKS may escape the fate of other cult television shows because of its almost timeless setting. Despite the show being set in 1988, TWIN PEAKS seems like a town trapped in the '50s.

"It's not really informed by contemporary trends," Peyton says of PEAKS. "I don't think it will seem dated unless it gives birth to a lot of shows that try the same kind of storytelling and the audience gets tired of it after a while. MIAMI VICE was a show I liked a great deal when it was on but it's bound pretty particularly by a certain time and place and PEAKS has certain moments where you feel its set in 1955. It has this kind of weird timeless quality which, in fact, may be why people have that obsessive interest in the show that they do. It's great watching THE AVENGERS to see what Diana Rigg was wearing, the hippest in '60s fashion, but that dates it and we don't really have anything like that.

"I remember writing a line for Albert," Peyton says, "and it wasn't a particularly good line, but it was one of his jokes where he was referring to someone as a sort of two-bit Marcus Welby and the note that came back from David immediately is that they're not going to watch television like we would and they would never say that."

INVITATION TO LOVE

The residents of TWIN PEAKS do watch television. Only its not STAR TREK, THE SIMPSONS or JEOPARDY that they're watching, but INVITATION TO LOVE, a soap opera that seems to be broadcast in perpetual repeats. Only twice has anything else been seen on TWIN PEAKS television besides the ubiquitous soap and that was the news; once when Laura was killed, and once in the wake of the mill fire.

Mark Frost laughs about the soap within a serial. "It's their favorite show," he says. "It's on constant reruns. I think that watching television is a big part of people's lives in this country and you very rarely see that treated in television. We thought it would be kind of fun for the folks up there to have one favorite show that they were always tuning in for."

"Mark Frost directed all those and we had a great time doing it," Harley Peyton says of the INVITATION TO LOVE soap which once aired regularly on a TWIN PEAKS TV in your neigh-

borhood until being cancelled second season. "It's just so hard to try and get these stories straight and it finally became too much. At one point, we were toying with having the lead actors coming to town but we were really never able to go through with that. We shot a lot of that stuff but whenever we were looking to edit our shows down to running time, those INVITATION TO LOVE segments were always the first thing to go." Unlike the soap opera which has captivated the townsfolk, TWIN PEAKS has a depth and intelligence that eludes not only the average soap, but television as a medium in general. What it mimics in form, it masters in content.

"I don't think we've had a car chase yet," says Warren Frost. "The way Mark and David look at telling a story is different — and I think it's hard to put your finger on why it's different. It's still about people and about people who have problems and people who cause problems for themselves and for others and it's still about good and evil. There are no new ideas in terms of the story, it's just the way that the writer sees that. That's the difference between a hack and Faulkner, I guess."

TWIN PEAKS FORM

TWIN PEAKS director Holland agrees, "It is bold in all its plotting and supernatural elements.

"It challenges the viewers to embrace a whole rack of concepts including deep space messages about owls. I roll my eyes when I get the scripts, but it manages to all find a shape which is TWIN PEAKS. You're always amazed at each new turn. How are they going to pay this one off?"

TWIN PEAKS adherence to form and not formula intrigued actress Madchen Amick when she first read the script.

"When I read it, I knew it was something very different and very special," she recalls. "I knew David's reputation and so I knew the critics would like it, but I had no idea it would be this big although I thought the script was really incredible. I went in to read for Lara Flynn Boyle's part and David said 'no, Shelly.' At that point Shelly wasn't supposed to be a character. She was just going to be in the pilot to add a little color."

Deschanel, who directed one of the season's finest installments, was also attracted by the eclectic mix of genres.

"No one has ever seen anything like it before," he says. "It operates on a lot of different levels, the pure soap opera level where all the stories are intertwined, the relationships are very much like a soap, but on the other level there's a strangeness and a mystery that doesn't exist anywhere on television. There's also wonderful music, great actors and for people who are interested, there's a subtext that recalls old movies and other things that are part of people's culture and history. It's sort of the Bullwinkle Moose show of the '90s.

"It's sort of hard to picture David Lynch as a contemporary Jay Ward, but Deschanel's analogy seems particularly appropriate considering the many levels that the BULLWINKLE AND ROCKY show worked on. Imagine that, Ben Horne as a modern day Boris Badenov.

"It was a very hip show," he continues. "It would make references to the Brill Building in New York which was the big center of the music industry, but how would you know that if you were ten years old. It was just another one of the thousands of layers that made it appeal to so many different people."

FOCUS ON DIRECTORS

Deschanel agreed to shoot an episode after seeing the pilot. His wife, Mary Jo, stars in the series as Mrs. Hayward, Donna's mother, and the director jumped at the chance to participate despite his reservations about working for television. Both the technical and aesthetic considerations seemed daunting to one of filmdom's premiere visual stylists.

"I asked how much time I had and he said seven days and I was kind of shocked," he remembers. "I'd never directed anything that fast in my life but I thought it would be fun to try. In the end, you really end up relying on the actors. They make it possible to get it done. My prejudice against television had been alleviated by David having done the pilot and I thought if they could show something of this quality on television than my prejudice is not against the medium, but with

what's being presented now which is not very good. I don't think there's anything inherently wrong with it."

Despite television's reputation as a producer's medium as opposed to film which is known as a director's medium, TWIN PEAKS was very user friendly to its cast of behind-the-camera talent which director Lesli Linka Glatter says is not surprising.

"Mark and David are both directors and there's a real focus on the director," she says. "You see the piece all the way through."

"TWIN PEAKS is satisfying for feature people because they want a director who's willing to put in the time to bring his own vision to it and stick with it to the bitter end," adds Todd Holland. "They're all used to catering to what David wants and as a result the director is important there and you really do have influence and they expect you to be there through the entire post production process which is relatively unheard of in episodic television. Usually the producers take the show over, you get your three day cut and you're gone. When I worked on MAX HEADROOM they tried very hard to accommodate me in post-production, but the system didn't know how to keep me in that process. Here you go through it all; the film to tape and then the layback of the final mix onto videotape and you feel like its yours. They were very supportive of the things I wanted to do, and it wasn't recut after I left."

By allowing the director to remain in the post-production process, TWIN PEAKS benefits from their ability to work on their episodes long after principal photography is completed allowing for them to alter, edit and, hopefully, improve upon their initial rough cut.

Glatter, who shot Episode 4, was able to create one of the first season's finest scenes. In it, Sheriff Truman, Agent Cooper, Deputy Hawk and Doc Hayward discover the cabin of Jaques Renault where Laura went the night of her murder. The Julee Cruise song "Into The Night" plays on the soundtrack emanating from what we later find out is a turntable in the cabin and not simply a song laid in to score the scene. The imagery is effective as is the superb scene in which the four line up in one shot to face the house as they come upon it.

"What happened with that whole sequence is I put that together and put the music onto of it," says Glatter. "It was not something that was scripted nor was the raven looking over them when they're approaching the cabin. That came out in the editing process. I wanted a sense of an omen watching them. You're given a lot of leeway to go where you want. Basically what was written in the script during the dance sequence in that episode was Catherine starts to dance with Leland and I choreographed this totally queer movement and got to play with it."

One of the advantages first season was that when the episodes were shot, an air date had not been determined by ABC and as a result the directors were allowed to spend a greater amount of time refining their shows in post-production. "Things sort of came by osmosis," she adds. "We were in post forever. We also came on really early even though you're only paid for one week to work. Everyone started earlier on their episodes to get to know everyone, what the storyline was, working on script and preparing for the idea of having to shoot that fast which was quite horrifying and the only way to approach it was to be as prepared as you could."

"Seven days is seven days," says Producer Harley Peyton. "If you don't get a shot, you don't get a shot and that's where the reality of television intrudes. Fortunately because of the lengths of the scripts we were shooting four to five fewer scenes than most shows which allows us to concentrate and focus more and it's not as though we have to work on any big dance numbers every week. We've kept it fairly simple. It's usually a couple of people talking in the diner. Heaven forbid we ever have to do a big action sequence. We had a couple second season and they're an incredible pain in the ass. It's much better to do a kind of weird dream sequence."

In the series twelfth episode, aired second season, TWIN PEAKS had one of its most ambitious action scenes filled with gunplay and fisticuffs. When Cooper discovers that Jean Renault is holding the kidnapped Audrey Horne at One Eyed Jacks, he and Truman raid the brothel to rescue her. "It was very difficult," says director Graeme Clifford. "The producers knew going in this should've been an eight day show because it had more action than any of the previous episodes so they were worried about how we were going to do this in seven days."

When Cooper and Truman approach the building, they discover a guard patrolling the perimeter and disable him allowing them to proceed inside. "We were planning to go location to shoot all the exteriors of One Eyed Jacks," says Clifford. "Everything with them breaking in, overpowering the guard, breaking into Blackie's and Hank watching them escape as they come down the stairs was all going to be done on location, but we decided if we built all those exteriors on stage we could save time going to and from location. So we built the staircase and the hallways and created all the exterior shots on the sound stage, but even with that time savings it was still incredibly difficult to do in seven days. We did a little more overtime than usual and we got it done."

Peyton says that when the action isn't so dramatic the production crunch is alleviated by the slightly shorter nature of the scripts for the show. No, not because the credits seem to go on for ten minutes — they're actually four minutes and forty-five seconds—but because the average TWIN PEAKS script runs 38 to 42 pages as opposed to the usual dramatic hour whose scripts range from 56 to 60 pages.

"It's because of the way its stylized," he says, " and because so much of it is about dialogue and the pacing of the show. When I tell people in television they're amazed because they have 24 pages more than we do to put out. It's one of the reasons it's a little easier for us because you get to polish these little gems and take more time doing that. It's a real advantage to know you're only going to have to go 40 pages, 10 pages per act. The producers are all writers and, in certain instances, very fast writers so I think that's probably a good part of the show's strength and one of our secret weapons."

FIRST SEASON PACE

Even with the writer's aptitude for working quickly, the actors and directors don't often see their teleplays until only a few days before shooting and sometimes given even less time to look over the material. "The pages come out rather wet," says Miguel Ferrer. "I haven't had much prep time with the scripts, certainly enough, but never more than a couple of days. With this show it's really been right down to the wire." The writers benefit from the long and detailed outlines which are drawn up at the beginning of each season outlining the year's events in great detail so even with the large degree of creative freedom afforded to the directors, the writers who are responsible for seeing that all the pieces fit into an ever more confusing puzzle remain close to the blueprint which has been drawn leaving little room for embellishment.

"It was very detailed first season," says Producer Harley Peyton. "If there's a change you wanted to try you could try it but there's a pretty detailed blueprint to follow. There has to be so your teleplay fits in with all the other puzzle pieces."

Peyton points to one of TWINS most titillating cliffhangers, a story in which Agent Cooper returns to his reasonably priced room at the Great Northern to find an unclothed Audrey Horne in his bed as the credits begin to roll.

"You don't really have the option of saying I think I will have them sleep together," he says. "It really is a house of cards. In a way, I found that liberating only because I still find working on plots, as much as I do it now, a pain in the ass. I just love to write characters. I'm certainly more involved with structuring plots now though and thinking of ideas and watching them blossom is kind of fun."

"It's not written down anywhere but we talk about it at the beginning of each story cycle," says co-creator Mark Frost. He's speaking of fashioning the various interweaving storylines. He continues, "We don't try and etch them in stone because during the process of writing and developing a story some wonderful stuff can happen"

An example of TWIN PEAKS's twisted creative process giving birth to its own demented offspring was the day Ben Horne's brother, played by David Patrick Kelly, was born.

"Jerry just came out of the ether one day," Frost says. "We just said Ben has a brother...and he's different from Ben. Suddenly Jerry was born; he

was there in the room with us and he was obsessed with food. It's a strange thing in the creative process when the characters suddenly tell you about themselves and its a lot of fun when that happens. To me, Ben and Jerry are a kind of bizarro version of Jack and Bobby Kennedy." Executive Story Editor Robert Engels agrees that his initial outing on the series as a freelance assignment for Episode 4 was challenging and that the rigid story structure with its few allowances gave him even greater opportunity to explore the depth of the many characters.

"The more structured outline lets you have the most leeway," says Engels. "It can specifically say Hawk has a wonderful poem about love and it can be anything and its eight lines long and if you're tuned into that it's great. My recollections of that were that we were starting to gas the show up, trying to figure how these people are going to talk and see what the boundaries are. Like having Andy shooting the gun and Catherine finding the chip from One Eyed Jacks. When they were so new it was fun trying to get things right and finding that reality that we go so comfortable with eventually. Once you get the reality down, it gets easier. We were really concerned that four looked like three and three looked like two. You kept looking at the pilot. When you write for another show you can look at fifty episodes whereas with this there was nothing to go back to."

WRITING TWIN PEAKS

Since joining the show as Executive Story Editor, Engels has brought in several freelance writers to script TWIN PEAKS later installments. This allows the producers greater time to spend on other matters than scripting.

"We actually have found three real good writers that took to the show wonderfully," says Engels. "We walk them into TWIN PEAKS and let them get to know it and warm themselves to the town. It's a great relief that we've found these people because it would take even longer if we hadn't...I'd have a cot here. Without having people who know it you end up with a very lonely feeling when you're weekend is devoted to 48 pages. We're probably over the big hump in that there are now people familiar with the show even though it's an awfully tough show to write for."

"Every writer certainly gets a blueprint to follow and writing within that blueprint is really the fun of writing a TWIN PEAKS episode," adds Peyton. "The challenge is not so much in plotting but in the dialogue and in the presentation of character."

One constant thorn in the writers sides is that each episode of TWIN PEAKS represents a day as opposed to the week most viewers assume has passed between each episode. Many questions during the first summer hiatus seem silly in light of this. After all, in TWIN PEAKS time, Ronette Pulaski had only been in a coma for a week, Mike Nelson, Bobby's best friend, had only disappeared for a few days, and several of the dangling subplots didn't seem forgotten about, only slow to unfold.

"At one point we were talking about Lucy being pregnant," Peyton says. "We were joking that we would have to be in our fortieth season when she gave birth. We stuck to that pace that every episode is a day in TWIN PEAKS for a very long time. In that sense things we seem to have forgotten about are just a week and we haven't really forgotten."

Among the writer's many responsibilities on the show is acquainting themselves with a wealth of bizarre and obscure knowledge. "All the stuff about Tibet is factual," says Peyton referring to the country that FBI Agent Cooper is so fond of. Cooper displays a spiritual wisdom gained from that country that you would have never found in Robert Stack. "I have my ancient Tibet book on my desk. My brother- in-law is a doctor, so particularly for the early shows when everyone was in the hospital, I found myself getting on the horn to him frequently. In one episode, we needed the name of a fly fishing lure and we wanted to find the weirdest, but one that actually existed. There were some fishing stores in the Northwest getting some weird phone calls for a while. You do little things like that."

One of first season's most memorable images will remain in the iconographical landscape of '90s television long after TWIN PEAKS has faded from memory. In Audrey's audition at One Eyed Jack, she deposits a cherry in her mouth and ties the stem with her tongue and plucks it out of her mouth and deposits it on the desk of the brothel's madame, Blackie O'Reilly.

"A friend of mine performs it," says Peyton. "That's the great thing about writing for television. Something happens at dinner over the weekend and suddenly it's on the screen in a month. You really are allowed to take things you see on a daily basis and put them in your work. It's a lot of fun and the cherry stem is a perfect example. As a writer, it never ceases to amaze me that you write about someone tying a knot with a cherry stem and you still read about it in articles six months later. That's a nice kind of thing to get used to. It's gratifying and certainly one of the things that helped keep us on the air."

TWIN PEAKS MANIA

As the momentum built, TWIN PEAKS mania raged. "I couldn't pick up a newspaper without seeing something about TWIN PEAKS," says director Graeme Clifford. "I thought it was unbelievable. I thought that if it became obsessive and excessive, it was actually going to hurt the show. Once there's that much written about it, the people who are going to watch for the first time are going to say, 'Yeah, that was good, but not that good.'"

TWIN PEAKS parties became the rage as grown adults showed up costumed as their favorite characters eating donuts and drinking coffee. Restaurants paid homage to the fad by incorporating TWIN PEAKS motifs into their decor.

At Mike's American Bar & Grill on Tenth Avenue in New York, the entire establishment was covered in PEAKS paraphernalia. Laura Palmer wrapped in plastic could be found hanging from the ceiling and donuts adorned the walls along with Laura's picture, a chalkboard with the names of the murder suspects and a sign at the door proclaiming, "Welcome To Twin Peaks."

One of the producers of the feature film TUNE IN TOMORROW, starring Peter Falk and Barbara Hershey, recalls that during a test screening of the film, half the audience ran out in the middle. Turning to one of his associates for consolation fearing he had a bomb on his hands, he was told, "Don't worry, they're only rushing home to see TWIN PEAKS."

Even the venerable SATURDAY NIGHT LIVE got into the act. For the show's season premiere, Kyle MacLachlan hosted and starred in an outrageous TWIN PEAKS spoof in which Leo is apprehended as Laura's murderer.

"It was very good," says Producer Harley Peyton. "Kyle was a great host. I liked what they did. When we get ribbing, it's fairly affectionate."

In the skit, Leo confesses to Laura's murder. It is a hilarious spoof on the slow-going investigation of Laura's murder which insists that Cooper doesn't want to find her murderer so he can stay in town.

COOPER: Tonight Harry, you and I are going to do a little spelunking.

LEO: I'm ready to do my time, get me a beer.

COOPER: Harry, this certainly puts him high on the list of suspects. See that he doesn't leave town.

LELAND: Special Agent Cooper, I want to thank you for finding the man who killed my daughter Laura. Now that it's all over, I'm going to miss you. Dance with me, dance with me!

COOPER: Leland, I'm afraid your celebration may be a bit premature. Laura's killer is still at large.

LELAND: What?!? Oh, ahhhhhhhhhhhhhhhhhhhhhhhh!

TRUMAN: Cooper, why did you say that. Leland was just starting to make a recovery.

COOPER: Don't worry about Leland. His dancing is actually getting quite good.

When Audrey enters she gives Cooper a farewell present and ties a piece of string into a bow with her tongue and hands it to Cooper. Cooper asks if she's gotten any new leads while Leo shows pictures to the Sheriff of him killing Laura. Cooper is still not convinced.

COOPER: Harry, tonight we'll stake out the graveyard disguised as altar boys.

TRUMAN: No, no we won't and I'll tell you why. The crime has been solved. Leo has confessed.

COOPER: Harry, I've got it. I'll throw this rock at the window. If it breaks, Leo is innocent...(of course, the window breaks). Leo, you're free to go.

The skit ends as Truman takes Leo away in cuffs. Cooper desperately tries to get them to stay.

COOPER: Wait! Maybe Leo did kill Laura Palmer, but we still haven't figured out who shot me.

LEO: I did...geez, you saw me!

As the media pondered TWIN PEAKS future, the producers began to considered future plans for the show. Not surprisingly, word came down from ABC that the series had been picked up for the fall. TWIN PEAKS would live even if Laura Palmer didn't.

"We had a fair amount worked out," Mark Frost says about the plans at the end of the first season. "As soon as we got officially renewed we started writing like crazy."

44

CHAPTER THREE:

Second Season— "The Owls Are Not What They Seem"

The seven episodes of the first season became a hot topic of national discussion. All summer people questioned the meaning of Cooper's dream featuring the dancing midget, what the R underneath Laura's fingernail meant, who was the father of Lucy's baby, what was the evil in the woods, what the heck 'Fire, walk with me' meant, and whether Laura slept with Ben Horne. If the mystery of Laura Palmer's murder wasn't enough to keep viewers hooked, there was now the equally intriguing mystery of who shot Agent Cooper...and whether he would survive into season two.

"We were poking a little bit of fun at the 'Who Shot J.R.?' syndrome," says co-creator Mark Frost. "He was on an undercover assignment so, of course, he was wearing a bulletproof vest. He's an FBI agent. I wasn't trying to present it as a mystery; it was just where the story stopped at the moment. It was the end of the chapter."

For still bored cocktail partiers, there were other questions: whether Leo was really dead, Nadine successful in her suicide attempt, Pete, Catherine and Shelly Johnson killed in the fire at the mill, and whether the sleazy Jaques Renault was truly dispatched by Leland Palmer.

"Walter Olkewicz, who played Jaques Renault, was suffocated to death in the last episode," explains director Caleb Deschanel. "He was talking to David at the wrap party at the end of filming the first season and David said see you next year. Walter said he was just killed in the last episode and wouldn't be coming back and David said, 'Oh yeah, well there are always dream sequences.'"

Peyton laughs at Deschanel's anecdote. "We're kindhearted here," he says. "We never want to kill off a friend. I think there'll be more deaths in the future. You have to start killing off people; you have too many to deal with. There are certain characters you never want to kill off. Even with all the exposure the actors are getting, its inevitable that we'll start to lose characters based on what's going on with their careers. There was a soap opera where the actor had to be kidnapped and off the show every summer because it was in his contract that he could do summer stock and so every spring his storyline would end with him being kidnapped or in a coma until the fall. Any serial is not that far from those problems and I'm sure we'll get to that point too."

Surprisingly, the cloak of secrecy which shrouds TWIN PEAKS has even extended to actors not knowing when their characters are going to be knocked off. In Episode 5 of the second season, Jean Renault, the vengeful brother of Jaques and Bernard played splendidly by Michael Parks, plunges a knife into Blackie O'Reilly, the madame of One Eyed Jacks.

Tom Holland directed Episode 4, one episode before she was killed. He recalls, "Victoria Caitlin, who plays Blackie, said to me, 'I don't die, do I?' I had read ahead to Episode 5 and I just sort of winced when she asked me. My face turned white; I didn't know what to say. She got really upset because she was having fun on the show and I said 'I'm sorry, I feel like the Grim Reaper'.

Holland continues, "I would have been more clever if I had been prepared for it. I assumed she knew. People are dying right and left and they don't know until they crank open their script. It's a little like the hand of fate. No one takes them aside and says, 'Sorry, you're dying this week.'"

TOO MANY PLAYERS

Even with the fates that befall many of the townsfolk, the writers still face a daunting task. Not only did new characters arise to take the place of the deceased almost as quickly as they were ousted from the show, but all of the cast, with the exception of the late lamented Jaques Renault, returned. They had not all weathered adversity well.

Nadine Hurley awoke from her coma thinking she was still in high school and now possessed superhuman strength. Pete Martell suffered from severe smoke inhalation. Wife-beater Leo was a mental vegetable carted around by Shelly, who had survived her own brush with death. Even Catherine was back, disguised as a Japanese businessman, Mr. Tajimora, to avenge herself on the treacherous Ben Horne.

TOO LITTLE TIME

Cast considerations aside, the producers faced a potentially insurmountable problem. In seven episodes they had created a show unique in the annals of television history.

Inevitably, the sophomore year would be compared to the first. It would have to expand upon the virgin territory explored in the show's ground-breaking season. In addition, the leisurely pace at which the show's first seven episodes were meticulously assembled would be only a fond memory. The second year would require a full year's worth of programming allowing little room for refinement. The new pace would prove fast and furious.

"Obviously it's a trend-setting program," says actor Warren Frost. "They're attempting to do something that's a cut above. It's very difficult to churn it out week in and week out. It's possible to write a darn good script and do a good show, but to repeat it 22 more times is a big order."

His boss, and son, Mark Frost elaborates, "We're under a little bit more time pressure second season and it's going to be more difficult to do 22 hours than seven. It's a concern, but on the other hand, we also have more people on the staff this year. We've got a better producing staff and there are more people able to work on the show and we know how to do the show a little bit better. We're trying to not let down what to us is the fun and quality of the show and that's the intricacies of the stories and the strange twists and turns that we take with the characters and plots."

"He only works about 18 hours a day," laughs Frost's father. "Maintaining the show is the hardest thing to do. Once you've found the holy grail or whatever it is in television, to be able to maintain the luster is mind-boggling."

"Mark says it's kind of like marathon running," says Robert Engels of Frost's comparison of the show to a 22 episode run. "You have to be in shape for it. You have to know there are going to be periods when it seems harder and periods when it goes longer and it's a blast. We're so unique and our franchise is to stay that way."

TIMESLOT TROUBLES

Another potential hurdle facing the show's producers was ABC's decision to remove PEAKS from its time slot on Thursday nights and move it to Saturday evenings, the least-watched television night of the week. Given the weak lead-in of CHINA BEACH, the gamble seemed a risky one at best. Early ratings seemed to bear the naysayers right. Although the demographic groups the network most coveted were tuning in, the show's ratings were mediocre. Considering the press the show had garnered during the off-season, it had to be considered a disappointment although the shows producers, including Robert Engels, don't see it that way.

"I feel people will come to trust that hour on Saturday and what it's going to be," Engels says. "It's just a weird thing. You can't look at the ratings and tell who's watching. We're going to keep working as hard as we can and say here it is, hope you guys like this. There's always the reaction that we're so quirky or this or that people will think we're doing weird things to be weird, and we really don't. My feeling is there is nothing we can do about the ratings as long as we're not saying we're *so hip* and making fun of the audience."

"I think it was actually a very good idea," Mark Frost says of the change in time slots. "Everybody says Saturday night is a wasteland, and that nobody's home watching television. Yet the research all indicates there are millions of people home watching cable and renting movies. I know my generation is getting too tried to go out on Saturday nights, because we're all having babies and sleeping in and getting kind of lazy. So there's no rule that says people can't watch television on Saturdays.

"It wasn't that long ago that Saturday was the night of MARY TYLER MOORE and ALL IN THE FAMILY and BOB NEWHART, and that was the most-watched night of the week."

AFTER LAURA PALMER

Another issue facing the show's creative team was whether the fizz in TWIN PEAKS would die out once the Laura Palmer murder was solved. Would viewers lose interest once her killer was

apprehended? Alternatively, could the mystery go on forever without alienating the audience? The mystery had taken on a life of its own beyond the show. Even people who had never watched an episode knew who Laura Palmer was and that her killer was still at large.

"The snowballing of the mystery was something we couldn't do much about," says Engels. "We had decided how we were going to resolve our story. I'm sure there were people who thought we were a bunch a bozos when they saw it though, but I think it was a good resolution, pretty wonderful. After we plotted out the first seven and the pick-up came for second season, we again began to solve it and pretty quickly decided to continue where we were going. It wasn't so much that we didn't want to reveal the murderer as people would have been disappointed if it had been a 'book 'em Danno', which required us to do what we did over the course of several episodes."

With a season full of plot twists ahead of them, the producers laid out the framework for the storylines beyond the resolution of the Laura Palmer mystery.

"We sat down before this season and started throwing ideas back and forth about possible directions to take characters," says Harley Peyton. "It was a pleasure to contribute to that, watching the ones that stuck to the wall and watching them develop. We all have our notebooks full of scripts, but Mark somehow miraculously keeps the whole thing in his head. What we don't remember, we can figure out in terms of what's come before.

"There's a woman who works in the wardrobe department who specializes in what the day and the date is. None of us can ever figure that out, but she knows that if Laura was killed on a Thursday, then today is Wednesday and all that kind of stuff."

"Planning helps when things go right," adds Robert Engels. "If no one gets sick and no one gets hurt and all the scripts come in good you would never have to vary. All you need is for something to go wrong or someone to get hurt and those plans pretty much go right out the chute."

Engels knew from his days on the show WISEGUY that unforeseen circumstances could often throw even tightly plotted storylines into turmoil. Such was the case with WISEGUY's own TWIN PEAKS-like story arc about a company town in Washington run by a bizarre family patriarch obsessed with the William Castle anticlassic, MR. SARDONICUS. During shooting, Ken Wahl, the series star, was injured, bringing production to a halt.

"We had it all planned out until Ken Wahl got hurt," explains Engels. "Then we had nothing. We did the best we could. We had well made plans and somehow they stopped and then you ask who's still left in the story. That's when Roger Laccoco came out of nowhere. Here we've pretty much been able to proceed at what we set out to do. There are broad strokes we've always stuck to and then there are lesser things which are delightful surprises which we've followed down the road. We do some of that and it's essential because you'll get a wonderful actor that everybody loves and you say this guy is so swell how can we make him or her last longer?"

Despite the meticulous planning even TWIN PEAKS was not free of its own small calamities. As season two went into production, Sherilyn Fenn, who plays Audrey, came down with pneumonia.

"It looked like it could give us some really serious problems," recalls Harley Peyton. "It turned out all right. She was tremendous and recovered rather quickly and came back sooner than she had to. We had different directors shooting each day and two directors shooting in a single day and, in fact, got all of her scenes done."

TIME AND MONEY

The other problems that the show encountered early on in its sophomore year were dilemmas which typify television production regardless of content or merit.

"You learn pretty early on about time and money constraints," says Peyton. "You can't write a scene in a football stadium. Both Mark and David are very good and if it comes down to a money question versus the quality of the show, the quality of the show wins. Usually those arguments are over little things like why we can't bring in another actor for an episode because we'll be x amount over our budget, but usually the good of the show is what comes first. We do pretty well and Greg Feinberg, the supervising producer, does an amazing job to balance all that stuff. Of course, there are always going to be times when you wish you could do more exteriors or location stuff. There are times when you see things where you would like to make improvements, but that's part of it. Unlike a feature, where you can go back and reshoot and change something, in television you have to let go and move on."

Not surprising it is the directors and not the writers who have the toughest time dealing with problems inherent in a rapid pace. Having hired all feature directors with little or no background in episodic television, the coterie of ambitious auteurs had little experience working at the brisk pace a television shoot demands.

"You have a production meeting and you start shooting," says Todd Holland. "You have your seven day schedule and its fast and furious and most of the directors were grumbling they needed that eighth day but you find a way to make it work in seven. You pick the places that are important to you where you want to spend time and the rest you fly through and get in a master shot."

Most of the first season directors returned to repeat their directing chores for the second, alleviating a lot of the problems. This allowed the writers freedom to realize that their work would be brought to the screen by talented and capable artists who would not destroy it.

"Coming back the second time they can say 'let's do this' and it's really healthy," says Robert Engels. "You know you're in such good hands you don't have to couch how you write. You don't have to write defensively. The directors get what you're writing and bring things to it that you've never dreamed of and make it look like aces."

"You're given seven days to prep it," says Caleb Deschanel. "During the second year I found that was more than enough time. The most important thing is knowing all the scripts that come before you and where the characters fit in. Each episode does not operate independently; they're all dependent on what comes before. I'm a director of a television show and you accept those limitations. You realize the weight of the show is really on the characters and getting across the subtext as best you can. The words are on the page and as you go through a scene you realize there's all sorts of subtext. What you focus on when you're trying to shoot a scene is the same thing the actor studies in terms of the beats. You don't use grand visual elements to tell the story. To a limited extent you get to use visual images and sound, but most of the time is taken up with dialogue.

"You learn there are complicated things you can't do," he continues. "You have to study each scene and get to the heart of it and know what you want to get across. The biggest thing you can't do is allow something to reach its own resolution by rehearsing. You have to dictate where people are going to go and what they're going to do which is the unfortunate aspect of the schedule. It doesn't give actors freedom to find their character and what they would do in the scene in relation to the other characters. Hopefully, if you made the right choices and if the actors are comfortable with the way you think things should be played, it will work."

"Caleb knows exactly what he wants," says Harley Peyton commenting on the director's work on the show. "He is tremendous. He has a great attitude and the cast loves to work with him. He is relaxed, but very firm about getting what he wants. His manner is such that everyone feels very at ease with him. It's great to watch his dailies because he's very economical in the way he shoots. He doesn't shoot a frame longer than he needs. Most people will do the take and remove what they need, but with Caleb you can almost see him cutting in the camera."

RETURNING HOME

"It's like coming home," says Lesli Linka Glatter, who also returned to direct during the show's second season. "It's a terrific crew and the cast is a joy to work with. The shooting schedule was the same, but everything is moving quicker because you know it's going to be on the air in a month and it's sped up by three so you just sort of hopped on this train and were just on it."

"The first year we would go long hours," says Deschanel. "The second they've tried to keep it down to twelve hour days. After the shoot, I work with the editors and decide what takes we like and we start to put it together and I sort of come and go, but the directors are allowed to finish it. When I did Episode 6, it was finished exactly the way I wanted it except for adding one thing back in which I didn't think we had time for. It was the scene in the hallway of the Great Northern with Audrey walking down the hall and an Oriental gentleman entering his room. It's one of those things you can do in the show that doesn't seem to have any significance but is textural and contributes to the show. It's a mysterious moment that makes you wonder: What does it mean?"

As fans examined the earlier episodes under a microscope and foes waited for PEAKS to burn out in the hot spotlights of its own lofty intentions, the producers began the second season with a bang. Under the direction of David Lynch, the two hour season premiere aired on September 30th, 1990. It would prove an important indicator for how the series would unfold in the year to come.

"We wanted to make sure we came out of the box as brilliant as we possibly could be," says Bob Engels. "That way as the production monster ate up our momentum you can deal with it when the next episodes become a blur."

Lynch's first installment unfolded slowly. The film's opening scene in which Cooper is discovered lying in a pool of blood by a senile room service waiter clocked in at almost ten minutes...and felt like an eternity. By the time the episode's disturbing climax exploded onto the screen as Bob, the killer, attacks Ronette and Laura in the train car, it had seemed like the phenomena had lost its momentum. Only the character moments really seemed to work; Big Ed explaining how his wife lost her eye while a wisecracking Albert Rosenfield looks on barely able to contain a guffaw and, in one scene, MacLachlan is just terrific interrogating a bedridden Ronette Pulaski who has just awoken from her coma. Even as she lapses into paranoid hysterics, Cooper just keeps prodding, 'Was there anyone else in the train car?' in monotone."

Unfortunately, the premiere's biggest drawback was its compulsive need to try and explain everything that had happened previously. PEAKS always assumed its audience was cogent enough to know what was going on without retreading on old ground, but in the premiere Lynch employs some very traditional flashback techniques to bring the audience up to speed.

"It had to start all those engines again," says Harley Peyton. "It was a real difficult one to write and direct. We were trying to get all that information out there. It's almost less for new viewers than for us in starting all those new stories so even if we left one of those stories out in the second episode it got us going with a kickoff for the third and the stuff in the train car is just very disturbing imagery."

RETURNING CAST

Frank Silva portrays Killer Bob, the wild-eyed, long haired psycho menace featured in the show's climax and integral to the resolution of the Laura Palmer storyline. In keeping with the show's eccentric nature, Silva was discovered not by casting director Johanna Ray, but by director David Lynch during the filming of the PEAKS pilot. Rather than being on the set as an extra, Silva was in actuality the series prop man and was noticed by Lynch while rearranging set dressing in Laura Palmer's room. Struck immediately by his appearance, Lynch recruited Silva to play Bob in the series ever-growing cast of characters. Only in Hollywood.

Also returning to the show well equipped with witticisms for another year was Albert Rosenfield. Reintroduced in the premiere, Miguel Ferrer reprised his role as the sarcastic urbanite in the backwards, country town.

"It's amazing how three scenes last season have made them willing to bring me back," says Ferrer. "It's a thrill for me. Mark sent me a very nice letter after my last episode last year. He said if we got our pick-up we're certainly going to want you back because we love what you do. I said to myself that's nice and forgot about it because talk is cheap. Isn't it?

"So I was thrilled when they brought him back," he continues. "The response to Albert was more than any of us anticipated. I was recognized and spoken to on the street moreso than any time since ROBOCOP from three scenes in a television show. That's unheard of and I've done more than 40 episodics and nobody has ever come up to me and said anything. I'd be walking down the street and people would yell from cars, 'Hey, who killed Laura Palmer?'"

NEW FACES

Holland was recruited for the show's second season and was impressed with the atmosphere on the TWIN PEAKS set. Despite all the attention and acclaim the show had garnered, both cast and crew remained extremely level-headed about the phenomena.

"They're all great," says Holland. "It's like a college environment, sort of like living in a dormitory. They all have a a great time together. They get along like college buddies and have a real repartee. It was more pronounced when I came aboard during Episode 4 because they were up for their Emmys and everyone was sharp and fresh and into the season having a good time. Later on the grind of the episodic machine wore on them a little bit because it is a big deal to turn out 22 episodes of television."

"It is fun," agrees Lesli Linka Glatter. "When you're working with really terrific people and you've got really good material, as hard as it is, it is really fun."

Holland, a friend of Glatter's from their days working on Steven Spielberg's AMAZING STORIES, owes his involvement on TWIN PEAKS to her intervention.

"Lesli and I met on AMAZING STORIES and our careers kind of tracked," Holland says. "She went on to do HBO's VIETNAM WAR STORIES and recommended me there and I followed her to that show and then she recommended me to Mark and David when she got to TWIN PEAKS. Johanna Ray casts the show and also cast AMAZING STORIES. She was a big fan and that with Lesli's recommendation led to me being interviewed by Mark and then I met David the same day on the set where he was shooting the premiere and I was hired to direct the fourth episode of the second season."

In preparing to direct his first episode, Holland, who most recently directed THE WIZARD starring Fred Savage, went back and reviewed the show's entire storyline. "I watched all the tapes that existed," he says. "Then I outlined all the scripts to get up to speed and went to what is called a concept meeting. At the meeting, you talk about the script and the tone of each scene and what it means and I asked a ton of very pointed questions that really tracked the mystery in a way that's hard to do when you just watch. Mark revealed a ton of secrets, which I was told was unusual. It was because I came to the door organized with a lot of homework so he told me a lot of backstory with characters that helped me a great deal."

Holland has been excited at the chance to meet many of the other directors who have worked on the show. "I had the best time of my life on AMAZING STORIES and its been very similar on TWIN PEAKS. Now I've met Tim Hunter, Duwayne Dunham and Caleb and on AMAZING I met directors like Tom Holland, Paul Bartel, Steven Spielberg and a whole smorgasbord of names, and that's fun. I had come right out of film school and it was the most wonderful finishing school you could imagine. It was slow enough that it didn't freak me out and the people were just the most gracious. They had to teach me how long lunch lasts on a union crew and all the production realities in the real world that you don't learn in film school."

"He would be our one young turk," Harley Peyton laughs.

Holland is one of the only directors on the show to come out of film school. This is very unlike Steven Spielberg's AMAZING STORIES, where the directing roster was mainly comprised of established talent like Robert Zemeckis and a host of California film school students, "the film brats" as they're called in the business.

"The nice part about TWIN PEAKS for me is that it's all designed," says Holland. "Episode 4 had no locations, which was daunting at first. I loved it in the end because it gave a lot more flexibility on a seven day schedule. I was able to walk fully dressed and designed sets and design scenes which were both efficient and elegant of which 50% was scrapped once you get there with the actors. With a feature film you have to design it all so you can't be on the sets; they're not all dressed and waiting for you. It was a real luxury to have the space to walk through."

One of the elements that Holland was able to incorporate into his episode was an ominous thunderstorm in the town which was added to the last twenty minutes of the episode as a result of his input into the story.

"I spent time coming up with approaches to the material like the thunderstorm," he says. "Leland confesses to murder (of Jaques Renault) and I convinced them to add the storm because it would reveal the Oriental man watching Josie and Truman while they're making love and enhance the fight between Hank and him at the end. It would be a wonderful addition. Of course, rain is a difficult production reality and on a short schedule its the first thing that gets dumped, but it hadn't rained in TWIN PEAKS in a long time."

Holland was also determined to make new use of the extensive library of stock footage at his disposal. Shots like that of the exterior of the Great Northern and the changing traffic light were familiar to the audience. They were originally filmed by Lynch for the pilot in Snoqualmie, Washington and frequently utilized in the course of the series.

"The footage was all very TWIN PEAKS and it was great fun to use it," says Holland. "I kind of keyed into all the stuff. I come from a real small town in Pennsylvania so I liked the traffic light a lot and I wanted to take it and rotoscope sheet lightning behind it and use a familiar image in an unfamiliar way since I had the storm but there wasn't enough money to do that so I made my own attempt to use it. Instead, I used the daytime traffic light which had never been used before. I really relate to that image and being a fan of the show there was a thrill in using those icons. I poured through the stock footage trying to find new images which you hadn't seen. There's a choice between the icons that have value because they're cliches now and a limited amount of footage which was shot for the pilot which was story specific. They had footage of the front drive of the Great Northern which is something you don't see often, but everyone had gotten to know the hotel as the waterfall side so using the unfamiliar side of the building was something I wasn't interested in."

One of the aspects of the show which also appealed to director Graeme Clifford who directed his first episode second season, was the opportunity to work with the writers in refining the material. Clifford never worked with Barry Pullman who had written the early drafts of his episodes, but rather the producers in devising his episode's chilling conclusion.

"I had a considerable amount of input on the screenplay which is unusual from a director's viewpoint on episodic television," Clifford says. "That tends to make you want to go back and do another one and makes you forget about the fact that it is television."

Originally at the end of his episode, Harold Smith catches Madeline trying to steal the secret Laura Palmer diary and raises a vase over his head to stop her from leaving. With input from Clifford, the ending was changed. "I thought that Harold, being this sort of introverted, closeted person, would take real anger out on himself. So I suggested he should pick up one of his gardening tools and just when you though he was going to attack one of the girls with it, he drags it down the side of his face. To me, that is much more horrible and gives greater insight into the man's persona and his problems. It fit in quite well eventually because since then he's hung himself."

LYNCH IN FRONT OF THE CAMERAS

Joining the ever-growing cast of characters inhabiting the town of TWIN PEAKS was a new visitor, Agent Cooper's FBI director Gordon Cole. The role is played by his creator, David Lynch. In the episode directed by Lesli Linka Glatter, a hearing impaired man in a trenchcoat arrives in town looking for Sheriff Truman.

Glatter says, "I thought David was terrific in it. I was on his set one day because I love watching him work and he was joking around with me and said there was a wonderful actor who was going to be in show 6 and that I really should direct it since it hadn't been decided which episode I was going to direct at that point. I asked him who was coming in and he started laughing and said it was

him. I immediately said, 'absolutely, I wouldn't pass that up in a billion years' and he explained what his character was about and I said, 'this is going to be a riot.'"

In shooting that episode, one of the season's best installments, Glatter benefitted from the willingness of the cast to put in extra time to rehearse scenes not allowed by the confining shooting schedule.

"You call them up at home and say, 'can we meet and go through a scene for an hour,'" she says. "They're not getting paid for that but are more than willing to do it. They want to do it, which is terrific. I want to leave it open for something magical to happen but because you're moving so fast you have to go in with a very clear plan."

Glatter roped in Joan Chen, who plays Josie Packard, and Richard Beymer to rehearse a scene. In it Packard, who has to leave for Hong Kong the next morning or risk seeing Sheriff Truman killed, confronts Benjamin Horne demanding the money she is owed for signing over the Packard Saw Mill lands to him. He plans to build the Ghostwood Country Club and Estates on them.

"I love working with Joan Chen and we had three scenes together in thirteen," she says. "One of the things that had been going on with her character, for me, is she had started to become this dragon woman and I had three scenes where I wanted to play it at different levels. I wanted to show that she had been manipulated, that she's not in control of her situation and that she really is in love with Sheriff Truman and can't do anything about it. We wanted to bring some of that stuff out and I feel we did.

"They have this whole scene that he has a safety deposit box and a lot of that came out of just getting together and working on it," she adds. "We got together and rehearsed and things started to happen that you could have never thought of in a room alone, and that's kind of exciting. The scene was written quite seriously and there was this moment when we were rehearsing where she started laughing and then Richard started laughing too. It was just great, a wonderful accident. One of the challenges is you have to make this interesting, but practical and its tough because the time is so short. If you had more time everyone feels they would do it differently, but you don't. You always feel like you're pushing the edge of the envelope. If you can get five or ten more minutes, you're going to go for it. If they'd give me five more hours, I would take it happily."

HOLDOVER SCENES

One of the advantages of the shows serialized format is that scenes trimmed from one episode due to time limitations can often find their way into another and still have great relevance to the story.

"If we're too long we'll try and find a place to put it in the next episode," says Bob Engels. "That's one of the great things about an arc with converging plotlines. You can delay it another ten minutes. Whether its the 55th or 88th minute, you can always move it as long as you keep the drama going. Ultimately it helps because it helps you to go into the next episode. You keep sliding things forward or backwards as may be the case."

Sometimes scenes never make it in. Madchen Amick has found many of her scenes with Norma at the diner left on the cutting room floor.

"I had lots of scenes with Norma about how I'm living the life that she lived and how we were both in the same situation," she says. "We both had married bad guys and were in love with this other guy. She was a best friend in sort of a motherly way. There's a scene where I came in and brought the gun which I was going to shoot Leo with and she saw it in my purse and warned me to watch it."

A scene that did make it back into an episode was when Shelly is forced to quit her job at the diner in order to take care of Leo. The previous week, Shelly told Bobby she had to quit her job at the diner and the following episode she is seen actually telling Norma she is going to quit. A scene featuring James Hurley's much talked about alcoholic mom has become a running joke on the show.

"We always laugh that we can always just throw that scene in when we're running short on an episode," Peyton says. "It was a scene Tim Hunter shot and Bob Engels wrote that was cut twice

since we've tried to use it. We had a story about James' mother which I'm sure we'll get to at some point."

"I had to drop it because of time," says Glatter, who was going to add the scene to one of her episodes early second season. "It also didn't make any sense because too much had happened on the show since it was shot. It's unfortunate because the actress did a great job and it was a wonderful scene."

Many scenes are dropped even before they're shot because of expense. Sometimes a scene can be filmed and not used because of something as simple as the performance of the guest actor or technical problems.

"I did a whole scene in Episode 3 where Cooper goes to the graveyard where Laura Palmer is buried," says Harley Peyton. "I had written it with an old caretaker who gives a very long and rambling speech that if you put your ear to the ground you can hear them singing beneath the sod because the wood in the casket expands. At the time, it was my favorite thing that I had written, but as is often the case, you're talking about a day player and it's hard to get people to do that stuff. When the person came in and didn't work out, that scene was cut."

Another aspect of the show that Peaks Freaks never saw was the promised introductory episode Mark Frost had touted throughout the summer. The show, which would be removed from the series, would recap the first seven episodes and lead into the new season on the Saturday before the premiere. It never materialized. What aired instead was a dreadful promotional program the network put together touting the return of TWIN PEAKS and a segment on the creation of the greatly hyped (and now cancelled) COP ROCK. The show was hosted by Alan Thicke.

"ABC wanted to know if we could do it and if we would do it," says Peyton. "Production reasons made it impossible. Thank god we didn't. It would have been a production nightmare although we would have loved to have done it because no one had ever done it before and it would have been completely different. Among the different ideas we were talking about was an hour of the cable access station in TWIN PEAKS."

CHAPTER FOUR:

The Cast—
"I Hate Cherry Pie...really"

It was Lara Flynn Boyle, star of the awful POLTERGEIST III and the even worse HOW I GOT INTO COLLEGE, who plays the straitlaced Donna Hayward who told ROLLING STONE she hates cherry pie, but she does love Special Agent Dale Cooper. Romantically linked to the jut-jawed FBI agent of TWIN PEAKS, Kyle MacLachlan, the two are Hollywood's hottest couple even if it's Audrey Horne who lights his fire when he's on duty.

Speaking of fires, Sherilyn Fenn practically ignited the nation with an arousing PLAYBOY pictorial in the December 1990 issue of the men's monthly. It wasn't the first time either. The last time TWIN PEAKS saddle shoed vixen cavorted in her birthday suit was in an otherwise forgettable film called TWO MOON JUNCTION directed by Zalman King. He managed to drench the heat of Mickey Rourke and the stunning Carrie Otis in the allegedly erotic adventure WILD ORCHID.

"They offered me a great deal of money," Fenn told ROLLING STONE about her PLAYBOY layout. "The pictures look like paintings." Actually, they look more like someone looking to be the next Marilyn Monroe echoing the poses in the Kirkland photographs of the late lamented sex goddess who continues to capture the imaginations of post-pubescent males everywhere.

"In the scene where Sherilyn Fenn is supposed to be drugged with heroin while she's being held for ransom I wanted her to look pretty beaten up," says Todd Holland who directed her. "She wanted to look a little better. I told her 'no, you're America's sweetheart, your America's favorite character' and finally she said 'alright, alright.' She's one of my favorite characters because you thought she was such a big slut and she's probably the most moralistic person in TWIN PEAKS and that's all tremendous fun. The ones like her father feign morality and are incredibly treacherous, but they carry on a good business front."

No doubt long after Fenn's pictorial has vanished from newsstands, images of the lovely lass in her One Eyed Jacks lingerie will linger on.

"It's a funny little place," Harley Peyton says of the brothel owned by Ben Horne. "One Eyed Jacks becomes kind of a paradigm for a particular variety of sin that you can play out in certain stories in a certain location. I suppose in a film critic way you can talk about it as a metaphor for a lot of things, that it's the place where all young girls go sooner or later...certainly Laura did."

QUICK AND DEAD

You remember Laura Palmer? She also turned up naked, but she was wrapped in plastic. Her complexion was a mess and her lips were blue. Fortunately, actress Sheryl Lee stayed on among the living as Madeline Ferguson for the stories first arc and also appeared on the cover of ESQUIRE magazine as woman of the year. Reportedly Lynch asked her during auditions, "How do you feel about being wrapped in plastic in the cold?" She went for it, although by now Sheryl Lee is no doubt tired of being draped in saran wrap every time she does a publicity piece.

"If it were a quick dead scene, then it would have been easier," Sheryl Lee revealed in SOAP OPERA WEEKLY. "But it was a lot more difficult than I realized — the hours (I had to) lay perfectly still, especially the one outside where Laura was found. It was cold. It was all me, pretty much, in my birthday suit and panties."

MacLACHLAN

One person who has nothing to complain about is Miguel Ferrer, star of the CBS series BROKEN BADGES, and best known for playing the amoral corporate flack in ROBOCOP. He has had a blast working in the land of TWIN PEAKS.

"It's a very happy set," Ferrer says. "They work very, very long hours and there's an awful lot of cast members. There's a feeling on the set from the crew and the cast and the guest directors alike that it is very different working on this show. It's certainly different than any other episodic I have ever done and I think everyone has the sense that they're doing something very special."

Can you blame him? Anyone with lines like "By the way, you were shot with a Walther PPK...that's James Bond'S gun," can't be miserable. There's been talk of not only bringing the acerbic Albert back in the future, but of giving him his own spin-off series.

During the filming of DUNE, director David Lynch, showing the ability for understatement which has defined his career, said that MacLachlan is "an actor with immense mental and physical power and at the same time a genuine spiritual quality, a sort of innocence. That's a rare combination. He could play any role."

Neither could have guessed that several years later it would come down to Kyle throwing rocks at bottles to determine who the murderer of the homecoming queen was.

"He eats vast amounts of foods and he's as thin as a board and a great guy," Ferrer adds about MacLachlan. "He has a very quick mind and boundless energy and the metabolism of a bumble bee. We try to crack each other up on the other's close-ups. I read my Albert lines as if I were Captain Kirk and he's absolutely unshakable, solid as a rock. 'I'm gonna get you this time,' I say, 'I'm going to go deep and do my best Kirk' and he just says 'I'm ready for it, go ahead' and I do it and he just looks at you with those clear blue eyes that radiate sincerity.

"I, on the other hand," he continues, "will crumble completely when he so much as cocks an eyebrow. I don't play that game with him anymore because I lose."

OUTKEAN

Ferrer is equally laudatory of Kyle's partner in crime-solving, Michael Ontkean. "All of my scenes in the beginning were just with Michael and Kyle and they're just such absolute gentlemen," Ferrer says. "They're gentle, wonderful, giving, and terrific people. I know it sounds like a lot of crap, but they're really just extraordinary men. I like them both enormously and they made me feel so much at home and so much a part of it from the first second."

Ontkean began a memorable career playing ice hockey. Learning how to check people into the boards at four years old in Montreal was something he couldn't easily resist. His father was a coal miner turned boxer and Ontkean, who went to the University of New Hampshire on a hockey scholarship, discovered acting when road-tripping it cross country with two girlfriends from Boston.

Bluffing his way onto the old Goldwyn lot, he hit up Norman Jewison, a fellow Canadian, for a job in FIDDLER ON THE ROOF. Although he didn't get the part, Ontkean ended up appearing in a number of movies and shows. His big break came when he was cast in the ABC series THE ROOKIES. After the series ended, Ontkean segued into a starring role in the outrageous Hollywood hockey hilarity of SLAP SHOT starring Paul Newman and Stephen Mendillo.

Since then he's starred in a number of forgettable films including MAID TO ORDER, WILLIE & PHIL and the potentially career ruining film MAKING LOVE. He holstered up for TWIN PEAKS as Sheriff Truman to become one of the few bastions of sanity in an insane world.

LAURIE

Piper Laurie, best known for her starring role in DAYS OF WINE AND ROSES, is a familiar face on the New York stage. She delivered a terrific performance in THE HUSTLER, in a role which earned her an Academy Award nomination. Laurie earned an Emmy nomination for her part as the unscrupulous Catherine Martell, but really didn't have a whole lot to do in the show's first season except spend an inordinate amount of sack time with Ben Horne. She did create an impressive turn as a Japanese businessman in the show's second year.

Feared killed in the fire, Catherine exacts her revenge on Ben Horne who had betrayed her and was actually in cohoots with Josie Packard, by dressing up as Mr. Takiyama, a mysterious Japanese businessman. The clever producers actually credited a fictional actor, Fumio Yamaguchi, with the role until the unveiling in which Piper was given her due as the man in black.

CHEN

Joan Chen (Jocelyn Packard) is best known for her role in THE LAST EMPEROR as Empress Wan Jung, the wife of Pu Yi, China's last emper-

or. She was kept busy while Dino De Laurentiis was in business, in myriad forgettable films including TAI-PAN.

Chen was raised in Shanghai during the Cultural Revolution. Now she is one of PEAKS wildest cards as the secret lover of Harry Truman. She seemed vulnerable until we discovered her secret agenda.

The future will reveal where Chen is heading in the role originally designed for Lynch's main squeeze, Isabella Rossellini.

ANICK

Madchen Amick stars as Shelly Johnson, the abused wife of trucker Leo who, as Albert Rosenfield so aptly put it, is now doing his impersonation of "Mr. Potatohead". Born in Reno, Nevada, Amick always had dreams of the big-time. With TWIN PEAKS under her belt, she's on her way.

"People have begun to look at Madchen and say, 'who is it?' — like they kind of missed her the first time," Robert Engels says. "To me, she's very hard to miss."

The frequent fornication of young lovers Bobby Briggs and Shelly steam up the screen. Who can forget the classic scene first season when Shelly tells Bobby she doesn't know hoe to use a gun and beckons him to "teach me, teach me" as she unbuttons her blouse and caresses the gun against her breasts? Well, Amick would like to.

"I found Shelly and Bobby's relationship in the beginning to always be hot and kissing and making out and I really wanted to see more than that," says the actress. "A lot of things have come up that I'm happy about now dealing with Leo and at home with Bobby being a jerk. I would like to see her become a little more strong and dominant which I have kind of seen happening, but I've always found her very sheltered in a bad way. Now that's she's having to take care of Leo, she's really finding out where she stands with Bobby and what her true feelings for Leo are now that he's not just this horrible guy that she has to take care of. She's becoming very close to him as if he's her baby, sort of. I'd like to see Shelly and Leo start a new life one day and may be have them be a happy couple. If he comes out of his coma, I hope he won't kill me."

The actress' resume includes starring in numerous music videos, guest starring roles on STAR TREK: THE NEXT GENERATION and the lead role in the BAYWATCH pilot.

"I was the guest lead in the pilot and my agent, Abrams Artists, sent my picture into Johanna and she wanted to meet me," recalls Amick. "I came down and met with her and she went to David Lynch and said, 'I think you should really meet this girl' and I was actually set to meet him at a certain time when I ran over on BAYWATCH. It was 9 at night and so I called and said I'd be late. He said he'd wait for me and it was after 10 when I got there. We sat and talked for over two hours and went over the script and the scenes and really hit it off. He told me I got the part right then. I was surprised because I thought he would be a lot stranger than he was.

"I thought he would be very serious and not very funny. He was a lot nicer than I thought he'd be. He had a good sense of humor and really made the interview comfortable and was very giving."

ASHBROOK

Shelly's not-so-secret boyfriend of late is Bobby Briggs, played by Dana Ashbrook.

"He loved Laura Palmer," Ashbrook says. "It's not so much a passionate, sexual love but a friendship love and then Bobby started seeing Shelly...." Ashbrook, whose father is head of Palomar College's drama department, worked on a number of episodics including CAGNEY & LACEY and 21 JUMP STREET. In TWIN PEAKS as its resident rebel without a cause, Bobby's a troublemaker with a sensitive side. One episode he's howling in warning to James Hurley, "When you least expect, expect it!" and the next he's crying in Dr. Jacoby's arms that Laura laughed at him when they first made love. He's a contradiction in terms, but maybe if you're father wore an Army uniform around all day and couldn't tell you what he did for a living while delivering secret outer space messages about owls, you'd be a little off to. "He doesn't like hypocrisy and that's something I find in my life I don't like either," says Ashbrook. "All the secrets in the town piss

him off because everyone lies to themselves and to each other."

"All you good people," Bobby yells in the series third, Emmy award nominated episode, "you want to know who killed Laura? You did! We all did! And pretty words aren't going to bring her back, so save your prayers...she would have laughed at them anyway."

Yeah, Laura really messed this boy up. When he wasn't selling drugs, he was off partying with Leo and Laura and even, as we're told in her secret diary, shot a man dead after stealing drugs from a gang in Lowtown.

HORNE

Crime is a little more upscale for Ben Horne...or was. That was until he was arrested for the murder of Laura Palmer. Richard Beymer, star of WEST SIDE STORY and multi-talented artist/ actor and film-maker, plays the town's resident baddie. When arrested for the murder of Laura Palmer, he says, "I think I'll go out for a sandwich now if you don't mind." Among Beymer's many talents are that of cinematographer and editor. His acting credits include PAPER DOLLS, DALLAS, MURDER, SHE WROTE, MOONLIGHTING and Gary David Goldberg's THE BRONX ZOO.

He meditates regularly, something of which David Lynch heartily approves. "What they say about meditation is that you expand your container," the director said to MOVIELINE magazine. "Everybody is a certain amount aware or conscious. If you make yourself more conscious, you might be able to capture ideas at a deeper or higher level. And to me it's about capturing ideas. They're right out there. Right there. For me, I don't want my container to stay the same size. I want it to get bigger."

WARREN FROST

"Mark called me and said him and David were going to do this show and they had a part for me," recalls actor Warren Frost who plays kindly Dr. William Hayward. As the town doctor, he's the physician who takes care of everyone in the town.

"I was in New York doing something at the time he called, but he wanted me to meet David and I did and that's how it started. I've spent my life working in the theater for 25 years. I only worked on AS THE WORLD TURNS for six months."

Among Frost's other credits are guest starring roles on TATTINGERS, BEAUTY AND THE BEAST and ABC's short-lived series CAPITAL NEWS. Frost's daughter is Lindsay Frost, star of MANCUSO FBI, an accomplished actress in her own right.

KELLY

David Patrick Kelly is no newcomer to playing lunatics. As Ben Horne's weird little brother Jerry, he has a wide and diverse range of screen psychos behind him. Kelly starred in DREAMSCAPE, 48 HOURS, THE WARRIORS and most recently WILD AT HEART during which David Lynch cast him in TWIN PEAKS.

"I'm an altar boy type...really," says Kelly. "Maybe I just have an angle of perception on these kind of crazy people that let's me be creative and enjoy composing them more than anything else. I tend to be a kind of arty guy and I like to work from theory rather than method. When I was doing a small part in WILD AT HEART David kept looking at me in a way different than he would have for just the film. When I came back (to my trailer), there were these six scripts and they were the funniest things I have ever read in twelve years of making movies. I don't why, they were just this baguette and cheese thing.

"The thing about Jerry and Ben came from an idea about David's work which I was working on," he says. "I came in for this meeting about WILD AT HEART and I was spouting on about this other character and talking about Robert Graves theory of poetry in WHITE GODDESS, a scholarly work about the nature of poetry, which says all true poetry is in homage to the goddess and there are two gods competing for the goddess and you can see this in all great poetry. My theory about Ben and Jerry comes about because I think all men who are thirty and over are laboring under the archetype of this '50s version of a man's man. It was sort of artificially demarcated by Kennedy's assassination and after that we're sort of floundering around for the new archetype of what a man should be. Ben and Jerry are sort of before that idea of a conquest and search for that. They're competing for the goddess figure which is Laura Palmer with the man that she was always looking for, but never found, who was Dale Cooper."

When this Peakster isn't pontificating on his theories, he's playing lead guitar, a skill which may show up one day in an episode. "I was too sensitive about my music. I couldn't fire the guys in the band," Kelly says of his many late-night gigs at a dumpy New York nightclub preceding his excursion into acting. "I'm CBGB's class of '75. I've always believed in heroes like John Lennon who said don't do this, it's a golden prison."

LIPTON

Peggy Lipton knows what its like to be a hipster too. She starred on THE MOD SQUAD for five years as Julie Barnes, a comely campus born cop. Once married to music producer Quincy Jones, Lipton pretty much fell off the face of the earth until her career was resurrected by PEAKS. As the shows elder stateswoman, she has made quite an impression on fans during her tenure on the show.

Lipton, whose character Norma Jennings is in love with Big Ed, is married to Hank Jennings, the recently released con who has been the long arm of the lawbreakers on the show. In order to express the hatred she feels towards Hank on the show, Lipton has stayed clear of actor Chris Mulkey who portrays him.

"Norma is depressed," she told EGG magazine. "Maybe not depressed, but she has to pin everything down. Because when a husband like hers gets out she has to feel like she's living on the edge, constantly on guard. One of the techniques I used to convey that edge was not to talk to Chris Mulkey at all. Because if I established anything friendly with him, that fear I tried to create would go away."

Amick, whose character Shelly faces similar problems with her on-screen spouse, Leo, played by Eric DaRe, feels differently about her off-screen activities.

"Eric and I hung out during the pilot," she says. "I'm able to separate myself once it's time to act so I like to stay friends with people and really get to know them and have fun and make it feel comfortable. He's a really nice, funny guy. I feel that if my character didn't completely have feelings for him maybe I would try to separate myself a little, but I think deep inside Shelly still has a love for him and sometimes when we're working we'll come from eating and go into a scene and he messes with me on purpose when I'm acting. When it's my close-up and he's behind the camera, he'll make faces and try and crack me up."

MARSHALL

James Marshall is the James Dean of TWIN PEAKS, or rather the James Hurley. Quiet, introspective but articulate, he's also a motorcycle enthusiast. Born in Queens, the son of a movie producer, Marshall started playing guitar as a kid. His idol is guitar master Jimi Hendrix.

Having starred in a CBS schoolbreak special about Date Rape and MY PAST IS MY OWN, a made for TV movie about racism, Marshall also appeared in CADENCE, a film directed by Martin Sheen set during Vietnam. He actually had a chance to show off his guitar skills in a bizarre installment of the show when he sits in his living room with Laura and Maddie, Laura's cousin, looking at her longingly while strumming on his six string.

McGILL

Everett McGill plays Ed Hurley, the unhappy spouse of Nadine, the drape obsessed woman with the patch, whose eye he shot out on their honeymoon. McGill joined the show with an impressive filmography having played lead guitar with his own R & B band and studied drama at the Royal Academy of Dramatic Arts in London. He starred on Broadway in WHOSE LIFE IS IT ANYWAY? and A TEXAS TRILOGY. McGill is better known for his starring, but extremely reticent role, as a primitive man on the QUEST FOR FIRE and DUNE where he met David Lynch. More recently, McGill played a dirty DEA agent in the James Bond flop LICENCE TO KILL and starred in HEARTBREAK RIDGE

and the acclaimed TV miniseries DRUG WARS.

ROBIE

Wendy Robie plays his whacked out wife. She starred in a myriad obscure theater pieces in the Northwest before becoming one of the most familiar staples of this trendsetting TV show. "TWIN PEAKS has changed my life," Robie says. "Prior to David and Mark coming into my life Seattle was sort of base camp for me and all my work was in theater and I was making as much as you would with a real good paper route...and loving it. When they came to Seattle to shoot the pilot, I was sent in to read and I got a callback. Mark and David asked me which was my good eye, and I wanted to answer everything right, so I pointed to my right and David said that was the correct answer — and I was Nadine."

Robie is also a competitive 100 Mile Endurance Runner which perhaps accounts for her character's newfound super strength. "It's everyone's dream," she says. "I get to be 18, have superhuman strength and kiss boys. I think it has something to do with the adrenal glands which are working overtime and pumping adrenaline through her system," Mark Frost jokes. "It's like she constantly thinks her child is under a car."

NANCE

Jack Nance is a Lynchian veteran famous for his lead role in the cult classic ERASERHEAD. Nance went on to appear in a number of films including CITY HEAT, JOHNNY DANGEROUSLY, HAMMETT, BARFLY, and COLORS. On television he appeared in Michael Mann's CRIME STORY which ENTERTAINMENT WEEKLY dubbed one of the ten best series in syndication and has worked with Lynch on a number of other projects including DUNE, BLUE VELVET and WILD AT HEART. In TWIN PEAKS he plays Pete Martell, the man who uttered the immortal Lynchian lines, "She's dead...wrapped in plastic."

ROBERTSON

Kimmy Robertson has skyrocketed to acclaim as the overly specific secretary at the Sheriffs office. Suffering through her own problems, her character, Lucy Moran, is pregnant at what may be the hands of the sleazy manager of Horne department store's home furnishings section and is still on the outs with lovable Deputy Andy Brennan. A member of the Groundlings, the noted improv theater group, Robertson has appeared in such films as HONEY, I SHRUNK THE KIDS, TRUST ME, BAD MANNERS, and THE REAL WORLD.

WISE

For a while he seemed strange...but in a nice way. That was until we found out "it was happening again" and lovable Leland Palmer had been possessed by the not so lovable apparition, Bob, and he smashed the head of Madeline Ferguson into his apartment wall after strangling her. Played by Ray Wise, Leland Palmer is one of the strangest in a very strange array of characters.

After suffering in grief-stricken agony over the murder of his daughter, dancing around with his hands in the air to Pennsylvania 6-5000 screaming "Dance with me", Leland seemed to finally get a grasp on reality...even if his hair had turned prematurely grey. His alter-ego, Ray Wise, has been considerably more successful, winning an Obie in 1983 for his performance in the off-Broadway production of Sam Shepard's "The Tooth Of The Crime". Wise worked in the more mundane world of dramatic serials on the soap opera LOVE OF LIFE. Born in Akron, Ohio and a drama major at Kent State University, Wise has also starred as a Nantokian who thinks Picard is a god in STAR TREK: THE NEXT GENERATION, MOONLIGHTING, BEAUTY AND THE BEAST, HART TO HART, KNOTS LANDING, LA LAW, and the classic DYNASTY spin-off, THE COLBYS.

Wise has also been featured in Wes Craven's SWAMP THING, Paul Schrader's erotic remake of CAT PEOPLE and Paul Verhoeven's gory sci-fi thriller ROBOCOP.

TAMBLYN

Russ Tamblyn stars in this North Side Story as the eccentric Dr. Lawrence Jacoby, the strange town psychiatrist obsessed with Hawaii and golf. When Cooper approaches him about assisting with the investigation, Jacoby is not loquacious.

JACOBY: Agent Cooper, I'd like to help you but I have a little problem here. Maybe there's some sort of hula we can do around my doctor-patient confidentiality.

COOPER: Is it safe to say she came to you because she was having problems.

JACOBY: Oh my yes.

COOPER: Were her problems of a sexual nature?

JACOBY: Agent Cooper, the problems of our entire society are of a sexual nature.

COOPER: Dr. Jacoby, I understand that you care deeply for Laura Palmer. Why is it that you won't help us?

JACOBY: My own personal investigation I suspect will be ongoing for the rest of my life...Laura had *secrets* and around those secrets she built a fortress that in my six months with her I was not able to penetrate and for which I consider myself an abject failure.

Tamblyn starred in the musical classic SEVEN BRIDES FOR SEVEN BROTHERS and received an Academy Award nomination for PEYTON PLACE and also starred in TOM THUMB, HIGH SCHOOL CONFIDENTIAL and THE HAUNTING. He's most famous for Robert Wise's WEST SIDE STORY which also featured Richard Beymer. Tamblyn is also a renown artist whose work is not only featured in the L.A. Institute of Contemporary Art and the Los Angeles County Museum of Art, but in Dr. Lawrence Jacoby's office in TWIN PEAKS.

GOAZ

He's a crybaby. Deputy Andy Brennan confronts the face of crime without the stoicism of Sheriff Truman or the detached reserve of Harry Truman. He immerses himself in the emotions of the moment and lets out a stream of tears. From the moment that he is asked to take pictures of Laura Palmer's corpse, Andy is a wreck. When Truman discovers recluse Harold Smith's body hanging from the ceiling in his apartment, he says, "I'm glad Andy's not here."

Harry Goaz stars as Deputy Andy Brennan. He was born in rural Texas and wasn't bit by the acting bug until after he graduated from college at the University of Texas at Austin. When he decided to pursue a career as a master thespian, he traveled to Los Angeles and studied at The Loft with acting coach Bill Traylor. While working as a driver rather than a waiter, he was assigned to pick up David Lynch. Lynch was on his way to a memorial tribute to the late, great singer Roy Orbison whose career he had inadvertently revived with the use of his songs in BLUE VELVET. The two started talking and the rest is TWIN PEAKS history.

HORSE

Michael Horse had been expected to become a legend in his own time with the release of the long-awaited big budget adventure of the masked man, THE LEGEND OF THE LONE RANGER. He took over the role that Jay Silverheels had made famous as the Lone Ranger's faithful Tonto. While LONE RANGER died a quick death at the box-office, Horse starred in a succession of forgettable films. With TWIN PEAKS it looks as though Michael Horse will escape the anonymity which greeted Klinton Spillsbury when THE LONE RANGER galloped quickly into the sunset. (Spillsbury was the Lone Ranger as was Clayton Moore). Horse, an internationally known American Indian artist of Zuni, Mescalero Apache and Yaqui descent, is passionate about his cultural upbringing. He is one of the first Indian regulars to appear on network television, playing Deputy Tommy "The Hawk" Hill.

STROBEL

One of the most shockingly good performances in the ensemble began as a walk-on part. Al Strobel was featured as the One-Armed Man in the pilot. Most people thought it was just another stab at self-reflective humor by the show's hipper-than-thou writers when in fact Philip Michael Gerard, sometimes known as Mike, a spirit from out of town, was actually a character intricately linked to the resolution of the mystery.

"He's an amazing actor," says Lesli Linka Glatter who directed Strobel during the scene in which he transforms himself into Mike and tells Cooper where he can find Bob. "He was a great surprise. He's just amazing. They realized on the pilot this guy was an incredible actor and when he did that scene we were all on the set going whoa, this guy is incredible."

WRITING PEAK RELATIONSHIPS

To the writers, the challenge of writing for this encyclopedic array of characters is exciting. It makes HILL STREET BLUES look like MY DINNER WITH ANDRE.

"James and Donna is always a fun relationship to write," says Harley Peyton. "I wrote a lot about kids in that age group when I was writing features like LESS THAN ZERO. In a way, I feel like I can make up for some of the mistakes I made in that. There aren't any characters I start a scene and don't like to write. You have Pete Martell or the things that Piper Laurie does with her character. There aren't any stiffs."

Robert Engels agrees. "Sometimes I love Andy and Lucy and sometimes you love Agent Cooper because he cuts through life like we all would like to," he says. "When you're feeling ornery you like to write Ben Horne. The characters are designed well enough that you can always find something interesting to work on.

"You try to get a feeling and stay in concert with them," Engels continues. "We have a pretty swell group in that sense, lot's of fearless people in the cast who trust us. It's just a case of trying to keep that trust up. The most important thing about working with actors is that they trust you, that you're not going to make them look bad and are going to find good things for them to do. We've been plotted so tightly that there hasn't been a chance for the actors to have much input, but they know their characters inside out and that's a great help. What would they wear to a carnival? He would do this. You have good actors and they trust each other and they trust us and that comes back in spades."

TOO MANY CHARACTERS

The one problem confronting all the members of the cast has been the lack of screen time they have been afforded. With such a large cast, it's difficult for the actors to have the opportunities to explore their characters that they hope for in the beginning.

"We have a troupe," Peggy Lipton told EGG magazine. "It's like a repertory and that's what acting is really about. What makes it more amazing is that all of us really like each other. Some of the kids on the show are feeling a little bit hurt already because their characters are not going the way they want them to go and though it's not easy for David and Mark to juggle about 25 characters, we've become very connected to these people, so it's difficult to adjust to certain things."

"It's frustrating at times," says Warren Frost. "You don't get to work that much. If you're not in the mainstream of the story, you sit around and do very little and actors like to work. It's like Peter Falk said, 'An actors job is looking for work'. Well, in this case, we're looking for a plotline."

Despite the desire among the cast to secure as much screen time as possible, the ensemble is extremely positive about their roles in the continuing saga of the show.

"I think it's a wonderful group of people," Frost says. "I've had a wonderful time working with this group of people. I haven't run into any problems in terms of working with them. Everyone seems to pitch in and have a good time. It sounds silly and high schoolish but its important that you're involved and enjoying it because I think that comes across."

Eventually members of the ensemble will pursue options resulting from their newfound fame possibly reducing cast of characters. Yet it might not work that way.

"Yes, it's a big cast," agrees Robert Engels. "And it's getting bigger every day. We're trying to have 300 regulars. That's the whole motivation for me doing TWIN PEAKS."

CHAPTER FIVE

The Creative Team—
"Look, It's Trying To Think"

In 1980 David Lynch was nominated for two Academy Awards for THE ELEPHANT MAN, one for Best Director and the other for Best Screenplay Based on Material From Another Medium. The film also received six additional nominations. THE ELEPHANT MAN was David Lynch's second feature film.

He was uncomfortable with the subject, the story of a horribly mutilated man who tries to fit into society. Photographed in stark black and white and starring John Hurt, the film was a triumph for the director whose name had resonance only among a small group of cinemaphiles taken by his first film ERASER-HEAD. This earlier work continued to play the "midnight circuit" successfully for years after its release.

LYNCH GROWS UP

Lynch was born in Missoula, Montana on January 20, 1946. His father served in the Forest Service and his paternal grandfather was a wheat rancher. Two months after his birth, Lynch's parents took him to Sandpointe, Idaho, where the family remained for two years. During this time his brother was born. From there, they moved to Spokane, Washington, where his sister was born, and then moved on to Boise, Idaho, where Lynch went to elementary and junior high school. His family finally settled in Alexandria, Virginia where he spent his high school years.

Lynch recalls his childhood as "'Good Times On Our Street.' It was 'See Spot Run'. It was beautiful old houses, tree lined streets, the milkman, building forts, lots and lots of friends. It was a dream world, those droning airplanes, blue skies, picket fences, green grass, cherry trees. Middle America the way it was supposed to be. But then on this cherry tree would be this pitch oozing out, some of it black, some of it yellow, and there were millions and millions of red ants racing all over the sticky pitch, all over the tree. So you see, there's this beautiful world and you just look a little bit closer and it's all red ants."

In keeping with a philosophy which has manifested itself in his films for over a decade, Lynch says, "there is a goodness like those blue skies and flowers and stuff, but there is always a force, a sort of wild pain and decay, accompanying everything." That paradox continues to prove a consistent theme for the director.

"Since I was little," he says, "I've dissected a cat, a mouse, a rat, a frog, moths, birds, ducks, a chicken and a fish. That was the whole thing about THE ELEPHANT MAN. There's the surface, there's a whole other world — and different worlds as you go deeper and deeper.

My parents didn't drink," he continues. "They didn't smoke, they never argued. And I wanted them to smoke, I wanted them to drink, I wanted them to argue, but they never did. I was ashamed of my parents for being the way they were. I wanted to have strange things happen in my life. I *knew* nothing was as it seemed, not anywhere, but I could never really find proof of it. It was just a feeling."

Lynch suspects that "because I grew up in that very beautiful sort of perfect world, other things became a contrast. I went to Brooklyn as a little kid, for instance, and it just scared the hell out of me. I remember being with my father and brother in the subway and I could feel this wind coming from the train, down the tunnel. First the wind and then a smell and then a sound. It was frightening. I had lots of tiny tastes of horror every time I went to New York."

If fear is what he felt in New York, than it turned to disgust when he went to Philadelphia. "It's a very sick, degenerate, decaying, fear-ridden place where things are totally absurd and confusing," the director told TIME magazine. "There is violence in the air at all times. It's definitely the sickest town I've ever been in and it's called The City Of Brotherly Love."

While Lynch rebelled against his parents, he possesses nothing but warm feelings for his paternal grandfather. "He was a tremendous influence," he says. "I though he was one of the coolest guys. He always drove these big black cars and he'd wear these thin leather driving gloves, and real, real good suits and engraved cowboy boots. He was fantastic". The image of TWIN PEAKS Judge Sternwood played by vet-

eran actor Royal Dano comes to mind; the adventurous and independent travelling judge who despite his advanced age is one of the hippest and wisest characters to visit the town in a long time.

At the age of 15, the possibility of becoming an artist first entered Lynch's mind. "I'd been drawing since I was very small. My mother refused to give me coloring books, but she gave me lots of blank pieces of paper and all the stuff I needed to draw with. So my imagination was never ruined, never limited by preconception. I could just go free. But it never occurred to met that was something adults did. Not till high school. I had a friend whose father was an artist. And I went to his father's studio in Georgetown and became unbelievably excited. Because until then, I really hadn't thought of any adult being an artist in this day and age. He got me into painting."

In 1964, Lynch graduated high school and enrolled in Boston's Museum School. At the completion of his freshman year, he departed for Europe. "I went to study under one of my least favorite painters, I don't really know why, but I meant to stay in Europe three years."

Instead, Lynch returned to the United States in fifteen days. "I remember lying in a basement in Athens and lizards were crawling up and down the walls. I began contemplating how I was 7,000 miles from McDonald's. And I really missed America. I knew I was an American and wanted to be there. On the other hand, I'd been to Salzburg first and it was too clean. So wholesome and sterile and beautiful. It was uninspiring. If I'd had to choose, I preferred Athens."

Upon returning to the United States, Lynch headed back to Alexandria, Virginia. "My parents disinherited me, sort of. They said, 'Okay, you're not going to school, you're not taking things seriously, we're not giving you any more money. You'll have to get out and find a job.'"

Lynch started work at an art store, working on commission. "I made 3.9 cents per hour," he recalls. "That's 15 cents per day. I wasn't fired, but I couldn't live on that, so I quit."

After leaving the art store, Lynch suffered through a series of mundane jobs that didn't quite work out. At a frame store he was fired for scratching a frame; he got a job making blue prints but was axed for tardiness. "It was horrible. Then the frame shop hired me as a janitor."

Since his parents had moved to California, Lynch was forced to move in with a friend who soon after threw him out. As a result, Lynch took up residence above the frame shop. "Two stories up," he says. "They hung a bell in my room to wake me up in the morning, I couldn't get up. But I was given paint and food — I was painting away like crazy, and then I'd sweep up. The owner's name was Michelangelo. Honest."

Despite the myriad obstacles Lynch encountered he continued to face each setback with a positive face. "Each time I was fired, it led me to somewhere else where I had a new experience. So I could see it all had a rhyme and reason. I mean, each time I was fired from a job, I was ecstatic. I remember when I was fired from the engineering office, Michelangelo put me to work digging clay, and I was digging right under the windows of the Holland engineering firm who'd fired me. And there I was out in the sun, digging up this clay, really beautiful stuff, great color, while all the Holland guys were inside having to slave away. They kept coming to the windows to watch me!"

Finally, fed up by a series of low-paying, menial occupations, Lynch decided it was time to return to school. "By the time I'd cleaned a stopped-up toilet that no one else would touch, the worst job I'd ever done, for $5, I'd have gone to any school to get out of there."

Lynch turned up at the Pennsylvania Academy of Fine Arts in Philadelphia. "I turned in my portfolio to be graded for entrance and they accepted me," he recalls. "I was super happy. I started in January of 1966 and that New Year's Eve a friend named Jack Fisk and I were moving all our stuff in a wheelbarrow to a place we'd rented at 13th and Wood. A man stopped us. He said, 'You're moving — moving on New Year's Eve! You need money!' And he began to put his hand in his pocket. And I said, 'Oh no. Thanks, but we're rich.' And we didn't have any money at all! Isn't that strange — I always felt like I was rich! The strangest thing."

DINERS AND ART

The house into which Lynch and his friend Fisk moved was "kitty-corner from the morgue and next door to Pop's Diner. And that has influenced more things." Without a doubt, Lynch's proximity to the two in his formative college years has had a great impact on his work. Diners have become a spawning ground for the director. Lynch and partner Frost formulated many of the ideas that became TWIN PEAKS in a diner. Indeed, the Double R Diner has played an important role in the series as well.

"They're very well lit, safe and clean places," Lynch told USA TODAY. "You can let your mind go into serious areas, frightening areas or new areas and if it does get strange you can bob back up to the surface and you're in a safe place."

Diners were safe havens for the director whose disgust for the city of Philadelphia in which he lived for many years has set the tone for much of the grotesque imagery found in his films. "It's a very sick, degenerate, decaying, fear ridden place where things are totally absurd and confusing. Violence is in the air at all times. It's definitely the sickest town I've ever been in and it's called the City of Brotherly Love."

The director's obsession with diners carries over to a fascination with morgues and what was contained within. These have ranged from the battered and bruised Dorothy Valens of BLUE VELVET to the penultimate Lynchian icon of Laura's blue corpse.

Looking back at his art school days in Philadelphia and the memories of morgues and the mundane, Lynch terms them "the best times of my life — and one of the worst times, too. The area had the greatest mood, an unbelievable mood. It was an industrial part of the city, with the strangest characters, the darkest nights. Factories, smoke, railroads, diners, true factory people — you could see strange stories in their faces. You could see plastic curtains and windows held together with band-aids, things stuffed into holes in the windows. Associations like that."

There was the morgue "with what we called the 'smiling bags of death' that they brought bodies in with. We'd always go through the morgue gar age in route to the hamburger restaurant. I only lived at night then."

Years later, giants would point to clues to a bizarre murder in a smiling bag. The past continues to affect the present and many of the long nights of hard work that typified his daily existence then still color his work today. "The art comes first. In the art life you don't get married and you don't have families and you have studios and models and you drink a lot of coffee and you smoke cigarettes and you work mostly at night. Your place smells like oil paint (the smell of Bob?) and you think beneath the surface of things and you live a fantastic life of ideas. And create stuff."

Exploring underneath the surface is exactly what Lynch has done throughout the course of his feature film career whether it be the seamy underbelly of seemingly normal suburbia in BLUE VELVET or the darkness in the woods of the sleepy little town of TWIN PEAKS. Underneath the surface of its residents are secrets and spirits. A seemingly normal, perhaps a little off-kilter, father is actually possessed by the evil spirit of a maniacal killer.

Lynch, although considering going to film school, rejected the lure of the commercial grooming schools of Hollywood at USC and UCLA and stayed in Philadelphia where he married a fellow art student in 1967. They gave birth to a daughter, Jennifer, in 1968.

"We were living in a house with 12 rooms, three stories, the bedroom alone was 25 by 25 feet, giant high ceilings. And this huge place cost $3,500. That's all! A whole huge house and only $600 down. So you know what kind of neighborhood it was in. A kid was shot to death a half block from our front door and the chalk marks around where he'd lain stayed on the sidewalk for five days. The house was broken into twice; two windows were shot out. I saw horrible things pretty much every day. My car was stolen. It starts getting to you. I thought I'd never get out of there, ever. I thought that was it. There was tremendous fear in Philadelphia, fear I didn't realize I was living under until I eventually moved to California and the fear left."

FILMS

It was in Philadelphia that Lynch began his filmmaking career in the Academy's annual experimental painting and sculpture contest. For the first year's contest, Lynch built a kinetic sculpture which won second prize. The second year he constructed "a sculptured screen with three-dimensional heads. He recalls he made "a film to be projected on it, of six people getting sick. First their heads and then their stomachs animated in. It was all on a big loop that went up into the ceiling and came back into the projector. The whole thing cost me $200 to do and took several months."

It was Lynch's first experience with the world of cinema, but far from his last. "I always sort of wanted to do films," he recalls. "Not so much a movie-movie as a film-painting. I wanted the mood of the painting to be expanded through film; sort of moving painting. It was really the mood I was after. I wanted a sound with it that would be so strange, so beautiful, like if the Mona Lisa opened her mouth and turned, and there would be a wind, and then she'd turn back and smile. It would be strange."

Lynch's film sculpture won him a shared first prize. "And then a millionaire saw the show, a former Academy student. He asked me if I'd build another film sculpture for his living room and gave me $1,000 to do it. I thought I was a millionaire!" To pursue his craft Lynch purchased a used camera which he didn't know was broken. After two months of tedious animating, he found the developed footage to be "one solid blur". His benefactor, however, was not disappointed. "He told me to do whatever I wanted with the rest of the money and whatever I came up with, just give him a print."

Soon afterwards, Lynch quit the Academy to pursue painting at home since he didn't feel he was still learning anything and went to work on a four-minute movie combining animation and live-action. It was called THE ALPHABET and he presented it to the American Film Institute, hoping to get a grant. "This was one of the bleakest times of my entire life," he says. "I had about as much chance of getting a grant from the AFI as flying to the moon."

He was working as a printer for an artist and his wife making just barely enough money to get by. "We'd watch soap operas while we printed, and then I'd drive home in the dark and my wife would have dinner for me and there was my daughter and my wife and me and my Falcon car and this house. Right? And this dark world."

Life seemed even bleaker to the young film-maker when he received notification from the AFI of its grant recipients. "On this list were some of the real heavyweights in experimental movies, all in their 40s. I looked at the list and I said, 'That's it, there's no possible way I'm going to win one of these things. It was a horror I ever thought I would, I wish I'd never applied!' So I gave up then."

AFI hadn't given up on Lynch. A few days later he received a phone call from George Stevens, Jr., the son of renown film-maker George Stevens and head of AFI, asking if Lynch could make his proposed $7,200 film on a budget of $5,000. The answer was an immediate yes and Lynch began work on his next film, THE GRANDMOTHER, about a disturbed boy who plants a seed which grows into his own grandmother, a wonderful, loving and caring woman. "I painted the entire third floor of my house black. It was very abstract."

In 1970, AFI accepted Lynch into its Center For Advanced Film Studies. There he worked on a script for a film called GARDENBACK, a tale about adultery.

Lynch says, "I always hide all my fears, and then sometimes my films hide them too, but in different ways. When I first finished the script of GARDENBACK it was 45 minutes long, enough for a short film, and was just what I wanted, all feelings and mood. But they wanted me to stretch it out to regular feature length."

After attempting to lengthen the film, Lynch realized expansion was impossible. The film fell apart but he learned a lot from his experiences in trying to get the movie made. "Mostly about film structure, about what not to do. And mostly from a guy named Frank Daniel, who was the Dean of the Film School and who now teaches at NYU. But still, GARDENBACK became uninteresting to me and I was ready to quit the AFI."

ERASERHEAD

Lynch was asked to remain and he presented his next idea, ERASERHEAD. That began what he calls a "wonderful long journey." The journey started in 1971 and continued through 1976. During that period, he separated from his wife (they were divorced in 1974) and for almost eight months, lived at AFI's headquarters, the Greystone mansion, in secret.

"It was totally illegal," he recalls, "but my wife had the car. We'd set up a sound stage in a whole complex of buildings on the school's estate and it seemed a good idea just to sleep there too."

Ironically, Lynch slept in Henry's bedroom. This is the character with the outrageous afro played by Jack Nance. "I'd lock myself in there in such a way that from the outside it looked as if no one could possibly be inside. We'd put these special blankets up on the walls to deaden the sound for shooting and it was quiet. The air was bad, but it was really inspiring there too. I was actually sleeping in a room that existed before only in my mental world and that would exist afterwards only on film. And there I was, dead broke, living in a mansion in Beverly Hills, surrounded by millionaires!"

Working with a crew of four at night and supporting himself with a WALL STREET JOURNAL paper route during the day, he ran out of the money AFI had given him after a year's work on the film. "All the money I had or made during that time had gone into the film. I had money for food and cigarettes for myself and that was it."

Unable to complete the film on his earnings from his paper route, Lynch took on a new role — that of fund raiser. "I finally raised the necessary finish money from about ten people — none of whom required I screen a frame. They jut all made a leap of faith."

In June of 1974, Lynch started work on the film again and wrapped two years later. "On the last day, the grounds' caretaker appeared. I think he knew I'd been staying there and wanted to catch me. I said, 'Look, we've been here four years and we've got one more scene to shoot. We're not going anywhere!' He said, 'Okay then. Sorry.' And that was it."

Lynch unsuccessfully tried to have the film screened at the prestigious Cannes and New York Film Festivals, but neither accepted the project. Finally, in late 1977, Filmex screened the film and the project opened at New York Cinema Village to a slow start. "There were 25 people in the audience the first night and 23 the second. But it never died. Finally it began rolling."

The movie's run expanded to include Los Angeles, San Francisco, and other houses in New York where it is still a popular midnight attraction.

After the successful launch of the small, wildly experimental cult film, Lynch moved into a garage and continued his paper route and began building sheds to add onto his apartment. During his free time, Lynch began writing his still-unproduced script, RONNIE ROCKET.

"I was in heaven," he says. "I only had to work at my paper route one hour a day. Then at 2:30 in the afternoon I'd go to Bob's Big Boy and have a chocolate shake and coffee. That's when I discovered that sugar made me happy and gave me ideas. Sugar for me is granulated happiness. I'd sit and think at Bob's and get so inspired and so wound up that when I got home I'd be rearing to go!"

ELEPHANT MAN

After two years of this, even Lynch began to find his daily existence monotonous. "I decided it would be better to make someone else's films than not make films at all." When he talked to a friend who was working for Mel Brooks, his friend mentioned that Mel was looking to develop the popular Broadway show, THE ELEPHANT MAN, into a feature film.

Lynch met ELEPHANT MAN's producer, Jonathan Sanger, and began to work with two writers who had worked on the first draft of the film. "We finished it and all the studios turned it down flat. They said, 'No one wants to see a film about a hideously deformed guy; it's a downer, forget it!'" Mel Brooks, however, remained committed to the project, but Brooks was wary of putting a complex film like THE ELEPHANT MAN in the hands of a novice director. After he saw ERASERHEAD, Brooks came running out of the screening room yelling "You're a madman, I love you, you're in!"

DUNE AND BLUE VELVET

After THE ELEPHANT MAN'S success, Lynch tried to launch BLUE VELVET and RONNIE ROCKET, both to no avail. Then De Laurentiis phoned and offered him DUNE.

Unfamiliar with the Frank Herbert novels, Lynch quickly acquainted himself with the books and plunged headlong into the big-budget monster which would consume three and a half years of his life and result in his most critically lambasted project. In exchange for Lynch taking on the ambitious assignment along with its projected sequels, De Laurentiis agreed to finance Lynch's small dream project, BLUE VELVET.

BLUE VELVET was the film which gave the Lynch name marquee value and although not a huge financial success, it turned David Lynch into a high profile director with an enormous personal following. Although the director's bizarre, eclectic and sometimes extremely violent style alienated some, it intrigued many more. It was truly an American original that ultimately ranked high on many critics' best of the decade lists.

"Nietzsche said in order to write like a lion, one must live like a lamb," TWIN PEAKS' Russ Tamblyn told SOAP OPERA WEEKLY. "And I think that's true in David's case. He's so healthy and he's an artist, too. He has no fear in exploring those dark sides, rather than worrying about what people are going to like or not going to like. He has no fear in delving into those areas and exposing, which I'm all for. He's an observer. And it doesn't take much of an observer to look at this society and see that it's screwed up."

Despite the considerable clout Lynch had gotten as a director resulting from the artistic triumph of BLUE VELVET, he was unable to get two of his other pet projects launched, ONE SALIVA BUBBLE, co-written with Mark Frost, and RONNIE ROCKET.

TWIN PEAKS AND WILD AT HEART

In the interim, Lynch teamed with Frost on the creation of TWIN PEAKS. Soon thereafter

Lynch received the unpublished manuscript of Barry Gifford's upcoming novel, WILD AT HEART. Captivated by the story of the story of Sailor, a recently released prisoner, and Lula on a cross-country odyssey pursued by Lula's vengeful mother, Lynch turned the film into a postmodern WIZARD OF OZ. WILD was honored at Cannel with the prestigious Palme d'Or and in the NEW YORK TIMES, Vincent Canby called the film "a cockeyed epic that goes back to the early days of Pop art".

Other critics were less kind, calling the film self-consciously weird and an attempt by Lynch to live up to his own inflated reputation.

In a way, they're right. The film boasts an impressive array of cultdom's finest thespians: Willem Defoe as the sadistic Bobby Peru; Harry Dean Stanton as Johnnie Farragut; and Crispin Glover as Lula's eccentric cousin, Dell, who enjoys dropping cockroaches in his underwear. This all from a director who is still trying to adapt Kafka's METAMORPHOSIS.

WILD AT HEART is filled with PEAKS people as well, including Jack Nance, Sherilyn Fenn, Sheryl Lee, Grace Zabriske, and Daniel Patrick Kelly. VELVET veteran Laura Dern plays Gifford's protagonist, Lula, who is truly "hotter than Georgia asphalt" and her mother Diane Ladd gives a wildly over the top performance as Marietta Fortune. The film is strangely disjointed and characters come and go without rhyme or reason. Stanton is wonderful as Farragut . He's killed soon into the second reel, lending impetus to some bizarre goings-on with Bobby Peru and his involvement with Perdita Durango played by Isabella Rossellini. One of the strongest performances and most compelling characters is that of Mr. Reindeer, the porno king don surrounded by a bevy of topless handmaidens played by W. Morgan Sheppard is best known for his role as the alien scientist who possesses Data in the STAR TREK: THE NEXT GENERATION episode, "The Schizoid Man".

The films random campiness is one of its biggest failings, but like all of Lynch's work, there is enough originality and sophistication to make it more than engaging.

Boosted by the popularity of PEAKS, the $9 million film has grossed over $15 million domestically. "My mother called me and said she went to see WILD AT HEART and said it was pretty good," says PEAKS producer Harley Peyton. "For my mother to say that, believe me, that's amazing and, I guess, the positive effect of her son being on TWIN PEAKS. Just the fact she went to see WILD shocked me. I loved her calling up and saying I heard these bad things about it and I liked it. I found it hilarious that my mom had suddenly become a huge defender of David Lynch when she used to yell at me for using curse words in my scripts."

Peyton feels that the critical drubbing the film received in some circles had a positive effect on PEAKS, allowing it to avoid the inevitable backlash from all the hype it had gotten over the previous summer. "David got a little bit of the TWIN PEAKS backlash," he says. "It came out right after we had started getting this huge amount of publicity. In a way it took a lot of the heat for us and than, once we lost at the Emmys, that really pretty much destroyed the backlash.

"The media, by definition, creates emperors so they can later declare they're not wearing any clothes. That's certainly happening with TWIN PEAKS. The Emmys retarded that process since the perception was that we were cheated and not given our due. We became an underdog again, and believe me, we were happy to do that."

MARK FROST

Lynch's collaborator on the series, Mark Frost is not only the Co-Creator, but serves as Executive Producer and has written and directed installments of the show. After Frost got his start in television working on the SIX MILLION DOLLAR MAN for Universal, he returned to Minneapolis, where he became a literary associate as the Guthrie Theater and playwright-in-residence at the Midwestern Playwright's Lab. His play, THE NUCLEAR FAMILY, was produced at Chicago's St. Nicholas Theater while his HEART TROUBLE was staged at a writing workshop at New Mexico State University.

Frost began work on a series of documentaries for PBS and wrote, produced, and directed THE ROAD BACK, about a rehabilitation program for young felons. He also worked for three years as writer, story editor, and executive story editor on

HILL STREET BLUES, for which he won a Writer's Guild Award and received an Emmy nomination. The show was created by noted television innovator Steven Bochco and inevitably led to Frost comparing Bochco and Lynch. "One's an earthling," he said. "The other's a Martian."

His screenplay for the voodoo cult thriller, THE BELIEVERS, paved the way for the supernatural side of TWIN PEAKS and his incredible sense of humor is readily apparent in the yet-unproduced movie, GOOD MORNING CHICAGO, the sequel to GOOD MORNING VIETNAM he scripted. Frost will soon make his directing debut on a feature film called STORYVILLE, and with David Lynch, he co-created the Fox documentary series AMERICAN CHRONICLES, a unique blend of Americana.

Frost reveals that unlike his alter-ego Cooper, Lynch doesn't remember his dreams. "I'm sure if he did they would be lalapaloozas," says Frost. "Most of his visions are waking visions. He called me up early second season after we started and said, 'Mark, there's a giant in Cooper's room.' I said, 'I believe you.' So that kind of stuff happens that way. I have long vivid dreams almost every night and there are things from that which I constantly use."

PEYTON

Producer Harley Peyton was brought on to assist Lynch and Frost in the difficult day to day production responsibilities on the show. "I did exactly what freelance writers do now and got a pretty by the numbers outline of most of what the episode is going to be in order to fit all those interlocking pieces of the puzzle. You've got to be pretty exact about it. Even though you get a blueprint to follow, the real fun of writing a TWIN PEAKS episode is the different character things you can come up with. The challenge is not so much in plotting, but in dialogue and the presentation of character."

Peyton has primarily worked in features, and despite having worked on two unsuccessful pilots, he is thrilled to be a part of the TWIN PEAKS team. "It's really just kind of writing and working on stories or enjoying the company of the people here," he says. "It never seems like an ar-

duous task. For a writer, it's a kind of heaven. You get to know these characters so well that it just becomes a lot of fun to write them everyday. It's the first job that's gotten me out of my robe before noon in many years having worked in features for the last several years. In television, since you're always in production, you develop this sort of family. There are a lot of good people here and I enjoy the work. It's a fun place to hang out as well.

"Most of my work is involved with writing and some casting and working on stories. I'm not necessarily here every minute that we're physically in production; it's a pretty sane work day. I get in around 9 or 10 o'clock and go home when I'm done which could be at 6 or it could be at 8. A producer is really a very well paid writer who works every week. That's where my job starts and that's how I want it to be although I am involved with some casting, plotting of the stories and going down to the set at six in the morning because an actor wants to change a line and my phone will ring."

Peyton says that if he had a hero, it would be the legendary screenwriter Ben Hecht. He is a film connoisseur and numbers an eclectic mix of movies among his favorites, including ODD MAN OUT, THE PHILADELPHIA STORY, THE DEER HUNTER, 1900, STRANGE CARGO, LAST TANGO IN PARIS, OUT OF THE PAST, and "all of Preston Sturges' films".

ENGELS

Robert Engels is the show's Executive Script Consultant, recruited during the show's first season by Mark Frost. "I've known Mark for a long time," says Engels. "We are old friends. His father, Warren, was my college advisor. When they got the order for the first seven episodes, Mark asked me to do one and it seemed to turn out okay and he asked me to come aboard."

Engels, whose career began as an actor, was born and raised in Minneapolis, Minnesota. His father was CEO of the Northern States Power Company and his mother was the first woman architect to graduate from the University of Minnesota. Engels graduated with a BFA in theater from the University of Minnesota and won a Bush Fellowship to continue his acting training at the Guthrie Theater. Aside from appearing in numerous commercials, he also played recurring roles on THE EDGE OF NIGHT and ANOTHER WORLD. Despite his previous soap work, Engels is not anxious to use TWIN PEAKS as a vehicle for his return to the acting profession.

"Everyone jokes I should do something on the show," he says. "I think, at this point, I would be terrible. Although I certainly can play parts on the show, I would prefer an actor get it. That's a hard side of the business and I would prefer someone who really need the job get the part...and if I did it, I'd be terrible, so that's probably why I have that rationale."

Engels reluctantly concedes that if INVITATION TO LOVE returns to the air in TWIN PEAKS he would have to consider a cameo in front of the cameras again.

Engels directed a Broadway production called TYKES. Now he kids that the show "came very close to being the first Broadway play to ever close at intermission." Since that time, he became Associate Artistic Director of the Cricket Theater, a regional theater in Minneapolis and continued working in New York and Los Angeles where he directed the hit show THE BASEMENT TAPES.

On the basis of his screenwriting work, which includes a documentary on Michael Jackson called THE LEGEND, he became story editor on the third season of the CBS series WISEGUY. Like TWIN PEAKS, the series features extended storylines and a serialized format.

"On WISEGUY there were four writer/producers," says Engels. "TWIN PEAKS only has three, so I have more to do which makes it more fun. You get involved with everything including casting. Because I acted and directed so many plays, I have a natural affinity for which isn't a story editor's job. Since I've done that for so long, its just something I can do quickly and enjoy. So that comes under my responsibility, while the best I could do at WISEGUY was suggest friends.

"Stephen Cannell (WISEGUY'S creator and producer) is much more organized and formal since it has been running a while. When you come into the job there, your job is defined since you're replacing someone. At TWIN PEAKS, you learn every day. A problem is new to the series because the series is new. Who'll do this and how does one do it. It's fun. There isn't a pat way to solving the problems."

TWIN PEAKS AND WISE GUYS

Similarities have been drawn between the last arc of WISEGUY's third season and TWIN PEAKS. In the WISEGUY arc, Steve Ryan (CRIME STORY) plays Mark Volchek, the unelected ruler of a small, backwards and strange Washington industrial town. When Vinnie Terranova (Ken Wahl) comes to town as Vince Kozak, pretending to be an ex-cop, he is invited to join the police force by Sheriff Stemm (David Stratharin). Vinnie soon learns that Volcheck is totally crazy, obsessed with an old William Castle film called Mr. Sardonicus, and wants to construct a hospital in the town at all costs. The viewer later learns he wants to house his parents who are in cryogenic freeze. The town also boasts a brothel, suggesting One-Eyed Jacks, and a serial murderer who is killing young girls. It is discovered to be Stemm, who electrocutes himself with a stun gun, and sends WISEGUY's Agent Cooper (Ken Wahl) running off when memories of the violent death of Sonny Steelgrave, subject of a previous investigation, are reawakened. The incident was actually a way of getting Wahl out of the show when he suffered serious knee problems during the shoot. "We had well made plans and somehow they stopped when Ken got hurt."

The similarities between the two series were so striking that it led the press to speculate on the possibility that WISEGUY had plagiarized its story arc. Frost vehemently denied the possibility at a press conference during the show's first season hiatus. "It's true we had a writer who did one episode for us who went onto WISEGUY," he says of Engels, "but he came onto that show after the arc had already been written. I'd prefer to think of it as a homage."

"It was very odd," Engels agree about WISEGUY's similar storyline. "Yet Cannell had planned for almost a year and half before to do a small company town in the Northwest and so when I came on the show they said let's make it a homage to David. There were all sorts of coincidences and people kept assuming there was some reason it looked the same whereas Cannell was up in Vancouver and that whole area before we were."

A TYPICAL DAY

Engels typical day on the show consists of re-writes and meetings. "You write and rewrite and rewrite," he says. "You can't write for television unless you can write pretty quickly. It's pretty workmanlike in that sense and can be pretty tedi-ous.

"I like to stay until the last shot is blocked and rehearsed. One of us always tries to stay until they're all set up to go home. I'm usually the last one in and I'm usually gone by 8 or 8:30 and then I'll go home. If I have pages due I'll go home and write until 2. If you don't have pages to write, then your day is indeed done at 8. It's a real hands-on job. That's the fun part. You get to see it right away. You write it, and a month later, sometimes two days later, they shoot it and then two days later you see the dailies and a month later it's on television."

In addition to his substantial writing chores and meetings with the shows ARTIO award winning casting director Johanna Ray, Engels sits in pro-duction meetings for each episode. "Every de-partment is represented," he says. "You work your way through the script with all the prob-lems, ranging from whether someone is going to be wearing a wig to what the props are for about two hours.

"If he's going to be reading a newspaper, what newspaper do we use and what's the headline? We've already established a newspaper for the town so the director will ask me to come up with a headline and I'll make a note and the next day the prop guy will call me and I'll give a headline. All that stuff makes for the reality of the town and needs to be dealt with piece by piece, item by item. You try to look for all the problems. One of the stunt guys is there, the set designer, one of the camera operators, and everybody just sits around and it gets pretty tedious plowing from scene to scene and you just hope everyone has read the script, but sometimes they haven't.

"I'll also go over— with the director— logistic rewrites. For instance, little things like in the script where it says hand me the cup and now they're going to be using cans of beer. I have to change it to hand me the can...not unlike stamp collecting. That kind of falls under my job de-scription since I'm the lowest man on the totem pole. It's not exactly the most challenging task and the next writer we hire gets to do that."

THE REST OF THE TEAM

Among the other members of the production team that put the show on the air are Supervising Producer Greg Feinberg and Co-Producer Bob Simon. "Greg is involved with just about every-thing," says Engels. "We wouldn't make it with-out him. From the budget to the talent, he is the heartbeat. He does everything. Bob Simon is a co-producer. Basically the Unit Production Man-ager, he's the person who controls each episode to stay on time and budget episode to episode. He coordinates the real hands-on stuff like stunts and extras casting."

Phil Neal serves as the show's editor and is in-tricately involved with every aspect of the show's post production from cutting through foley walk-ing and the looping of dialogue.

Another vital component of the TWIN PEAKS creative team is Angelo Badalamenti, the show's composer whose film scores include TOUGH GUYS DON'T DANCE, COUSINS, NA-TIONAL LAMPOON'S CHRISTMAS VACA-TION, BLUE VELVET, and WILD AT HEART. Badalamenti's long and fruitful collaboration with Lynch has emerged in the aftermath of the director's pairing with the rock-band Toto for the score to DUNE.

Born in New Jersey, Badalamenti is also an ac-complished songwriter. His songs have been re-corded by Nancy Wilson, George Benson, Shir-ley Bassey, Melba Moore, Patti Austin and The Pet Shop Boys. His work for Julee Cruise in-cluded co-producing and lyricist credits on her album FLOATING INTO THE NIGHT. He also co-wrote and co-produced the Brooklyn Acad-emy of Music production of David Lynch's IN-DUSTRIAL SYMPHONY NO. 1.

His music for TWIN PEAKS was released on a bestselling soundtrack album by Warner Bros. Badalamenti told MOVIES USA that he had developed a great creative relationship with Lynch through their collaboration on BLUE VELVET and TWIN PEAKS. Badalamenti said, "(Lynch) would come to my office, sit across the piano from me and describe what he wanted for a particular scene. I would improvise while he talked, developing the themes and melodies that matched the images or the mood he was describing."

Badalamenti created a wide array of themes for the show ranging from the evocative "TWIN PEAKS Theme" to the sad and wrenching melody of "Laura Palmer's Theme" to the surreal jazzy rhythm of "Dance Of The Dream Man" to the almost comically bombastic "Freshly Squeezed". Many of the themes appear with great frequency and have become inextricably tied to the success of the show. During post-production, the directors work from a library of themes and call on Badalamenti's services when a new piece of music is required.

"I had a number of conversations with Angelo," says director Graeme Clifford. "He lives in New York so its unusual for any of the directors to actually sit down with him face to face. I needed him to write a new piece of music to write for Harold Smith so I was very much concerned and it was used three times in my episode in different incarnations. Each director spots the show with music that already exists, and then when you can't find something that fits, that's when he writes new material. I track the show with his assistant and then talk to him when I need some specific ideas or if something needs to be written from scratch."

WARREN FROST

73590-X/$8.95 U.S./$10.95 CAN./POCKET BOOKS

A △ TWIN PEAKS △ BOOK

THE SECRET DIARY OF LAURA PALMER

CHAPTER SIX:

The Merchandising— "Dear Diary"

TWIN PEAKS' unprecedented success soon gave rise to a diverse range of entrepreneurs seeking to cash in on the show and its enormous cult following. Millions had been made off STAR TREK, BATMAN, STAR WARS and, more recently, THE SIMPSONS, and soon home-grown shirts bearing the words "I Killed Laura" began showing up all across the country. The fledgling production entity, Lynch/Frost Productions began to realize the value of the TWIN PEAKS name and created an executive position at the company to oversee merchandising operations. This soon gave birth to merchandising plans.

Frost and Lynch were determined not to simply cash-in on the TWIN PEAKS phenomenon, but to create a line of merchandising which was totally original. While they toyed with ideas for such products as a coffee mug shaped like a log and TWIN PEAKS cherry pie, they began to work with Pocket Books.

Pocket, which had tremendous success with their traditional STAR TREK tie-ins, was now embarking on a less familiar road with its TWIN PEAKS line. In early September Pocket issued an audio cassette, DIANE...THE TWIN PEAKS TAPES OF AGENT COOPER. Boasting not only all of Agent Cooper's recordings to Diane up until the second season premiere, the tape includes all new voiceovers written especially for the tape and read by Kyle MacLachlan. The new material serves as a prequel to the show, and starts when Cooper first finds out about his new assignment to go to Twin Peaks. The tape takes him through a rough plane flight to Seattle after which he begins his trip into town, and stops at the Lamplighter Inn on the way. The tape is often clever, informative, and proves a refreshing recap to fans anxious to be reacquainted with the mystery up through the premiere. It makes for surprisingly interesting listening and opens with the TWIN PEAKS theme music.

THE NOT-SO-SECRET DIARY

More popular and even more vital to PEAKS freaks is THE SECRET DIARY OF LAURA PALMER as seen by Jennifer Lynch. In this NEW YORK TIMES bestseller, Jennifer Lynch has put together an exceedingly provocative series of information which has since turned up in the show in the custody of agoraphobic Harold Smith who Laura gave the book shortly before she was killed. It is discovered by Donna while investigating the meals-on-wheels program when she is given a clue which leads her to play Nancy Drew and embark on her own personal search for information on Laura's killer.

In Episode 12, Donna confesses to Harold in exchange for information.

"Diary, I'm back. Sorry I had to stop. So I was dancing, and Donna saw what I was doing and looked at me like I was crazy. She looked around for a minute and I guess she wanted to be a part of the attention, too, or something because she looked at her watch and said, 'Let's go skinny-dipping!' That right there should tell you how drunk Donna was. Everybody got quiet and just listened to the music for a second, then said, 'Yeah, okay.' So Donna and I took off our clothes...all of them. We almost left our panties on, but we were afraid they would think we were stupid little girls (p. 37). The diary begins when Laura is twelve years old and first receives the diary as a birthday present along with a horse named Troy. We soon find out that the horse given to Laura from her father is actually a present from Ben Horne whose retarded son, Johnny, Laura tutors.

As time passes, Laura metamorphoses from innocent little girl into the enigmatic Laura Palmer who left so many mysteries when she was murdered. The really bad girl who desperately yearns to be good, but can't. In part, her development is made impossible by the intervention of BOB in her life, the mysterious apparition that constantly is mentioned in the diary admonishing her for her sins.

"Dear Diary, I'm sorry I haven't written, but so much has happened. Tonight as I began to undress for bed Bobby Briggs came to my window. A beautiful, dreamy sight that sent me reeling. He says there is a party we couldn't miss out at the end of Sparkwood. A friend of his, Leo — who I think I've heard of before in the air of gossip that I often hunt down — is throwing a party. I warned him, I had only thought seriously of curling up with him, and confessed that I was

missing more sleep than I need to be sociable.

"He promised me there would be no problem in the alertness department as he had a new treat for me to try that sometimes negates the need for sleep entirely. I'm out the window, Diary. Shhh! I'll tell all the moment I return. I'm hiding you...beware of BOB...he is sometimes tardy.

"Laura P.S. It just struck me that BOB's name is a warning in itself.... B. BEWARE O. OF B. BOB" (p. 75)

ENCOUNTER WITH BOB

As we would later learn, the true three letters that Laura need to beware of were DAD.

After the party, high on cocaine and having engaged in some outrageous sexual antics, Laura writes, "And I woke up. Ashamed. Horrified. Guilty. And I imagined him suddenly, right before me at the edge of my bed. YOU FORGOT, LAURA, I KNOW EVERYTHING, SEE EVERYTHING, GO ANYWHERE I WANT...I COULD TELL YOU MORE ABOUT WHAT YOU THINK ARE SECRETS THAN YOU COULD TELL YOURSELF! YOU LET YOUR GUARD DOWN, DIDN'T YOU. LET ME HAVE A NICE VACATION FROM THAT STENCH OF YOURS...THEN YOU HAD TO CALL ME BACK...RANCID LITTLE BITCH! YOU'RE PRETTY MEAN TO ME. SOMETIMES WHEN YOU WRITE, AREN'T YOU! WE'LL HAVE TO FIX THAT. MAKE YOU LOVE ME LIKE YOU USED TO. I REMEMBER THAT...SOON YOU WILL TOO? And then he disappeared. I need to do something that is right and good. Today! Who in the f-ck is he and why does he hate me so much? I want to die, and to forget everything else. I can't take it anymore! I begin to feel good and then someone makes me feel that I'm dirty. Then someone kisses me just right and I feel wanted and excited all over again." (p. 83)

Despite Laura's attempts to relegate BOB to the back of her subconscious, he continues to be an ever-present force, paying more frequent visits into her life.

"...I CAN DO WHATEVER I WANT.

"Stay away from this house! Leave me alone or I swear I'll find a way to make you sorry.

"CAN'T FEEL SORRY, LAURA PALMER.

"Look at where I am, because of you, and your sickness your weakness, you are an awful creature.

"NO CONSCIENCE. NO GUILT. YOU SAID SO YOURSELF. I SEE YOU GOT YOURSELF F-CKED LAST NIGHT. AN OWL TOLD ME. REALLY INTO THAT COKE, AREN'T YOU? DIRTY GIRL, LAURA PALMER. YOU SHOULD KNOW BY NOW THAT YOU CAN'T IMPRESS ME...I'M NOT INTERESTED IN WHAT YOU DO WITH YOUR LITTLE COKE FRIENDS. YOU ALL LOOKED RIDICULOUS OR SO I HEARD.

"Get out of my head. Now!

"NAH.

"Leave me alone you sick bastard. How dare you! I don't want you here! Get out! I'm tired of accepting you all the time...I hate you. Leave!

"IT ISN'T GOING TO STOP ME FROM STAYING EITHER. I'M IMMUNE TO YOUR EMOTIONAL, ADOLESCENT, F-CKING, LESBIAN WHORE WHINING AND SELF-PITY. I'M THE BEST THING IN YOUR LIFE.

"You aren't. It's not true!

"ISN'T IT?

"Stop lying to me. I have better things in my life than you. I know it.

"OH, YES? NAME ONE.

"My parents.

"DOUBT IT. THEY HAVEN'T KEPT ME FROM GETTING TO YOU. HAVE THEY? NEITHER ONE TALKS TO YOU THE WAY THEY USED TO. THEY STOPPED CARING A LONG TIME AGO. THEY PUT UP WITH YOU. NOTHING MORE. I'M BETTER.

"Donna.

"THE 'BEST FRIEND' YOU NEVER SPEAK TO? THE ONE YOU LEFT BEHIND IN EXCHANGE FOR DRUGS? YOU ARE SADLY MISTAKEN.

"I have myself. Me. I'm better than you are!

"NO. I HAVE YOU. YOU BELONG TO ME. YOU DON'T DO ANYTHING I DON'T ALLOW YOU TO DO. I RUN YOUR LIFE, AND I STEER YOU AS I WISH." (pgs. 105-107)

INTO THE ABYSS

Laura begins to sink further into the abyss and even as she initiates the Meals On Wheels program to bring food to indigent shut-ins with Norma and continues tutoring both Johnny Horne and Josie Packard, Laura's nights of kinky sex and drug abuse continue unabated. In the December 21, 1987 entry she writes "I have to go shopping for Christmas presents tomorrow. God, I have no idea what to get anyone. I suppose its bad for me to wish for coke for Christmas...A ton of white, fluffy snow all over me." (p. 116).

On page 168, Laura reveals the reasons for keeping two diaries, a plot point which would prove important later in the series when it is discovered that a second diary exists. The one found in Laura's room in the show's pilot has little of the information that gives us true insight into Laura's inner self and the demons that torment her.

"I think that in order to ensure my privacy I will need to start a second diary, one that if found will give the intruder 'the Laura' that everyone thinks lives inside of me. I will have to spend time filling its pages. I wonder if life is still something I can make up."

Later Laura describes her last days at One Eyed Jacks, when she has sex with Blackie O'Reilly, the madame of the Canadian brothel owned by Ben Horne. She says, "I smiled the way BOB would and thought to myself, I'll be the one teaching the lesson. By the time I left Blackie, she was on the floor, naked except for her jewelry, and was humiliated because I had been able to take total control and show her things she had never thought possible. I took her into a very dark erotic place...but I left her there alone.

"As I opened the door Blackie threw her final, and only remaining punch. 'You better watch that cocaine use, Laura. It could get you fired.' I knew right then that it was to be my last night at One-Eyed Jack's." (pgs. 174-175)

She ends that entry with what has proven to be one of the most important pieces of information discovered in her secret diary when read by Agent Cooper, "I'm going to have tell the world about Benjamin."

Soon afterwards, following a series of ripped out pages, the diary ends — just a few days before the night of Laura's death with only the vaguest of premonitions about what awaits her.

"I think of death these days as a companion I long to meet. Goodbye, Laura "

(p. 153)

GAPS

The diary lends vivid insight into the psyche of the tortured Laura Palmer and helps fill in many of the gaps left necessarily vacant by the television show. The diary not only gives depth to some of the cryptic allusions made in the show, but, unlike the television medium, is able to truly plumb the depths of depravity that engulfed Laura. On one series of pages, Laura lists all the men, women, and possibly even pets that she has ever made love to and, in addition, her many interludes with Leo, Jaques, and Bobby are recounted in, in some cases, nauseating detail.

Reluctant to elaborate, Jennifer Lynch only says some of the unfamiliar initials on the list of Laura's previous lovers include "our entire writing staff". She adds with a laugh, "Even I slept with Laura Palmer."

The diary explores uncharted territories in Twin Peaks, regions that the ABC Standards & Practices department would never allow any television fare to chart. Jennifer Lynch, who rejects the charges of "pornography" that have been levelled at the diary, believes that it not only lends insight into Twin Peaks but explores the dilemmas of many young women at Laura's age.

"She started out innocent, having all the same questions we all do," says Jennifer Lynch. "I think no matter what your situation, certain universal instincts are going to come to you. Laura, just because of her situation, reacted to them differently and drove down the wrong road." In this climate of repression and censorship, some bookstores refused to stock the book because of its erotic and, at times, sadistic content. More than anything else, the story of Laura Palmer is a tragedy in the tradition of such works as OEDIPUS REX and HAMLET (of course, it's not quite as good. Shakespeare never wrote "Maybe Dad knows BOB too, but Mom won't let us talk about him because it makes everyone...so upset...? I don't know." p. 111).

UNIVERSAL THEMES

The novel/diary explores universal themes that Lynch feels helped propel the book onto the bestseller lists in appealing to not only the Peaks Freaks but other readers as well. "Whether we have a Bob in our life or not, we usually all have something that causes us to believe we're not the way we're supposed to be," she says. "I think that is a fear that's fairly general and universal. Then there are people who are reading it just because it's juicy as hell."

ENTERTAINMENT WEEKLY gave the book an A rating in its Literary section, agreeing that Jennifer Lynch has done an extremely credible job in bringing Laura Palmer from screen to printed page. "I was given the freedom to go for it," she says. "It was a very strange experience and I could literally say I was almost possessed by who Laura is because she's so 180 degrees different from myself and, hopefully, the rest of us. She was wild and crazy, but hated herself. She wasn't able to enjoy any of her innocence or relish any of her day-to-day activities because she felt she didn't deserve to. She felt worthless.

"I went hunting for 12- to 17-year olds and I do this a lot with writing. I felt it was incredibly relevant that I not force Laura and I spent a few weeks just trying to find habits that young girls had and envision her in front of me so that I could write for her. I'm hoping the people who read the book don't say what a little slut Laura is because she never condoned, and I never wanted her to condone, the drugs or the sex and the way in which it happened for her. I think she regretted it in the end."

JENNIFER LYNCH

The 22-year old poet and writer, who is the daughter of David Lynch and his first wife Peggy Reavey, was the youngest poet ever published in the CARNEGIE MELLON THREE RIVERS

POETRY JOURNAL and will soon make her feature film directing debut with a movie for Columbia called BOXING HELENA. She told the NEW YORK POST that "I was approached (to write this book) by Mark and David in a way that I really was thankful for. It was my ability to do the project and not just my genes that got me the job."

She wrote the book in four days, delayed by a computer disaster in which the entire document and its later revisions were erased leaving only a rough first draft. She says if there's any moral in the book it's "don't do drugs and don't have sex with people you don't know."

"I read the Laura Palmer diary and its unbelievable," says PEAKS Producer Harley Peyton. "You typically think of that kind of stuff as just kind of rip-off merchandise and an attempt to get more money out of something, but I think Jennifer Lynch did a fantastic job. As for the tapes, I thought they were a very weird merchandising idea, but in a way it does kind of make sense. It sounds like something David would think of and even in writing the show those monologues of Cooper are often one of the things you most look forward to writing."

MERCHANDISING PEAKS

Now with the success of the Laura Palmer Diary, a slew of additional PEAKS paraphernalia is coming to a bookstore near year. Among the other merchandise planned for the future is a computer game, a TWIN PEAKS style autobiography of Agent Cooper, and a tourist's guide to the town.

"The whole idea of the books is to expand the world of TWIN PEAKS past the television screen and give people some background that this was a place that was real to us and give people a chance to experience that," says co-creator Mark Frost. "Cooper's autobiography will be in book form and it'll be every tape recording he's made since he was 17 years old. We're also doing a TWIN PEAKS Access Guide. There's a guy, Richard Werman, who does access guides for different cities including Paris, Los Angeles, Boston, London, all the great cities, and now, of course, TWIN PEAKS. It will have its own access guide which will have historic walking

tours, building by building, and things like where to get a really good donut."

SUMMER PLEASURES

Where to Go • What to Buy • What to Wear • Where to Eat • What to Read

$2.25 • JULY 2–9, 1990

New York

Twin Peaks'
Sherilyn Fenn

02475

CHAPTER SEVEN:

After Laura—
"The Woods Hold Many Spirits"

Finally the revelation everyone had been waiting anxiously for: who killed Laura Palmer?

Not surprisingly, the killer was indeed the spectral apparition Killer Bob played chillingly by Felix Silva, but more of a shock was the body which he was inhabiting, that of Laura's loving, but wild and crazy father, Leland.

It is only when the giant played by Carel Struycken warns Cooper that "it is happening again" that we see Bob in action. Drugged, Leland's wife crawls down the stairs of the Palmer household as Leland gives her little thought while he adjusts his tie obliviously. As Madeline comes down the stairs to return to Missoula, we see Bob's face reflected back in the mirror Leland is looking at and he attacks her. Pounding her several times, Leland dances with her inert body and smashes her head in a picture frame. The vision of blood on the carpet Maddie had seen earlier comes to pass. It is her blood, and like her cousin, Maddie is brutally killed.

Originally it was intended that the carpet was going to rearrange itself into a vision of Bob laughing, but it was rejected by Frost as "being too dumb. Instead it was just like something that was moving in the room to establish Madeline was a person who was sensitive to those things like Bob who had just moved by her."

POSSESSIONS

"It's kind of like the relationship between an artist and an agent," Mark Frost says of Bob's ability to possess a human soul. "He is a creature from somewhere else and maybe he's only from within Leland. We don't exactly say where he was belched up from. He is somebody who kind of went along for the ride.

When Leland talks about knowing Bob as a child and says this was someone who invited me to play and I invited him in, there's a certain classic type of vampire myth that comes into play when a soul that invites something into it to take part in its life cannot than refuse it anything. That's a myth that goes way back before pre-Christian times and that's one possible explanation...the other is that Leland is just completely whacked out of his mind."

The greusome ending in which Madeline was killed has come under fire for graphic violence which Mark Frost adamantly defends. "We wanted that to be a very violent scene because we were suddenly seeing the consequences of everything that had led up to it. In a way, you are kind of seeing Laura's death. You can tune into any show any night of the week and see people getting shot or stabbed or rotting and you don't feel anything, but here we felt it needed to be authentic."

CLUES

Even after witnessing the murder of Madeline though, many still felt that it was Ben Horne who had killed Laura and Bob had simply fled his body after the crime into that of Leland only to find out in the next episode that it really was Leland as Ben was with Catherine at the time of the murder.

The clues planted all along suddenly became evident. Leland telling Agent Cooper and Sheriff Truman that when he was a boy he knew a man who used to flick matches at him and say "Want to play with fire little boy." There are many references to her father in the diary although we are led to believe even Laura didn't know Bob had inhabited him.

"If she did, she masked it in a way that prevented her conscious mind from knowing it," says Frost. "She found out something very near the end of her life."

It may seem surprising that the producers who created all this seem equally puzzled as to their own intentions as is the audience, but to Frost that's part of the fun of TWIN PEAKS.

"We want you to decide what you think is right because I don't know for sure that things like that exist and I don't know that they don't," he says. "I don't think that Western Psychology which goes back 75 years on our planet can really presume to say these things do or don't exist when we're talking about these myths that go back 6,000 years."

"I've grown up around secrets and mysteries," says Jennifer Lynch. "I enjoy them and I don't feel like I've been cheated out of something when I have to wait to find out a little bit more. It's kind of an exciting process and it's a fun game so I think my father has allowed me to be very patient and enjoy the slow process of discovery rather than just the process of instant gratification which we so often find in television and life." Finally, the question which had plagued millions for the last several months had been answered, but many new questions had been raised. It still hadn't been answered as to Who Shot Agent Cooper. Or what the significance of the owls is. Or what the connection to the murder of Teresa Banks was. Or even what was going on with Josie Packard. And how did Catherine manage to change her voice to that of a testosterone-toting Chinese businessman. And would Leo come out of his coma. Or what does Major Briggs actually do for a living. The list seems endless.

AFTER THE CASE

Still, the most pressing of all questions, the Laura Palmer murder, had been solved. Now what would keep FBI Agent Dale Cooper in town? The answer was also soon revealed. In a town of 51,201, there are more than enough mysteries to keep the FBI busy for the next several years.

"TWIN PEAKS is perched on mighty fertile turf," says Story Editor Robert Engels. "There's is a lot of dramatic acreage that we will continue to plow. We're not going to change what our franchise is; we have a wide open landscape."

Engels compares the dilemma of crafting a new and engaging storyline in TWIN PEAKS, in the wake of the wildly successful Laura Palmer arc, to that of his tenure on WISEGUY, a show that faced similar obstacles in devising new missions for OCB operative Vinnie Terranova.

"After the Steelgrave story they had a problem," Engels says of the popular first season storyline of WISEGUY in which Ray Sharkey played underworld kingpin Sony Steelgrave. "After the less successful arcs, they had less problems. Steelgrave almost stopped it and the Seventh Avenue arc with Jerry Lewis almost stopped it again because you find ways to keep spinning it and then after a particularly good story you decide 'we're done now, (how do we top it)', but you're going to have to find another one. That's the challenge, and it's exactly the same on TWIN PEAKS.

"You have to find another factor to put into the town. WISEGUY was different in that we could say now Vinnie goes to Miami, but in TWIN PEAKS we have to stay in the town, probably. We could say that Agent Cooper is going, but that's a big decision. In the sense of cranking up another arc, and that's a harsh way to put it, the problems are very similar for us now and I think we benefit by WISEGUY having gone before us. I think the audience understands that when you start a new story you've got to give us some time to get some new people into it. The advantage of TWIN PEAKS staying in the town is that it doesn't take us nearly as long to introduce new people to story whereas in WISEGUY that first episode of an arc had to create a whole new cast of characters for eight shows and we have all these people who have dreams and ambitions and even as the Palmer saga was unfolding there were other things coming into play so we were able to slide into our next big story pretty seamlessly."

NEW FACES

As time passes in TWIN PEAKS one day at a time (or one day a week as the case may be), the continuing destinies of both old cast and new is always being worked out by the writers.

"We're bringing in a lot of people for three or four episode shots," says Harley Peyton. "Perhaps one day we'll even see Diane. With a cast there are certain commitments for a minimum number of episodes they have to appear in so there are those things to juggle, but there are also people you have to keep out of certain episodes and we do bring new people in because you can't simply have the same cast members interacting with each other all the time. You have certain couples which have been set up and you can only break them up and reunite them so many times. By bringing in new people or new storylines you can go off in a new direction which is a lot of fun, but it does get to be a problem when you find yourself trying to balance everything because you don't want to slight the people already working on the show."

Despite the end of first season where many of the characters were apparently dispensed to the great beyond only to return the following season, Mark Frost has said that death will be an ever-present force in the not so sleepy little town of TWIN PEAKS.

"We will never massacre Moldavia on this show," he kids referring to the infamous DYNASTY cliffhanger. "People will die in TWIN PEAKS, people that you've known fairly well."

OTHER MYSTERIES

Once Laura (and Maddie's) bodies were finally laid to rest, the many other complex mysteries of the town came to the fore, including the story of Cooper's old partner, Windom Earle, the only man the intrepid FBI agent has ever feared. At the same time Robin Lively plotted to kill the affluent Tony Jay for his money in much the way we suspect Josie Packard was able to inherit the estate of the late Andrew who was facing her own problems with Mr. Eckhert in Hong Kong.

There was little doubt that the creative team behind TWIN PEAKS which had been full of so many surprises (and secrets) during the Palmer murder investigation had many more ideas up their proverbial sleeves.

"The stories after the murder thing will be in slightly shorter cycles," says Mark Frost. "It's not unlike what happened in HILL STREET BLUES. On the second season, the story arcs tightened and scaled down a little bit so that people could come in and not feel quite so lost. (On TWIN PEAKS) there will be some things that will spill over from hour to hour. There will be very few episodes that we'll do that will be just one stand alone, self contained episode."

AUDIENCE

Since the second season began, the show has gradually seen its viewership erode in its Saturday night time slot. USA TODAY reported that "the cult following for this creepy soap has steadily dwindled in the ratings, now averaging a mere 14% of the audience on Saturday nights. Many bolted from the draggy pacing of the season's early episodes, gave up because it was too weird or not weird enough, turned it off when its touchstones (coffee, etc.) resurfaced or complained when they disappeared (like the soap-within-the-soap INVITATION TO LOVE)."

Harley Peyton admits that TWIN PEAKS faces that fundamental problem in television—that is, you can please some of the people some of the time, but never all of the people all of the time. With PEAKS' penchant for bizarre plot twists, quirky characters, and in-humor, it's even more difficult to appeal to a large audience.

"I haven't written a donut and coffee joke in some time," says Peyton. "Those things can go sour very quickly and I've even found that in writing Albert's wisecracks humor. The week in and week out scrutiny that an audience is going to give to what you're doing demands it and you do find yourself looking for new things since you can only make so many jokes about saying what phone call is coming in. You have to become careful of that stuff because it will become a cliche very quickly.

"There are certain members of the cult though who are happy with donut jokes forever and there was a panning shot in the two hour premiere second season of some donuts and I was watching it with a lot of people at UCLA and my initial thought was 'Oh God, donuts', but they went crazy and that's part of the balance. You want to satisfy yourself, but not get myopic about it either...so maybe I will write another donut joke."

Madchen Amick is encouraged by the response to the show and feels that the future will be bright despite its cult status and the implications of that being that the show only appeals to a narrow segment of the audience.

"I feel it's a definite trend and trends don't last," she says. "The difference between TWIN PEAKS and normal trends is that PEAKS has great substance and talent behind it and normal trends are just there and don't usually have much to offer so they don't last long. We have a large group of fans who will watch it every time it comes on even if it goes for five years and then there are the people who just don't get it and my parents are in that group."

"It's getting pretty weird," her parents told her. "I don't know, we're only watching it for you." However, Amick believes that when the show's stigma as a trendy must for hip television viewers wanes in much the same way that LA LAW, MIAMI VICE, and THIRTYSOMETHING changed from must-viewing for those in-the-know, the show will attract a whole new audience.

"A lot of people don't want to be doing the in-thing and rebel against it for that reason," she says. "Maybe once the people who are hot on it now just because it's the in-thing stop watching it, the people that don't want to be 'in' will come around and realize it really is worth watching on its own merits."

FUTURE TWIN PEAKS

If the show does last, Engels is not sure where TWIN PEAKS will be in five years. "Well, it'll be three weeks from Laura's death the way we're going," he laughs. "It'll be graduation if we continue at this pace."

Even as the TWIN PEAKS phenomena began to wane in America, leaving a core audience of only several million diehards, a whole new audience was getting acquainted with Laura Palmer and the residents of TWIN PEAKS abroad.

Just as the Laura Palmer mystery was being resolved in the U.S. on ABC, the series began its run in England where it was greeted by big ratings and mixed reviews.

"The garage man is having an affair with the lady at the diner," wrote Christopher Dunkley in THE LONDON FINANCIAL TIMES. "Laura has been dating at least two boys and having an affair with the psychiatrist, Leo is a wife beater, half the population snorts cocaine, there is a plot to raze the sawmill and claim the insurance, local girls dabble in prostitution at One Eyed Jacks and even the Sheriff is carrying on with a Japanese widow."

Even those who were critical of the new series like Brett Arends of the London paper, THE GUARDIAN, grudgingly acknowledged Lynch's sheer originality, if not necessarily in art, then in business.

"You could make many things of movies like these, but you should never make the mistake of Paul Morley, who in his review of TWIN PEAKS on THE LATE SHOW, said that David Lynch 'obviously doesn't know what he's doing.' David Lynch knows exactly what he's doing," Arends wrote. "No film-maker who's been making rubbish for 15 years while receiving massive critical acclaim, no film-maker who has made a bomb selling the world a TV series whose greatest catchphrase is, apparently, 'That's a damned fine cup of coffee' does not know what he is doing. We may not know who killed Laura Palmer, but we know who's making the killing now."

European viewers were not totally unfamiliar with the world of TWIN PEAKS since Warner Bros. homevideo had released a videotape of the ABC pilot a year earlier. Due to contractual obligations, it included an ending in which the killer is revealed to be none other than Killer Bob in the wildly surrealistic dream sequence that appeared in the series second episode.

"We had our contractual agreement with our distributor to give them a two hour version that could be released on homevideo in Europe,"says Frost.

"This was long before we had a series sale. So we came up with an ending. It was mostly Dale Cooper's dream, and that was how we had always designed it. It has important things in it to the plot of the show and Cooper's dream is very important to the eventual resolution. It ends, in Europe, 25 years into the future with the little man dancing."

As for whether the European audience was satisfied with the ending in which Bob is revealed to be the killer, Frost replies, "I don't think the Europeans care. You know, they just go on having coffee and smoking Gauloises and they're perfectly happy."

TWIN PEAKS BLEND

Of course, there's always the question as to whether the American audience was satisfied with the ending in which Bob is truly the killer also, but then the point of TWIN PEAKS is not really to be a second- rate COLUMBO, but rather immerse us in a world which in some ways is totally unlike our own, but in many ways very similar. By plumbing the depths of the everyman's subconscious, TWIN PEAKS enters a realm which has never been charted in television and explores a world unlike any which has ever been depicted in any medium. While the actual content of its storylines are certainly no more creative than your average PEYTON PLACE or FALCON CREST, it is the blending of these stories within this mythical world that makes them unique.

The audience gradually comes to accept the genre splicing. TWIN PEAKS' brilliant creative team has performed it well, combining the cliches of contemporary soap opera with the more outrageous world of the supernatural and the ethereal. Unlike the petty squabbles of multimillionaires over business dealings and beddings that typify the traditional soap operas which have preceded it, TWIN PEAKS' world is not immersed in money alone, but spirituality. It goes beyond the black hats and white hats of the oil barons of DALLAS and DYNASTY to explore the very nature of good and evil and the corruption of the soul. It doesn't always hit its mark, and the show can often segue into lightweight fluff as it often did during its ridiculous subplot with Nadine Hurley imagining to be 18 and in high school again, but at the same time the show probes the dual existence of the One Armed Man living both in this world and beyond, and the dynamics of power as exercised by Ben Horne.

CONSERVATIVE VALUES

As hip and progressive as the series is in form, it's philosophy is conservative, perfectly suited to the evolving America of the '90s in which traditional values have resurfaced. The townsfolk of TWIN PEAKS who have been most fortunate and free of tragedy include the doctor, Will Hayward, whose vocation heralds back to an earlier time and place. He has a beautiful and responsible daughter, Donna, and despite having a wife confined to a wheelchair, is relatively happy and content. Likewise, the outsider from urbania is burdened by the problems of contemporary society. Albert Rosenfield, who says "his concerns are global" and "walks in the footsteps of great men like Gahndi and King," is embittered and sarcastic. He criticizes the town and its people even as he embraces the values it represents.

In a world in of pressing global concerns such as AIDS, the town's resident sexpot, Audrey Horne, is a virgin. "I hope you aren't disappointed with me Agent Cooper," she says to her special agent in his hotel room. "I never slept with anyone at One Eyed Jacks." She's intent on letting him know that she has not been despoiled in the house of sin and that even though she can tie a cherry stem with her tongue effortlessly, she is really an innocent. Despite Cooper's protestations of platonic friendship between them, we realize its only a matter of time before the two end up together in bed. Audrey sees in Cooper the classic childlike dream of the knight who has come to her tower to rescue her. Her hope is that this upright, forthright man will deliver her from the confines of TWIN PEAKS and take her into the world. It is only then that she will gain an appreciation for the town she has all along wanted to leave. Cooper could only discover the unspoiled beauty of the town after having been to Philadelphia. Without the contrast, the world which is unique to him would be impossible to see. It is Audrey's hope to be granted access to Cooper's very special perspective on life which not only harkens back to the traditional '50s values of the one-note cops of yesteryear like the straitlaced Joe Friday but incorporates a post-'80s spiritualism which will become important in embracing the new world which has arisen in an altered geopolitical afterlife following the Cold War. Now the Soviets are friends, Eastern Europe has fallen to democracy, and the United States finds that it must share power with the Oriental businessmen of the Far East.

TWIN PEAKS FOREVER

"Jokes have been made about TWIN PEAKS conventions," says Harley Peyton. "Based on the effect the show has had already I would guess there will be. After each episode you hear about people talking about it and having parties, but I don't know if these are the kind of people who would want to go to conventions."

The idea that TWIN PEAKS will be with us for a long time to come is one that Miguel Ferrer firmly believes in, tidily summing up the phenomenon in a way that only the man who plays Albert Rosenfield could. "Thank God for this show," he says, "because you know, no matter what happens with my acting career, 20 years from now I'll be picking up a couple of grand in Atlanta doing a TWIN PEAKS convention. I won't starve."

The Ten Best Theories About Who Killed Laura Palmer

(And didn't we all know any way? Sure!)

1) THE BODY HEAT THEORY. Laura had actually killed Madeline Ferguson and come back to town pretending to be her cousin allowing her to assume a new identity. "There's a critic in LA," Harley Peyton says, "who came up with this incredibly Byzantine theory about double identities who killed Laura based on the names we had worked out. It was very clever."

2) THE BELA LUGOSI THEORY. Vampires. To some the darkness in the woods was because these bloodsuckers couldn't visit TWIN PEAKS during the day and perhaps explained BOB's easy access into her room at night. "In my particular episode when Jean Renault kills Blackie, he kisses her as she's dying and gets blood on his mouth," says director Graeme Clifford. "He comes up and sees Michael Ontkean through the window and shoots at him. I said to John when you come up I want you to lick the blood off you lips so that was immediately interpreted by all my friends who have this vampire theory as proving their point. In fact, it was something I had just thought of on the spur of the moment."

3) AUDREY HORNE. She wanted an excuse to get the hell out of TWIN PEAKS. That's as good an idea as any, I guess. Other reasons included the fact that Audrey was jealous of Laura because her father loved Laura more than her. Perhaps so, but could the dear departed Miss Palmer tie a cherry stem with her tongue?

4) BEN HORNE. Even after the unveiling of the murderer, some still clung intractable to their man, the town's resident Michael Milken, Ben Horne. After all without chemicals he points and it looked like the One Armed Man was pointing like crazy when Ben entered the lobby at the Great Northern.

5) AGENT COOPER. Aw, come on guys...

6) LAURA PALMER SUICIDE THEORY. As Sheryl Lee so put in eloquently in an interview once, she killed herself...and than wrapped herself in plastic and jumped in the water.

7) MR. POTATOHEAD. Leo Johnson? After all, he did kill poor Waldo, the mynah bird. "I thought it was Leo," says director Caleb Deschanel. "He was the obvious choice but I later dismissed him because he *was* the most obvious choice."

8) JAMES HURLEY. He had the broken heart (literally, figuratively and otherwise) and Laura didn't exactly think the world of this introspective biker as we later found out. "I was actually questioning more of the younger people like James because he was really mysterious," says Madchen Amick who as Shelly was never really much of a suspect to anyone. "When the series went on and new characters came in I thought of the possibility of Laura dressing up as Madeline and the whole switch thing, but the more we went along I thought it could be anybody. With David and Mark they could just bring someone in and say it's him.

9) DIANE. Out for revenge against Agent Cooper for leaving her in Philadelphia, Diane killed Laura Palmer giving him a case he could never solve trapping him in TWIN PEAKS forever (and thus solving the problem of how to keep Cooper in the town once the murder was solved). That's right out there with her being attacked by a flock of extraterrestrial owls (hmmm?!?).

10) DADDY DUNNIT. Leland Palmer? Don't be ridic-alic-olous! Nobody guessed Leland. Except me, yeah right.

An article in TV GUIDE running prior to the series second season premiere featured several bestselling authors personal speculations on their feelings about the beguiling mystery. Andrew Greeley, author of THE CARDINAL SINS guessed it was psychiatrist Dr. Jacoby, "because he's most like Waldo, the Clifton Webb character who was the killer in the 1944 movie LAURA...it makes me think that Madeline, Laura's cousin, is really Laura, and that, as in the movie, the killer murdered the wrong girl. I also think it's the real Laura who shot Agent Cooper because she believed he was getting too close to solving the murder." He jokes, "One thing I must say about TWIN PEAKS - it certainly has an extraordinary number of high school seniors who are gorgeous, certainly not like most high school seniors I've ever known."

The queen of soap literature, Jackie Collins, whose books include LADY BOSS and CHANCES guessed that it was Andy, Truman's deputy and dismissed Leland because "he's such a whiner and so hysterical that you can see his guilt coming out."

The reigning writer of romance also wrote that "it's obvious Cooper wears a bullet-proof vest because he eats so much he needs one to hold in his stomach" and that "if someone gave me the choice of watching KNOTS LANDING or TWIN PEAKS I would opt for KNOTS. The casting is brilliant, but the show is somehow like nouvelle cuisine — you can't really sink your teeth into it." Tony Hillerman, author of COYOTE WAITS and A THIEF OF TIME, was critical of the show dismissing it as "adolescent and shows an arrogant disregard for the audience. If you take out the dog-food commercials, you take out most of the intellectual content of the show. I really lost interest after the episode that finished with Cooper waking up from his dream and saying he knew who the killer was. The next week there was no real follow-up. It reminded me of those old Saturday matinees where Flash Gordon and heroes like him were left on the brink of death, and the next week they were back in a new adventure. Well, I'm not 11 years old anymore."

Hillerman though did manage to guess that it was Leland who killed Laura Palmer. "Given the kind of girl we now know Laura was, and what a neurotic guy Leland is, it's possible that he could have bumped her off in a rage after he found she was working at One-Eyed Jacks," he wrote. Frankly, he should have just stuck to guessing the killer without his off the mark explanation. They'd still pay off in Vegas though.

Esquire

Man At His Best
August 1990 Price $2.50

Women We Love

and women we don't!

SHE'S COLD! **LAURA PALMER** A little stiff at parties, but then, so are we!

SHE'S **BOLD! MARLA MAPLES**

Best sex we never had!

The results of our Perfect Woman Poll! Sorry, Marge, hair isn't everything.

NOW IT CAN BE TOLD!

STORIES

* TWIN PEAKS, unlike many dramatic series, does not title their episodes but rather assigns numbers to them. Executive Story Editor Robert Engels says that's because "we want to stay away from ever being though of cute or poking fun so we thought one of the solutions was let's just not title them."

** The two hour pilot is not included as an episode. Each installment is numbered sequentially starting with the first one hour episode.

Executive Producers: Mark Frost & David Lynch, Producer: Harley Peyton, Co-Producers: Robert Engels, Robert D. Simon, Assocaite Producer: Philip Neel, Supervising Producer: Gregg Fienberg, Coordinating Producer: Tim Harbet, Production Designer: Richard Hoover, Director Of Photography: Frank Byers, Editor: Mary Sweeney, Music By: Angelo Badalamenti, Created By: Mark Frost & David Lynch.

COOPER: .KYLE MACLACHLAN
SHERIFF HARRY TRUMAN: ..MICHAEL ONTKEAN
SHELLY JOHNSON: ..MADCHEN AMICK
BOBBY BRIGGS: .DANA ASHBROOK
BENJAMIN HORNE: ..RICHARD BEYMER
DONNA HAYWARD: LARA FLYNN BOYLE
AUDREY HORNE: .SHERILYN FENN*
DR. WILLIAM HAYWARD: WARREN FROST
NORMA JENNINGS: ..PEGGY LIPTON
JAMES HURLEY: .JAMES MARSHALL
BIG ED HURLEY: EVERETT MCGILL
PETE MARTELL: .JACK NANCE
LELAND PALMER: RAY WISE
JOSIE PACKARD: JOAN CHEN
CATHERINE MARTELL: ..PIPER LAURIE*
LEO JOHNSON: ..ERIC DaRE
DEPUTY ANDY BRENNAN: HARRY GOAZ
DEPUTY TOMMY "HAWK" HILL: .MICHAEL HORSE
LAURA PALMER/MADELINE: .SHERYL LEE
DR. LAWRENCE JACOBY: RUSS TAMBLYN
SARAH PALMER: .GRACE ZABRISKIE
LUCY MORAN: KIMMY ROBERTSON
JERRY HORNE: ..DAVID PATRICK KELLY
HANK JENNINGS: CHRIS MULKEY
ALBERT ROSENFIELD: ..MIGUEL FERRER
BLACKIE O'REILLY: VICTORIA CAITLIN
MAJOR BRIGGS: .DON DAVIS
BETTY BRIGGS: .CHARLOTTE STEWART
MARGARET, THE LOG LADY: CATHERINE E. COULSON
MIKE NELSON: ..GARY HERSHBERGER
NADINE HURLEY: WENDY ROBIE
EILEEN HAYWARD: ..MARY JO DESCHANEL
SYLVIA HORN: ..JAN D'ARCY
PHILLIP "MICHAEL" GERARD: .AL STROBEL
KILLER BOB: FRANK SILVA
GORDON COLE: ..DAVID LYNCH
RICHARD "DICK" TRELAINE: ..IAN BUCHANAN
HAROLD SMITH: .LENNY VAN DOHLEN
JEAN RENAULT: .MICHAEL PARKS
RONETTE PULASKI: .PHOEBE AUGISTINE
JANEK PULASKI: ALAN OGLE
SUBURBIS PULASKI: MICHELE MILANTENI
NANCY O'REILLY: ..GALYN GORG
JUDGE STERNWOOD: .ROYAL DANO
SID: .CLARE STANSFIELD

* - Nominated for Emmy Award

PILOT

Written By Mark Frost and David Lynch Directed By David Lynch

Airdate: 4/8/90

In the premiere episode of the show, Pete Martell (Jack Nance) discovers a body lying on the shore outside his home in the Blue Pine Lodge while on his way to go fishing. He rushes inside to call the police and says into the telephone, "She was dead...wrapped in plastic."

Sheriff Truman (Michael Ontkean) quickly responds to the call accompanied by the town doctor, Will Hayward (Warren Frost). Turning the body over, Truman and Hayward are shocked when they realize the identity of the corpse. It is Laura Palmer (Sheryl Lee), wrapped naked in plastic and bound by tape. Deputy Andy Brennan (Harry Goaz) begins to break down to the chagrin of Truman who asks him to leave the crimesight.

At the Palmer residence, Laura's mother, Sarah (Grace Zabriskie) realizes that Laura had not come home the previous night and begins making frantic phonecalls trying to find her daughter. The football coach tells her that Laura's boyfriend, Bobby Briggs (Dana Ashbrook) didn't show up at practice and his parents haven't seen him either.

At the Great Northern, a sprawling hotel overlooking a waterfall owned by the town's corporate big-wig Ben Horne (Richard Beymer), Laura's father Leland, is pitching a real-estate development with Ben to a group of Norwegian investors. The proposal they are proposing is the Ghostwood Country Club and Estates on the site where the Packard Sawmill now stands. Leland is called to the phone by a distraught Sarah Palmer who says Laura hasn't come home. As Leland tries to calm her, Truman enters the hotel. Leland leaves the receiver dangling as the Sheriff informs him that his daughter was murdered. Sarah screams as she realizes Laura is dead.

Across town at the Double R Diner, Bobby Briggs enters, not yet aware of his girlfriend's death. He offers to drive waitress Shelly Johnson (Madchen Amick) home. She takes him up on his offer and when they walk out we realize there's more than just a platonic relationsip here. Bobby drives Shelly towards her house and asks her if her husband, Leo (Eric DaRe), is at home. She assures him that he's in Butte, Montana and isn't back yet. As they turn the corner of the country road, they see Leo's rig, a massive truck, parked outside the house. Bobby brings the car to a screeching halt and Shelly rushes out.

At the high school, a state trooper enters Laura's homeroom class to speak to the teacher. Her best friend, Donna Hayward (Lara Flynn Boyle), looks at the empty chair and realizes something is tragically wrong. When a girl runs across the courtyard in tears, Donna turns to James Hurley (James Marshall), Laura's secret boyfriend fearing the worst as the teacher re-enters the classroom shaken with the news of Laura's death.

Bobby Briggs upon his arrival at the school is immediately taken into custoy by Truman for Laura's murder. Passionately denying his responsibility, Briggs is handcuffed and taken away to the Sheriff's Station.

On the school's public address system, the principal announces to the school that Laura has been killed as the camera slowly trucks in on a portrait of Laura, the school's homecoming queen, in the a place of honor in the school's trophy case.

At the Palmer residence, Sarah Palmer tells Truman that she last saw Laura go into her room at 9 the previous evening and that she received one phone call. Upstairs, Deputy Hawk (Michael Horse) finds Laura's diary and a video camera. As Truman continues his line of questioning, he is interupted by Andy who informs him that one of the worker's at the mill, Janek Pulaski (Alan Ogle), daughter has disappeared.

Josie Packard (Joan Chen), who became the owner of the Packard Sawmill after her husband's death in a mysterious boating accident, orders Pete, the husband of Catherine Martell (Piper Laurie) — the manager of the mill and Andrew's sister, to shut the mill down for the day. Catherine threatens Josie not to close down the mill, but she refuses and orders Pete to "push the plug". Disgusted, Catherine walks out and fires one of the millworkers, Fred Truax, out of spite. Josie delivers an announcement over the antiquated public address system that she is closing the mill for the day in remembrance of the memory of Laura Palmer and in lieu of the disappearance of Janek's daughter, Ronette. She urges the millworkers to go home and spend time with their families.

On a deserted train trestle stretching through the mountains around Twin Peaks, Ronette Pulaski staggers down the tracks in a ripped neglagie, her hands bound with rope, as a railroad foreman looks up and sees her.

James Hurley drives up on his motorcycle to his Uncle's gas station and hands Big Ed Hurley (Everett McGill) a note for him to give to Donna and says of Laura "She was the one" as he drives off.

FBI Special Agent Dale Cooper drives into town, dressed in a conservative blue suit, he speaks into his pocketsized taperecorder remarking about the beauty of his surroundings and his assignment in Twin Peaks, to find the killer of Laura Palmer.

Meeting Sheriff Truman at the town hopsial, Calahoun Memorial, he asks the sheriff about the magnificent trees in the town and than is taken to the room where the comotized Ronette Pulaski lays. Muttering "Don't go there, don't go there", Cooper, for some reason, checks under her fingernails and finds nothing. On their way to the morgue to examine Laura Palmer's body, the two are confronted by Dr. Lawrence Jacoby (Russ Tamblyn), the town psychiatrist. He explains that Laura was a patient of his and asks if he can join them. Cooper refuses Jacoby's request.

As they proceed to the morgue, they pass a One-Armed Man (Al Strobel) who is in the hospital to visit his friend Bob Lydecker. In the basement, as the fluorescent lights flicker above them, Cooper examines Laura's fingernails. Under one of her nail's he finds a tiny piece of paper with the little R inscribed on it. Truman is befuddled as Cooper turns to him and says, "We have alot to talk about."

Arriving at the Sheriff's station, Cooper opens Laura's diary and reads aloud several entries into his taperecorder. "Nervous about meeting J tonight," he says also finding a safety deposit box key and white powder he suspects is cocaine. Harry denies this possibility telling Cooper, "You didn't know Laura."

Interogating Bobby, Cooper shows him the tape they retrieved from Laura's room in which Laura and Donna are dancing in the woods while on a picnic. Bobby denies having shot it and Cooper asks him who the "J" in the note could of been. Was he the one shooting the video? Bobby denies knowing anything about a "J" and is released from custody. Telling his best-friend, Mike Nelson, that he has learned that James Hurley was actually Laura's secret lover and swears to deal with him. Cooper's secretary Lucy Moran (Kimmie Robertson), who overhears their conversation, tells Truman and Cooper that she found out that biker Hurley is the one responsible for filming the video according to Briggs.

Audrey Horne (Sherilyn Fenn), the sexy and mischevious daughter of Ben Horne, sneaks into the conference room where the Norwegians are assmebled and tells them that her friend Laura has been brutally murdered. When they flee the town in a panic, she laughs, as Ben desperately tries to keep them from leaving.

Cooper and Truman find the abandoned railroad car where Laura and Ronette were attacked. There, they find a mound of dirt with half of a golden heart necklace and a scap of paper on which "Fire, Walk With Me" is written inscribed in blood.

On a hill nearby, James Hurley looks out on the panaromic vista fondling the othe half of the golden heart in his hand. Investigating Laura's safety deposit box, Cooper is given the box by bank clerk Alice Brady and opens it finding $10,000 in cash and a copy of FLESHWORLD magazine featuring personal ads placed by Ronette Pulaski and Laura Palmer featuring a picture of Leo Johnson's truck.

At Leo's house, the trucker questions his wife, Shelly, about a different brand of cigarette he has discovered in the ashtray. He warns her that in the future she better only smoke one brand of cigarette because if he finds another brand in the future....

A Town Meeting is called that evening to discuss the disturbing events in the town and Cooper asks Truman about several of the attendees. Truman tells him that Josie inherited the Packard Sawmill from Andrew and that Ben Horne is the town's big-wig businessman. He also tells him that the Log Lady is a strange occupant of the town who carries along a log that possesses a special wisdom. Cooper tells those in attendance that the murder of Laura Palmer bears an unnatural resemblance to that of one which took place almost a year ago in another part of the state and that a serial murderer could be at work. He warns them that there is a chance that "the person who committed these crimes is someone from this town, possibly even someone you know."

Later that night at the Hayward residence, Donna overhears her father talking to her mother about the fact the police suspect that whoever has the other half of the heart necklace they found could be the killer. Intent on warning James, she sneaks out of the house to find James. Outside, Mike and Bobby show up to find Donna and when Dr. Hayward goes to her room he finds she has broken the curfew and snuck out of the house.

At the Roadhouse, the Twin Peaks bar, Julee Cruise sings "Falling" and "The Nightingale" and when Donna enters Bobby and Mike get into a fight with Big Ed and James biker friends. Billy Paulsen, one of James friends, escorts Donna out to James while Cooper and Truman wait outside having suspected that Donna would lead them to Hurley.

Rendezvousing with James in the woods, Donna tells him they suspect he may be responsible for Laura's murder and as they break down and share their grief over her death together, they begin to realize the passion and love which had lain dormant underneath their once platonic relationship. They decide to bury the necklace and as they leave the woods, the two are intercepted by Cooper and Truman who have been following them and James is taken into custoy.

Taken into a holding cell, Mike and Bobby who have been incarcerated for their barroom brawl, start howling at James and warn him that "when you least expect it, expect it". In the conference room, Cooper tells Truman that he wants to find a hotel room which is "clean and reasonably priced" and Truman promises to "get him a rate" at the Great Northern. When Cooper leaves to check-in at his hotel, Truman drives up to meet Josie Packard, with whom he is having an affair.

Catherine, calls Ben Horne from the adjoining room, and says "he's here again". At the Palmer house, Sarah screams as a gloved hand reaches into the mound of dirt in the woods to retrieve the broken necklace.

EPISODE ONE

Written By: Mark Frost & David Lynch Directed By: Duwayne Dunham

Airdate: 4/12/90

In Room 315 of the Great Northern Agent Cooper hangs from a chin-up bar remarking on the magnificent Douglas Firs that tower in the air outside his window and he wonders aloud to Diane, the recipient of all his taped recordings, "Two things that continue to trouble me — and I'm speaking not only as an agent of the Bureau, but also as a human being. What really went on between Marilyn Monroe and the Kennedys...and who pulled the trigger on JFK."

Cooper goes downstairs for breakfast and sipping a coffee looks up as the waitress and says, "Excuse me, this is a damn good cup of coffee" (Trudy, the waitress in the Great Northern is played by Story Editor Robert Engels wife, Jill Rogosheskie). Audrey sits down with Cooper trying to make small talk with him and he asks if she was close with Laura. "Not exactly," she says and as for her retarded brother Johnny she said "He has emotional problems, it runs in the family."

Arriving at the Sheriff's office, Cooper and Truman review the autopsy report on Laura. Dr. Hayward tells them that Joe Fielding from Fairville did the post mortem since he couldn't bring himself to do it and tells them that there were a number of shallow wounds and bite marks found on her body and that the toxological report showed she had sex with at least three men before she was killed.

Leaving for work at the Double R Diner, Shelly Johnson is given a bag of laundry by her husband. Bringing it inside, she prepares to throw the dirty clothing into the washing machine when she finds a bloodstained shirt and hides it.

Cooper interogates James Hurley who reveals that he shot the videotape of Laura and Donna and that he knew she was addicted to cocaine but tried to get her to stop. Telling them that he was with her on the night of her death, she jumped off his motorcycle at Sparkwood and 21 and he never saw her again. He tells them though he knows nothing about the necklace despite having a vivid recollection of the cold day on February 5th when Laura broke her golden heart necklace and handed it to him saying "now my heart belongs to you". Meanwhile at the Johnson residence, Leo is furious because he can't find the bloodstained shirt.

Still incarcerated, Bobby and Mike are distrubed because the $10,000 they need to pay Leo for a shipment of cocaine was in Laura's safe-deposit box, money they no longer have access to. Big Ed arrives to pick up James who is being released. He tells Truman that he fears his beer was drugged the previous night at the Roadhouse because even as he got up to stop Mike from grabbing Donna he almost collapsed. He tells them that Jaques Renault was tending bar. As James and Big Ed leave, James tells Ed that Mike and Bobby are after him now and he'll need the "Bookhouse Boys" to help protect him.

Nadine Hurley (Wendy Robie) runs into Norma Jennings (Peggy Lipton), the woman that Big Ed is secretly seeing, at the hardware store and tells her that she is hoping to build a silent draperunner.

"Can we offer you gentlemen a cup of joe," Josie Packard asks Truman and Cooper when they come to visit her, Pete Martell pours them coffee and inadvartently leaves a fish in the percolator resulting in a very unnatural tasting brew. Josie tells them that Laura was tutoring her in English and that the last time she saw her was the previous Thursday and that "something was bothering her". She tells them Laura said, "I think now I understand how you feel about your husband's death." When Josie leaves the room Cooper asks Harry how long he has been seeing her. Surprised, Harry asks, "How did you know?"

At the same time, Ben Horne and Catherine Martell, who are also sleeping together, discuss their plans to take control of the mill in order to build the Ghostwood estates. "A few more local tragedies and Josie might just run the old mill into the ground all by herself," Ben says. Catherine is reluctant to wait and Ben says, "Maybe it's time to start a little fire." Catherine asks, "Are you talking about business or pleasure?"

Visiting the griefstricken Palmer's Donna embraces Sarah who envisions her as Laura and then has a terrifying vision of Bob (Felix Silva), the long-haired and malevolent killer, and she screams in terror. Hawk sees the One-Armed Man again lurking around the hospital. We also discover that Ronette Pulaski worked at the perfume counter of Horne's Dpeartment Store.

Ben Horne enters his study where he finds Audrey dancing dreemily and confronts her about the exodus of the Norwegians. He chastises her and says, "Laura died two days ago, I lost you years ago." At the Briggs house, the Major, Bobby's father assures Bobby that while "rebellion is expected in a boy your age" smoking is a filthy habit for "a varsity athlete" and tries to establish a dialogue with his authority hating son.

At the Double R Diner, Cooper and Truman are talking to Norma eating the delicious pie when the Log Lady enters. She tells them that, "One day, my log will have something to say about this. My log saw something that night." Cooper is dubious, but does find out that Laura initiated the Meals-On-Wheels program with Norma to bring food to elderly shut-ins.

Leo Johnson, who is carving open a football hears Shelly enter. When she walks in, he immediatley confronts her about the blood soaked shirt which has disappeared and wields a sock with a bar of soap in it over his head and turns on the radio attacking her to a pulsating melody. She collapses against the transparent platic sheeting which hangs on an unfinished wall in the house.

At the Hayward residence, James visits for dinner while Mike and Bobby drive by. Bobby says, "Too bad we can only kill him once." In Dr. Jacoby's office, the psyhiatrist listens to a tape Laura made before her death and takes out the other half of the golden necklace. Listening to the tape, Jacoby starts to cry as he holds the broken heart in his hands.

EPISODE TWO

Written By: Mark Frost & David Lynch Directed By David Lynch

Airdate: 4/19/90

Jerry Horne, Ben's brother, returns from Paris, interupting the Horne's quiet dinner with delicious brie and baguette sandwiches. Ben and Jerry devour them, engaging in a completely incoherent conversation. Ben tells Jerry that Laura was murdererd and that the Norwegians left without closing the deal for Ghostwood. Jerry, depressed over Laura's death, is told by Ben that a trip to One-Eyed Jacks will help cheer him up. "All work and no play makes Ben and Jerry dull boys," Jerry laughs.

The two arrive in a motorboat at the bordello and casino north of the Canadian border and disembark where they are greeted by scantily clad women who escort them inside. Ben wins the chance to spend the evening with the new girl "freshly scented from the perfume counter" on a coin flip.

In the Hayward's house James tells Donna that their newfound love is not an offense against Laura. "What we're doing now would have worked out this way anyway," he says. Donna realizes that they "could never say how they felt when Laura was around" and the two lovers kiss. Cooper arrives at his room at the Great Northern and receives a phonee call from Hawk wo tells him that "the One-Armed man was snooping around intensive care" and Cooper asks him to "maintain watch". Picking up a note slipped under his door he looks at it: "Jack with One Eye," the note reads.

In the woods, Mike and Bobby go to pick up their cocaine filled football only to find it empty. Leo confronts them with a gun and demands to be paid, but they tell him that Laura had the money and her murder complicated matters. "You punks owe me ten grand, Leo needs a new pair of shoes," Johnson snarls at them. He tells them his wife has been cheating on him and Bobby scared, promises to get the money. Leo orders him "to go out for a pass" and Mike and Bobby flee back through the woods to the car where the football lands on their winshield.

Big Ed, while entering his house, trips on the drape runners Nadine has left on the floor and drips grease on them. She screams at him, furious over his clumsiness. Nadine is devestated and bends back the steel handles on her exercise machine in a rage.

Cooper assembles the sheriff's department outside where he explains to them how he intends to solve the case. After delivering an impassioned speech about the Dahli Lama in Tibet who was forced to flee to India in 1959, he tells them that by placing a bottle on a log, he intends to hurl rocks at them and if they break then the name of the person who has been called out is guitly. One pebble strikes a bottle when Dr. Jacoby's name is called, but it does not break. As Lucy checks off names on the blackboard and the deputies look on incredulously, a bottle shatters when the name of Leo Johnson is called out.

Donna approaches Audrey at the Double R Diner where they discuss Laura. "Agent Cooper loves his coffee, but he likes it black," Audrey tells Donna. She asks her, "Did Laura ever talk about my father. He used to sing to her". Confused by Audrey, Donna watches as Audrey segues into a sensuous, somber dance. "I love this music. Isn't it dreamy," Audrey says immersed in Badalamenti's music emananting from the jukebox.

Arriving at the Sheriff's Office is Albert Rosenfield, the sarcastic forensic pathologist who has come to examine Laura's body for clues to her murder. Cooper tells Truman that he's an extremely competent investigator but, "Albert is lacking in some of the social niceities". Big Ed returns home and is grabbed in an embrace by Nadine who thanks him. She's elated, when Ed's grease dripped on the drape runners it rendered them completely silent.

Up at the Blue Pine Lodge, Pete Martell takes Josie to a wall safe where Catherine keeps a second ledger secreted. In Laura's room at the Palmer House, her father Leland is listening to her old records. When Glenn Miller's "Pennsylvania 6-5000" starts playing, he yells, "We have to dance for Laura" and takes her picture and starts dancing. Struggling to retrieve it, Sarah prys the picture away from him and it shatters. "Leland," she screams. "What is going on in this house?"

Preparing for bed at the Great Northern, Cooper begins to dream. In it he sees images of himself as an older man, Sarah Palmer running down the stairs of her house and Laura's face in the morgue. Suddenly the One-Armed Man appears walking through the darkness saying, "In the darkness of future past, the magician longs to see, one chance heart between two worlds. Fire, walk with me." The rambling poetry of the One-Armed Man turns to clues about Bob, "We lived among the people," he adds menacingly. "How do you say...convenience store. We lived above it. I mean it like it is and it sounds. I too have been touched by the devilish one. A tattoo on the left shoulder. But when I saw the face of God, I was changed. I took the entire arm off...My name is Mike. His name is Bob."

The frighteningly scary Bob appears calling for Mike, "Can you hear me? Catch you with my death bag! You may think I have gone insane, but I promise I will kill again."

The image returns to a room with red drapes in which an aged Dale Cooper sits confronted by what appears to be Laura Palmer and a dwarf who dances and says, "Let's rock!" Talking to him in a garbled, but subtitled, dialogue. "She's full of secrets," the dwarf tells him. Cooper sits motionless as the man from another place begins to dance. Agent Cooper wakes from his dream and calls Truman, "I know who killed Laura Palmer," he says, telling the Sheriff that the answer can wait until morning...and the beginning of the next episode.

EPISODE THREE

Writen By: Harley Petyon Directed By: Tina Rathborne

Airdate: 4/26/90 EMMY AWARD NOMINATED EPISODE

"Good morning Colonel Cooper," Audrey says to FBI Agent Dale Cooper over breakfast at the Great Northern. "Just Agent, Special Agent," he replies. By comparing her handwriting to the note he received the previous night, he realizes she wrote it and asks Audrey what the note she slipped under his door meant. She tells him that One-Eyed Jacks is a place across the Canadian boarder where "women work". Cooper asks if Laura worked there, Audrey doesn't know but tells him that she did work at the perfume counter at her father's department store — like Ronette.

Truman charges in at 7 AM with Lucy in tow and Cooper asks Audrey to leave. The sheriff immediately asks who killed Laura Palmer and Cooper explains that in his dream, a girl who looked exactly like Laura Palmer ("she's my cousin but doesn't she look exactly like Laura Palmer" the dwarf said) whispered the murderer's name in his ear, but he forgot. "My dream is a code waiting to be broken," Cooper tells him. "Break the code, solve the crime."

At the county morgue where Albert Rosenfield is preparing to do a more thorough examination on Laura's body, Dr. Hayward intervenes refusing to let him keep the body which needs to be taken to the cemetary. "I am the sultan of sentiment," Albert tells the Doctor. Cooper sides with Dr. Hayward and insists that Albert who will release the body for the funeral and an angered Albert "who will suffer fools with badges never" is struck by Sheriff Truman who has taken as many insults as he could take from the city slicker.

Leland is watching INVITATION TO LOVE when Madeline Ferguson (also played by Sheryl Lee) arrives, his niece, "but doesn't she look exactly like Laura Palmer". She has come from Missoula to Laura's funeral and to spend time with her Uncle Leland and Aunt Sarah. Meanwhile at the Double R Diner, Mr. Moody, the attorney for Norma Jennings incarcerated husband, Hank, tells her that she will need to testify at his parole hearing to help obtain his release.

Leo Johnson is chopping wood when the Sheriff and Cooper arrive to question him:

TRUMAN : We'd like to ask you a couple of questions

LEO: So ask.

COOPER : Leo, is that short for Leonard?

LEO: That's a question?

COOPER: Did you know Laura Palmer?

LEO: No.

COOPER: You're lying.

Leo tells them that he was on the road in Butte, Montana the night of Laura's death and that his wife, Shelly, can corroborate his story. "I paid my debt to society," Leo says to the lawmen.

Bobby's father, Major Briggs, sits down to speak with him about his feelings about the funeral. He takes a cigarette out of Bobby's mouth, "It's a filthy habit especially for a varsity athlete." He goes onto tell Bobby that "responsibility is the lynchpin of our society" and that he understands Bobby's grief and emphathisizes about the pain he must be feeling over Laura's death and that there is no need to be afraid about the funeral, his family will be besides him. "Afraid," Bobby yells. "Afraid! I'm going to turn it upside down!"

In the conference room at the Sheriff's Office Hawk tells Cooper he can't track down the One-Armed Man and Albert sits down to brief them on his findings. He confirms that Laura had a cocaine habit and that she was bound with two kinds of twine before her murder.

ALBERT : Toxicology results also positive. News flash: the little lady had a habit. Next we have fibers of twine inbedded in her wrists and upper arms. Two different kinds of twine, fibers of twine found in the railroad car, I matched the sample from her wrists. The same twine was used to bind the wrists of the Pulaski girl. Conclusion: she was tied up twice at different locations on the night of her death.

COOPER : Sometimes my arms bend back.

Rosenfield goes on to tell them that the wounds on Laura's shoulder were bite and claw marks.

ALBERT: Distinctive wounds found on Laura's neck and shoulder appear to be claw marks. Bites of some kind.

TRUMAN : An animal?

ALBERT : Look, it's trying to think.

Rosenfield also discovered a fragment of plastic in her stomach, partially dissolved by digestive acids. "I'm taking it back to the lab for reconstruction as the local facilities give new meaning to the word primitive," he says. "I note with some interest what appears to be the letter J."

COOPER : Good work Albert.

ALBERT : A couple more days with the body who knows what I would have found.

Andy summons Truman, the funeral will be starting soon and as they start to leave, Albert calls Cooper back into the room for ruther consultation. He tells him that there is the additional matter of dealing with Truman having struck him earlier that day and wants Cooper to sign a letter of complaint against the Sheriff.

COOPER : Albert, I hope you can hear me. I have only been in Twin Peaks for a short time and in that time I have seen decency, honor and dignity. Murder is not a faceless event here, it is not a statistic to be tallied up at the end of the day. Laura Palmer's death has affected each and every man, woman and child because life has meaning here, every life. That's a way of living I thought had vanished from the earth, but it hasn't Albert, it's right here in Twin Peaks.

ALBERT : Sounds like you've been snacking on some of the local mushrooms.

Across town, Nadine and Ed prepare to leave for the funeral, Nadine admits that she has always been jealous of Norma and says "she's like a little brown mouse". Ed consoles her as they start to leave. At the Horne residence, Audrey enters one of the secret tunnels in the house and spies on Dr. Jacoby preparing Johnny for the funeral.

At the gravesite, Laura's coffin is lowered into the ground. A priest delivers the eulogy. "I baptized Laura Palmer, I instructed her in Sunday School and I, like the rest of you, came to love her with that special love we reserve for the headstrong and the bold. Laura was bright, she was beautiful and she was charming but most of all, I think, she was impatient for her life to begin and for the world to finally catch up to her dreams and ambitions. Laura used to say I talk too much, I'll not make that mistake today. Just let it be said that I loved her and I will miss her the rest of my days."

Johnny Horne lets out a reverberating "Amen" echoed by Bobby Briggs who gives his own personal epitath.

BOBBY : What are you looking? What are you waiting for? You make me sick. You damn hypocrites, you make me sick. Everybody knew she was in trouble, but we didn't do anything. ALl you good people. You want to know who killed Laura...YOU DID! We all did. And pretty words aren't going to bring her back, so save your prayers...she would have laughed at them anyway.

Bobby's speech serves as the catalyst for chaos, James charges at Bobby and Big Ed is forced to hold him back as Mike grabs onto Bobby as they flail their fists at each other. By the grave, Leland jumps onto the casket crying out in anguish as the mechanism goes haywire. "Don't ruin this too," Sarah screams at Leland.

A few hours later Shelly Johnson tells a customer about the coffin incident laughing as Leland was raised and lowered ontop the coffin in the grave while Truman introduces Cooper to the Bookhouse Boys, a Twin Peaks secret society at the corner table. "This must be where pies go when they die," Cooper says as he consumes a forkful of Norma's delicious cherry pie. Big Ed, who has been investigating drug trafficking in Twin Peaks is put off by the FBI invesitgators bizarre idiosyncracies and is reluctant to take him into the group's confidence until Cooper looks at him and says deadpan, "So Big Ed, how long have you been in love with Norma?"

TRUMAN : Cooper, you're going to have to go along with me on this even if it sounds a little weird. Twin Peaks is different, a long way from the world. You've noticed that.

COOPER : Yes, I have.

TRUMAN : That's exactly the way we like it, but there's a backend to that that's kind of different. Maybe that's the price we pay for all the good things.

COOPER : What would that be?

TRUMAN : There's a sort of evil out there. Something very, very strange in these old woods. Call it what you want, a darkness, a presence, it takes many forms and it's been out there for as long as anyone can remember and we always have been here to fight it.

Cooper smiles, "A secret society". Hawk suggests they take Cooper for a ride to the Bookhouse, the homebase of the Bookhouse Boys where they have Bernard Renault tied up. Bernard is the janitor at the Roadhouse and brother of Jaques Renault. He is his brother's accomplice in bringing drugs across the boarder. "Did you ever sell drugs to Laura Palmer," Cooper asks him. "I don't sell drugs," Bernard answers in a thick Canadian accent. Back at the Roadhouse, Jaques sees the buslight on, a warning to Jaques to get out of town. He calls Leo Johnson who agrees to pick him up in front of the Cash & Carry. As he leaves, Shelly secures a pistol in her secret hiding place in the house.

That night at Josie's, she tells Harry that she suspects Katherine Martell wants to kill her. "They're going to hurt me," she says. "Who wants to hurt you?" asks the sheriff. "Catherine and Benjamin Horne," she answers. When she takes Truman to the safe where she found the two ledgers, there is only one inside. Catherine listens in over a secret microphone hiding the duplicate ledger just as Pete enters the room.

At the gravesite, Cooper catches Jacoby paying a secret visit and asks him why he wasn't at the funeral. "I'm a terrible person, Agent Cooper," the psychiatrist tells him. "I pretend that I'm not but I am. These people think of me as their friends, the truth is I really don't care."

Back at the Blue Pine Lodge, Josie tells Truman that she thinks they want her dead to gain possession of the sawmill. "I believe they want to take the mill away from me," she says, "so Benjamin can have the land."

At the Great Northern, Cooper and Hawk sit at a table in the hotel sipping coffee. "Do you believe in the soul?" Cooper asks the Indian. "Several," he answers. "Laura's in the ground," Hawk says of a possible afterlife in which the young Palmer's questions could be answered. "That's the only thing I'm sure of." They are interupted by Leland breaking down on the dancefloor crying out "Dance with me". As they escort him home, a traffic light turns from green to red.

EPISODE FOUR

Written By: Robert Engels Directed By: Tim Hunter

Airdate: 5/3/90

Sarah Palmer helps the police create a sketch of Bob, the man she saw in her vision. She also tells the police about seeing a gloved hand take the broken necklace from its hiding place in the woods.

At the Sheriff's Office, the man who secretly has the necklace, Dr. Lawrence Jacoby has come to meet with Cooper but is vague and evasive and tells him very little of conseqenece. He tells Cooper that the night of Laura's death he followed a man in a Red Corvette but lost him on the Old Mill Road. "I'm planning a pilgrimage to Pebble Beach," he says waving good-bye. Truman tells Cooper that Leo Johnson drives a Red Corvette and shows him the police sketch that Sarah Palmer gave them of Bob. It is identical to the man in Cooper's dream.

On the phone, Cooper's supervisor, Gordon Cole calls. "Cooper, where do we start, the Palmer girl or Albert's new best friend, Harry Truman?" Cooper answers, "Laura Palmer". Albert's been very busy," Cole replies. He tells them Albert has determined the wounds on Laura's neck were bird bites and that Rosenfield is filing charges against Truman for assault. Cooper abruptly hangs up and tells Truman not to worry about Albert. Hawk says he's found the One-Armed Man and that he's checked-in at the Timber Falls Motel.

Staying at the same hotel are Catherine and Ben on a secret rendezvous while Josie spies on them from outside. Ben tells Catherine that he will make the fire look like arson and the headlines will read "Josie Packard Torches Bankrupt Mill In Insurance Fraud." When Ben gets out of bed to take a bath, a poker chip from One Eyed Jacks falls out of his pocket. Catherine picks it up.

Outside, Andy drops his gun and it discharges as they raid the hotel room of the One-Armed Man. When they burst in they find him standing in a towel. Once they interogate him, they disover the One-Armed Man is Philip Michael Gerard, a shoe salesman who was at the hospital to visit a sick friend, veterinarian Bob Lydecker. When shown the sketch of Bob,

Gerard denies knowing the man in the picture. He tells them he lost his arm in a car accident and that he did have a tatoo, but it read "Mom", not "Fire, walk with me." In the parking lot Hawk is able to determine from the tire tracks that Josie was at the hotel.

In the bathroom at school, Audrey approaches Donna and asks for help in investigating Laura's death so that she can continue helping Agent Cooper. "In real life there is no algebra," Audrey tells her. "Maybe you should go off and join the circus," answers Donna who is then told by Audrey that she has learned Laura was seeing Dr. Jacoby and that she may have been working at One-Eyed Jacks. Donna agrees to help Audrey as long as they keep their findings secret.

At the prison, Norma thanks Mr. Moody for all his help and visits with Hank. "You haven't been by lately," he tells her pleading for her to back him up. "I swear I've changed," he says. In the parole hearing Norma tells the board that she can give him a job at the Double R diner and Hank delivers an impassioned speech about fate and how he has benefitted from his time in prison. They promise to let him know their decision by 5 PM.

Arriving at the convenience store that Cooper envisioned in his dream they see Bob Lydecker's veterinary office across the street and enter. Cooper decides to confiscate the records guessing that the bird who attacked Laura the night of her death was a patient of Lydecker.

Shelly tells Bobby that she knows Leo has been spending time with Jaques Renault and that they are running drugs across the boarder and selling them at school and perhaps even sold them to Laura. Shelly shows Bobby the bloody shirt of Leo's she has hidden and he takes it. "Leo's not going to be a problem for us anymore," he says.

Truman asks Lucy to search the confiscated records and find all the people who own birds in Twin Peaks. Andy tells Lucy about how embarassed he is over dropping his gun, but she is treating him coldly and he's not sure why. Cooper decides that under the present circumstances they could all use some practice using their guns and they proceed to the shooting range.

Andy completely misses the target and as Cooper discharges several astoundingly accurate shots he tells Truman and the deputies stonefaced that he was never married, but knew someone once who "helped me understand commitment, the responsibility and the risks...who taught me the pain of a broken heart."

HAWK : One woman can make you fly like an eagle, another can give you the strength of a lion but only one in the cycle of life can fill your heart with wonder and the wisdom that you have known a singular joy. I wrote that for my girlfriend.

COOPER : Local gal?

HAWK : No, Diane Shapiro, Ph'D. Brandeis.

At the diner, Shelly and Norma share horror stories about their respective husbands. "I've definitely got plans for Leo," Shelly says of her spouse. Soon afterwards, Norma receives a phone call from mr. moody, Hank has been paroled. Madeline enters the diner and James is shocked when he ses her, she looks just like Laura (apparently he missed her at the funeral). She tells him they used to pretend to be sisters when they were children.

Riding an exercise bike in his study at the Great Northern, Ben Horne peddles furiously when Audrey enters. "Are you ashamed of me?" she asks her father. She tells him she wants to change and help him with the family business. Reluctant to believe her, she manages to convince him and agrees to let her have a job at the Department Store. Their conversation is intrupted by a mysterious phone call.

At the Sheriff's station, they find in Lydecker's files that Jaques Reanult owns a mynah bird named "Waldo". When they arrive at his apartment they see someone escaping out the window, but the stranger eludes them. Unbeaknownst to them it was Bobby secretly planting Leo's shirt in Jaques' apartment where the police find it.

At the river, Ben meets with Leo Johnson who has arrived at the covert meeting in a radiant red Corvette. Leo, who has just killed Bernard Renault to keep him from revealing any details of their cocaine smuggling ring, is instructed to torch the Packard Saw Mill. "Keep it simple," says Ben. "The insurance investigator should read ARSON in block letters about six feet high."

Having heard about Sarah Palmer's vision, Donna and James return to the woods to retrieve the necklace which has disappeared. They consider telling the police, but decide to pursue the investigation on their own as they embrace in a passionate kiss.

Pete Martell attempts to recuit Josie for a mixed-double's fishing tournament when Sheriff Truman calls to find out why Josie was at the Timber Falls Motel that afternoon. She tells him that she was following Ben and Catherine and after she hangs up she opens an envelope and finds a drawing of a domino from Hank Jennings who calls a few minutes later. "Did you get my message," he asks holding a domino in his hand. "Catch you later."

EPISODE FIVE

Written By: Mark Frost Directed By: Lesli Linka Glatter

Airdate: 5/10/90

Cooper is awakened from a restful night of sleep by a rollicking group of Icelanders who have moved into the Great Northern as the newest suitors for the Ghostwood Estates project.

While Ben Horne plots to close a deal quickly with the merry northerners by taking them to One-Eyed Jacks, Leland enters and starts crying again. At Jaques apartment, Cooper, Truman and Dr. Hayward determine that it is Renault's blood on Leo's shirt, AB Negative and not Laura's.

Andy arrives at Shelly Johnson's house looking for Leo and she tells him that she hasn't seen her husband. Norma, meanwhile, visits Big Ed and tells him that Hank has gotten his parole and is coming home. They agree to break-up since Ed isn't ready to leave Nadine and Norma still can't leave Hank.

At Horne's Department Store, Audrey insists on being given a position as at the perfume counter by Emory Battis, the store's manager, and is able to overcome his objections by telling him that she will tell her father that he sexually abused her if he doesn't relent. He gives her the job.

James confesses to Donna that his father isn't dead, but has run off and that his mother, a writer, is an alcoholic. "I don't want to have any secrets from you," he tells her. "It's the secrets that people keep that destroy any chance they have of happiness."

Back at Renault's apartment, Cooper finds another copy of FLESHWORLD with a picture of a nearly-nude Laura Palmer against red drapes and finds a picture of Jacques cabin which also has the same red drapes.

Madeline meets with James and Donna at the Double R where they recruit her to help with their "personal investigation" into Laura's death. She tells them that "I always felt close to her, but I didn't really know Laura that well, but I feel like I do." Sitting at the adjoining table is Hank Jennings, freed from prison, waiting for Norma to return.

At Dr. Jacoby's office, the Briggs are engaged in a family counseling session with the psyhiatrist. He asks Major Briggs and his wife to leave for a moment so that he can speak to Bobby alone. "What happened the first time that you and Laura made love?" Jacoby asks. "Did yu cry? And then what did Laura do, did she laugh at you." Bobby is shocked and braks down in a crying fit. "Laura wanted to die," he says. "Everytime she tried to make the world a better place, something terrible came up inside her and pulled her back down into hell and took her deeper and deeper into the blackest nightmare. And every time, it got harder to go back up to the light."

"Laura wanted to corrupt people because that's how she felt about herself," says Jacoby. Briggs admits it was Laura who made him turn to selling drugs.

In the woods; Cooper, Truman, Hawk and Dr. Hayward encounter the cabin of the Log Lady, whose log promises to reveal the secret clues of the case. Margaret has had the log since her husband, a woodsman, was killed in a fire the day after their wedding. "About time you got here," she says. "Come on then, my log does not judge!" She invites them in "for tea and cookies, no cake," she says. "The owls won't see us in here. Shut your eyes and you'll burst into flame."

LOG LADY: You can ask it now.

COOPER: What did you see that night, the night Laura Palmer was killed

LOG LADY: I'll do the talking. Dark, laughing, the owls were flying, many things were blocked. Laughing. Two men. Two girls. Flashlights passed by over the ridge, the owls wer enear. Footsteps. One man passed by. Screams. Faraway. Terrible, terrible. One voice, girl, further up over the ridge. The owls were silent.

From the cabin of the Log Lady, the team proceeds onto Jaques cabin where they find "music is always in the air". A turntable is skipping on the song "Into the Night" and in the cabin they find Waldo, the mal nourished bird that Jaques owns. They also discover twine, blood and a broken poker chip from One-Eyed Jacks.

That night at the Great Northern a celebration is taking place to welcome the Icelanders to Twin Peaks. Pete Martell is astonished to find out that their entire country is "above the Timber Line". What do you get when you cross a Norwegian with a Swede, asks Jerry Horne, "a socialist who wants to be King."

In one of the adjoining rooms, Catherine is admonishing Ben for the poker chip from One-Eyed Jacks she found in his pocket. "Let's burn the mill," Catherine says. "Let's do it tonight." Ben retorts, "I have retained the services of a qualified professional...breath mint?"

At the party, Leland arrives and starts dancing wildly crying out, "Dance with me, dance with me." Ben forces Catherine to dance with him and they wave their hands wildly in the air as everyone joins in with their bizarre routine.

Madeline calls Donna and tells her that she has found a tape concealed in Laura's bedpost which may reveal clues to the mystery of her death. Back at the Great Northern, Ben enters another room and starts speaking to Josie Pakcard who has brought the duplicate ledger from Catherine's secret hiding place that Ben has apparently told her about. "Then we proceed," Ben says. "Tomorrow night."

Outside the Johnson residence, the recently freed Hank Jennings clobbers Leo and says, "I told you to mind the store Leo, not open your own franchise. Do as your told Leo." Infuriated, Leo staggers into his house where he verbally abuses Shelly who pulls out her gun and shoots him. Leo flees into the night.

Returning to his room at the Great Northern, Cooper pulls his gun realizing someone is in his room. When he throws on the lights he sees Audrey lying naked under the sheets. "Please don't make me leave," she begs.

EPISODE SIX

Written By: Harley Petyon Directed By: Caleb Deschanel

Airdate: 5/17/90

Cooper tells Audrey who's in his bed that he feels they should remain friends. "When a man joins the Bureau, he takes an oath to uphold certain values," he says. "Values that he's sworn to live by. This is wrong, Audrey; we both know it." He offers his friendship and tells him they can talk through the night. Cooper goes off to fetch two chocolate milkshakes as Audrey gets dressed (In one of the script's early drafts, the episode simply opens with the two having breakfast: Audrey says, "I'm going to help you learn all of Laura's secrets. We'll learn them together." Cooper replies, "Stick to your homework, Audrey. A high school diploma is nothing to sneeze at." Foreshadowing her future responsibilities at One-Eyed Jacks, Audrey answers, about her first day of work at the Perfume Counter "Homework's for kids. I'm a working girl now. Syrup?")

At the police station, Lucy continues to give Andy the cold shoulder when Dr. Stanicek calls and she finds out she's pregnant. Cooper walks in and visits the conference room where Waldo is being kept. He's not fond of birds, but is positive that this particular bird who can mimic human speech when in good health, may hold the key to Laura's murderer. He places his voice activated pocket-sized tape recorder by the cage. At the same time, a picture developed from the roll of film they found at Jaques cabin clearly shows Waldo perched on Laura's shoulder. Peering at the poker chip, Cooper decides its time for a little undercover work at One-Eyed Jacks with the Book House Boys.

Leo Johnson spies on his house through the telescopic sight of a shotgun when Bobby comes to pay Shelly a visit. She's scared that Leo's still alive and will come after her and as Leo prepares to come in to exact revenge he overhears on the police radio that Waldo, the bird, has been found and taken into police custody.

Madeline plays the tape she found the previous night for James and Donna. "What's up, Doc?" Laura says on the tape to Jacoby. "I feel like I'm going to dream tonight...big bad ones, you know? The kind you like? I guess I eel I can say anything...all my secrets, the naked ones..I know you like those, Doc...Why is it so easy to make men like me? Maybe if it was harder..." James turns off the recorder, upset. They realize that one of the tapes is missing, the one dated February 23rd, the night of her death. The three plan to sneak into Jacoby's office and find the tape by having him receive a call from...Laura Palmer.

At the perfume counter of Horne's Department Store, Audrey sneaks off to follow a meeting Emory Battis is having with Jenny, her co-worker. He offers her a job at One-Eyed Jacks as a "hospitality girl" and tells her to "ask for Black Rose". When Jenny comes back to the perfume counter, Audrey pretends she was also recruited and manages to secure Blackie's number from her.

Hank, meanwhile is trying to find out who Norma's been seeing in his absence, and manages to find out from Shelly that Big Ed has been extremely helpful while he was in prison. Cooper and Harry treat themselves to a cup of coffee. "I'm gonna let you in on a little secret," Cooper says to the Sheriff. "Everyday, once a day, give yourself a present. Don't plan it, don't wait for it, just let it happen. It could be a new shirt and the men's store, a catnap in your office chair...or two cups of good, hot, black coffee."

Nadine is watching INVITATION TO LOVE, upset over being refused a patent. Ed tries to console her and urges her "don't give up." At Josie Packard's house, Truman arrives and Josie tells her when she was following Catherine and Ben she overheard something about them planning to set a fire at the mill.

At the Great Northern, Cooper and Big Ed are donned in tuexedo preparing to go undercover as two high-rolling oral surgeons from the Twin Cities at One-Eyed Jacks. Truman confides in Cooper that Josie suspects Catherine and Ben are plotting against her and are planning to burn the mill and murder her. "How much do you know about her?" he asks Harry. "Where she's from? What she was before?" Truman assures him that Josie's on the striaght and narrow to which Cooper responds, "That's good enough for me." Meanwhile Audrey tries to reach Cooper at the hotel with an urgent message.

Catherine Martell is surprised when insurance salesman, Walter Neff, arrives with an insurance policy on her life that she was not privvy too. The agent tells her that the policy was drafted and signed by Josie and Ben Horne who are the beneficiaries. Catherine tells him that she intends to withold her signautre from the contract until she has the chance to review it. When Neff leaves, she checks the safe for the secret ledger and finds it has disappeared.

In the conference room of the Sheriff's office, Waldo begins to speak when a shot rings out killing the bird and splattering his blood all over the donuts on the table below him. Leo flees the scene with shotgun in hand. Replaying the tape recording made of the late, lamented Waldo, Cooper hears an errie and disturbing recreation of the events in the cabin. "Laura? Laura?" the bird said into the recorder mimicking a female voice. "Don't go there. Hurting me. Hurting me...stop it! Stop it! Leo, no! Leo, no!"

With $10,000 in FBI money, Cooper and Big Ed show up at One-Eyed Jacks with Hawk monitoring Cooper's wire. They introduce themselves to Blackie and while Big Ed proceeds to lose some serious money at roulette, Cooper sits down with Jaques Renault to play blackjack.

At the Palmer residence, Madeline slips on a blonde wig and with Donna and James prepare a videotape which they send to Jacoby in which Madeline pretending to be Laura shows up holding that day's newspaper summoning the doctor to Easter Park. At the Great Northern, Ben anxious to close the deal with the Icelanders summons Jerry and decides to obtain their signatures at One-Eyed Jacks. Horne calls Josie telling her to lure Catherine to the mill that night and she turns to Hank Jennings who is standing next to her.

In Blackie's office at One-Eyed Jacks, Audrey is interviewing for a job at the brothel. She tells Blackie her name is "Hester Prynne" and when the madame asks her to give her one good reason "why I shuldn't air-mail your bottom back to civilization," Audrey takes a cherry from the desk and ties the stem into a knot with her tounge and places it delicately back on her desk. Blackie hires her.

Dr. Jacoby watching INVITATION TO LOVE is interupted by a phone call from Maddy pretending to be Laura. She tells him to retrieve the tape she has left by his door. He plays it on the video recorder and is told to go to Sparkwood and 21. Jacoby, however realizes that the gazebo the video was filmed at was in Easter Park. He runs out for the rendezvous and James and Donna sneak into Jacoby's office.

Outside, Bobby plants cocaine in the gas tank of James motrocylce while a mysterious stranger spies from behind the trees on Madeline who is waiting at the gazebo.

EPISODE SEVEN: SEASON FINALE

Written and Directed By: Mark Frost

Airdate: 5/23/90

Donna and James searchng through Jacoby's office find a coconut in which the tape they have been looking for is hidden and the golden necklace of Laura's that they had buried in the woods. At Easter Park, Dr. Jacoby arrives to see Laura and is struck on the head by the mysterious stranger.

Jaques deals Cooper a card at the blackjack table at One-Eyed Jacks and he gets "21". Talking to Jaques, he explains that he is a friend of Leo's and the financier for their drug operation. He gives Jaques the broken poker chip from the cabin and offers to buy him a cocktail.

Audrey enters Blackie's office in sexy lingerie and is told that the owner will be arriving shortly and would like to see her. "He likes to spend some times with all the new girls," says Blackie.

Cooper tells Jaques that "Leo played you like a violin" and that he hasn't "cut him in on a piece of the action". He says that he has a $10,000 job for Jaques without Leo to make a boarder run. He asks him as an aside, what really happened in the cabin. Jacques explains the bird pecked at Laura's shoulder and that Laura was tied up. He agrees to meet with Cooper.

In Audrey's room at One-Eyed Jacks, she prepares for her visitor that night while Shelly washes her hair in the kitchen sink. Leo grabs her towel and takes her hair in hand.

Preparing for Jaques, the deputies are staked out with Truman when he arrives. Two officers attempt to arrest him when Jaques gets free and aims his gun at the Sheriff. Andy aims his pistol and fires dropping Jaques to the ground. "Better call that ambulance," he says cooly.

James and Donna listen to the secret tape recording made the night of Laura's death where she chornicles her secret rendezvous with a mystery man who "if I tell you his name, then you're going to be in trouble — wouldn't be such a mystery man any more, but you might be history man. A couple of times he's tried to kill me...but guess what, as you know, I sure got off on it. Isn't sex weird? This guy can really light my f-i-r-e," she says of the sexy stranger in a red corvette. Dr. Hayward interupts them, summoned to the hospital for an emergency.

At the mill, Leo binds and gags Shelly and sets a timer to go off in an hour as he stalks off to kill Bobby. "You broke my heart," he roars. Meanwhile, Nadine Hurley is driven to suicide by her failure to secure a patent for her silent drape runners and dressed in her prom gown she pours sleeping pills into a bowl as she prepares to kill herself.

Josie, who is preparing to give Hank Jennings $90,000, is upset when he wants to renegotiate the terms of their deal in which Hank reveals that he accepted the blame for vehicular manslaughter to avoid being implicated in "a much greater crime - murder." He severs his thumb and hers and touches their bleeding hands together to seal their bond.

At the mill, Catherine enlists the aid of Pete to help her find the missing ledger and rekindles the flame of their romance in an impassioned speech about the attraction they once shared for each other. Pete, puts aside the years of enimity, and rushes to her aid.

The deputies share stories about how Andy saved the sheriff's life when Lucy calls Andy aside to reveal that she is pregnant. Shocked, Andy stumbles away. Lucy, answers a phone call from Bobby Briggs, pretending to be Leo Johnson tipping the police off to the fact there is cocaine secreted in James gas tank.

In Jaques room at Calhoun Memorial Hospital, Cooper interogates Jaques about the night in the cabin when Laura was killed. He confesses to them that Leo knocked him out during a fight and that when he awoke Laura and Ronette were gone and that it was Laura's ideas to take the pictures for FLESHWORLD, an assertion borne out in her diary. Dr. Jacoby is also in the room confined to his bed having had heart attack from seeing Laura.

Catherine receives a phone call at the mill that says she can find the ledger in the drying shed at the sawmill. At the Double R, Ed tells Norma their relationship can still work and upon returning home he finds Nadine laying inert on the floor and calls for an ambulance.

Back at the Sheriff's office, Lucy tells Cooper and Truman that "Leo" called and she could hear the clock at Easter Park. Leland confronts Truman having heard Jaques has been taken into custody demanding to know if he is the murderer of his daughter. They send him home. James arrives with the tape they recovered from Jacoby's office. "What kind of dangerous games are you playing?" Cooper asks James as he opens the package of cocaine they found in his gas tank.

At One-Eyed Jacks, Einar Thorson (Brian Straub), the Icelander signs his contract for the Ghostwood Country Club And Estates. At the Johnson residence, Bobby enters looking for Shelly and instead finds an axe-wielding Leo Johnson who approaches him menancingly when Hank Jennings shoots Leo through the window not realizing Bobby is also inside.

Catherine arrives at the mill and finds Shelly hanging from the rafters. Shelly desperate to communicate cannot be understood as she is gagged. "I can't hear a word you're saying, you have a thing in your mouth?" Catherine says removing it as the timer ignites the mill fire. Outside, realizing Catherine is inside, Pete charges into the mill to rescue his wife.

A sleeping Jaques Renault is bound with tape by Leland Palmer who suffocates him with a pillow and then stalks silently out while at One-Eyed Jacks, Ben Horne enters the room of the new girl, who unknown to him is his daughter. As he enters the room, Horne chillingly recites "Close your eyes, such are the stuff that dreams are made of" as Audrey is shocked to see her father's reflection in the mirror.

Back at the Great Northern, Cooper returns to his room for "some quality sack time". He picks up the note from Audrey upon arriving in his room, but before he can open it the phone rings. He answers it but is brought to the door by several knocks. Opening it, an unknown assaliant fires several gunshots into his stomach as Cooper collapses to the floor.

* * * *

PROGRAM NOTE: The assailant who attacks Dr. Jacoby was never revealed on the show, but it was indeed Leland possessed by Bob, according to Mark Frost. He sees Madeline leaving the house and follows her. Fearing that Jacoby is going to attack her, he strikes the doctor and is forced to leave when James and Donna arrive.

EPISODE EIGHT: SEASON PREMIERE

Written By: Mark Frost Story By: Mark Frost and David Lynch Directed By: David Lynch

Airdate: 9/30/90

Cooper, who is lying on the floor bleeding from his gunshot wounds, is attended to by the world's oldest and most senile room service waiter. As Cooper lapses into unconsciousness, a giant (Carel Struycken) materializes in his room telling him that "I will tell you three things. If I tell them to you and they come true, will you belive me?" The giant proceeds to tell Cooper that there's a man in a smiling bag, the owls are not what they seem and without chemicals he points. ("This all I am permitted to say. We want to help you?" Who?) "Give me your ring," the giant asks. "I will return it when you find these things to be true." He adds that "Leo is locked inside a hungry horse. There's a clue at Leo's house...you will require medical attention". He than disappears.

Ben Horne, who has entered Audrey's room at One-Eyed Jacks, is put off by the woman hiding behind the curtains and as he reaches in to her she puts a mask over her face so that her father will not recognize her. Jerry Horne interupts by summoning Ben to deal with a snag in their plans.

At the Great Northern, Cooper talks to his taperecorder and reveals he was wearing a bulletproof vest, but rolled it up to chase down a woodtick. He says that "being shot is not so bad as long as you can keep the fear from your mind." He notices his ring is gone as Truman arrives. and he lapses back into unconsicousness.

Cooper awakens at the hospital where Dr. Hayward, Harry and Lucy are hovering over him. Lucy brings the special agent up to date and tells him that Leo was shot, Jaques was stangeled, the mill was burned, Catherine and Josie are missing, Shelly and Pete are suffering from smoke inhalation and Nadine is in a coma from an overdose of sleeping pills. Staggering out, Cooper sees Jaques being wheeled away in a body bag and asks, "Is that bag smiling?"

In her hospital bed, Ronette calls Laura's name as she awakens from her coma while Madeline tells Sarah about her vision of blood on the carpet. Leland comes downstairs singing and his hair has turned completely white.

Ben and Jerry Horne discuss the whereabouts of Catherine and Leo's condition at the office back at the Great Northern when Leland enters signing. He announces to them that he is "back and ready."

At Leo's house, Hawk finds a funnel of gasoline in the back of Leo's car and when Andy rushes up the porch to warn Harry that Albert Rosenfield is back, he inadvertently sends a loose board flying striking him in the head. Underneath, Truman finds a new pair of boots and cocaine in concealement.

At the Double R Diner, Donna meets with Madeline who tells her how much she hates her glasses as she snaps them in half. Donna tells Madeline that James spent the night in jail and not to tell anyone about their plot to sneak into Jacoby's. Norma hands Donna a note she received, "Look into the meals-on-wheels."

Back at the Sheriff's office, Albert is telling Cooper that he was ordered back to town by Gordon Cole to investigate the person who shot him when Andy enters and tells Cooper that Leo Johnson was locked in a jail in Hungry Horse, Montana when Theresa Banks was killed. In the lobby, the One-Armed Man comes in with a suitcase looking for Sheriff Truman to sell him some shoes.

While interogating James, he reveals to Cooper and Truman that Laura once recited a strange poem about fire in which she said, "Would you like to play with fire little boy, would you like to play with Bob." He tells them he doesn't think the mystery man is Leo that she refers to on the tape, but Bob.

Donna visits the holding cell where James is being kept, wearing sunglasses and smoking. James is surprised to see Donna acting so strangely as she hangs on the bars and tells him she can't wait until he is released so they can make love. Upstairs, lovers Lucy and Andy are ordered to look through back-issues of FLESHWORLD for pictures of Teresa Banks, the first victim of the killer found one year ago.

Cooper interogates Dr. Jacoby at the hospital and demands to know how he got the necklace. "The night after Laura died," he says, "I followed Leo. I lost him. A motorcycle came by followed by the police." He followed them into the woods and saw them bury the necklace and took it. "The last time I saw her," Jacoby says of Laura,"she seemed ready to die." He mentions hearing the fire alarm go off the night Leo was killed and smelling a peculiar odor — like engine oil.

In Shelly's room at the hospital, Bobby pays a visit and offers to play doctor as he does his own personal examination on Shelly with a stethascope. He brings her flowers while in the hallway Albert, Cooper and Harry run into Big Ed who is waiting for news on his wife. Big Ed explains that Nadine's eye was shot out on their honeymoon and that the only reason he married her was because he thought his high-school sweetheart, Norma, had married Hank. Cooper and Truman start back to the station.

COOPER : I'm ready to lay the whole thing out

TRUMAN : Rocks and bottles?

COOPER : Chalk and blackboard will be just fine.

TRUMAN : Jelly doughnuts?

COOPER : Harry, that goes without saying

Bobby arrives at the Double R DIner where he finds his father having lunch. "Would you care to join me?" the Major asks his son who takes a seat at his booth.

MAJOR : How was school today?

BOBBY : Fine.

MAJOR : That's good.

BOBBY : How was work?

MAJOR : Work was good.

BOBBY : Dad, what is it that you do exactly?

MAJOR : That's classified.

BOBBY : Oh.

The Major relates a vision he had the previous evening (distinuished from a dream which is the sorting and cataloging of the day's events by the subsconcious, thanks for the tip Major) of standing on the veranda of a vast estate where he was born where he answers a knock at the door from his son who is happy and care-free "leaving a life of deep harmony and joy and we embraced a warm and loving embrace...and we at this moment were one. My vision ended and I awoke with a feeling of optisism and confidence of you and your future. That was my vision of you." Bobby is on the verge of tears as the Major says, "I'm so glad to have had the opportunity to share it with you. I wish you nothing but the very best of all things." Norma enters the diner after visiting with Shelly and when Bobby sees Hank salute his father he recalls that it was Jennings who had shot Leo.

Cooper reviews the case with Rosenfield at the Sheriff's Office where they have determined Laura met James on the night of her death then she met up with Leo, Jaques and Ronette. Laura had sex with Leo and Jaques that night and that there was a third man, who presumably, is the killer. The blood soaked rag with the letters, "Fire, walk with me" was written in the killer's blood, AB Negative. Andy starts crying and Albert turns to him and says, "I know, I know. It's what we call a real three hanky crime." Everyone else is dead or in a coma...only the third man remains.

Harry brings Pete Marttell home where he is still feeling queasy from smoke inhalation. They find a note from Josie that says she went to Seattle on an emergency business trip. Truman tells Pete that they haven't found Catherine. The phone rings, Harry answers it and the mysterious oriental man on the other end of the line hangs up.

"Have you seen Audrey today?" Ben asks Jerry when Hank Jennings enters the room. "Where's Josie?" Ben asks. "She left last night," Hank answers lying and telling them that he shot Leo while he was chopping wood. No one saw, he says. Hank asks them what they're going to do with the two ledgers to which Ben replies to let the Horne Brothers do the thinking, "You're a bicep, relax until we say flex."

At One-Eyed Jacks, Audrey asks Blackie why the door to her room was locked. Blackie tells her, "The owner was disappointed with your performance last night..I don't want to hear another complaint about you." He wasn't my type, Audrey says, and neither is Blackie she jokes. "No offense" Blackie slaps her, "Let's get one thing straight between us princess, when you work for me, everybody's your type."

Donna phones Norma to tell her that she's going to take over Laura's meals-on-wheels route. In the living room, the Hayward's entertain the Palmer family and Harriet, one of Dr. Hayward's three daughters recites a poem about Laura while Gersten (DUNE's Alicia Witt) plays Mendolessen on the piano. Leland gets up and starts singing "Come on, Get Happy!" and collapses.

As Cooper goes to bed, Audrey prays from her room at One-Eyed Jacks that Cooper get her note which has fallen underneath his bed. She thinks she might be in over her head this time. The giant pays a return visit to Cooper's bedside. "I forgot to tell you something," he says. "Better to listen than to talk, don't search for all the ansewrs at once. A path is lain by laying one stone at a time. One person saw the third man, but three have seen him, but not his body. One known to you. Ready now to talk..one more thing, you forgot something" and vanishes.

In Ronette's hospital room, she has a nightmare about the evening she was attacked in the train car of Laura being murderered before her eyes as Bob pounds on her stomach.

EPISODE NINE

Written By Harley Peyton Directed By David Lynch

Airdate: 10/6/90

Albert and Cooper meet for breakfast at the Great Northern Rosenfield tells him that agent Windom Mearl, his former partner, who was retired in an insane asylum has escaped.

Donna starts her meals-on-wheels route by bringing food to Mrs. Tremont whose grandson, a magician (played by David Lynch's son), mysteriously makes creme corn disappear from her plate and into his hands. Mrs. Tremont has little to say about Laura, but suggests she make inquiries with Harold Smith, a friend of Laura's next door. Donna knocks on Smith's door, but there is no answer. She leaves a note for him as he peers out through the windowshades.

In Ronette's hospital room, Cooper and Harry question Ronette. When Cooper shows her a picture of Bob she reacts violently and screams, shaking uncontrollably as Agent Cooper continues to try and question her. At the Horne's, Ben and Jerry try and decide which ledger to burn and decide on roasting marshmellow's instead.

At the Double R Diner, Andy is putting up Wanted posters of Bob when Major Briggs is approached by the Log Lady who tells him that her log told her to relay to him, "Deliver the message." At the Sheriff's Department, Lucy contemplates killing a fly while Andy paces outside. He confronts Lucy about her baby having found out that he is sterile and demands to know how Lucy got pregnant.

In Harry's office, Cooper finds out from the Sheriff that Hank Jennings used to be a Bookhouse Boy and a best friend of Truman's until he turned to crime when they receive a call from Ben Horne telling them that Audrey has disappeared.

Back at the Horne's, Jerry enters with an unsigned insurance policy when Leland joins them. He tells them that he's called Einar Thornson, the Icelander, about the fire when he sees the Wanted poster of Bob. "I know him," Leland says. "From my grandfather's house, he lived next door." As Leland leaves, Ben tells Jerry jokingly to "kill Leland".

Dr. Hayward takes Shelly to see Leo who is in a coma while at One-Eyed Jacks Audrey performs her own interogation on Emory Battis wrapping a rope around his neck and finds out that her father owns One-Eyed Jacks and that Laura worked as a prostitute at the bordello.

Once released from the hospital, Bobby tells Shelly that they can make a fortune from Leo's disability if he stays at home and he persuades her to allow her comotized husband to return home.

That night in Cooper's hotel room while he is telling Diane about his concern over Windom Earle, Major Briggs arrives. He tells Cooper that his secret job with the government involves the receiving of deep space transmissions at radar installations and that the night he was shot they detected a transmission in which scattered through the "space junk" was a message, "The owls are not what they seem" and then "Cooper...Cooper ...Cooper."

James plays a song to Donna and Maddie at the Hayward residence who sing along (which will hopefully never turn up on any soundtrack album). When James starts to look longingly at Maddie, Donna runs out of the room when she receives a call from Harold Smith who wants her to visit. Abandoned in the room alone, Maddie has a vision of Bob attacking her in the living room.

Back at Cooper's room, Cooper is interupted from a dream when he receives a phone call from Audrey calling from One-Eyed Jacks when she is abruptly cut-off by Blackie and Emory. "Trouble Miss Horne, you don't know what trouble is, not by a longshot," Blackie cackles.

EPISODE TEN

Written By: Robert Engels Directed By: Lesli Linka Glatter

Airdate: 10/13/90

At the hospital, Cooper discovers a "B" underneath Ronette's fingernail. Despite the protective guard, the killer managed to sneak in and place the letter under her nail.

Donna pays a visit to the reclusive Harold Smith. He tells her he knew Laura and wants her to place an orh-card on her grave. At the Sheriff's office, Rosenfield once again incites Truman to violence in one of the most astoundingly funny scenes in the series yet.

COOPER : Harry, I belive that these letters and the giant's clues are in some way related to the long-haired man. Mrs. Palmer saw him in a vision and called to say that Maddie had seen the man twice in the last two days, both times in a vision. I've seen him in my dream

TRUMAN : And Ronette?

COOPER : She saw him, physically, at the train car.

TRUMAN : Right.

COOPER : Four of us have seen him in different forms. This path is a psychic link that will lead us straight to him.

TRUMAN : So what did the giant sound like? Did he have a big booming voice or what?

COOPER : No, he spoke softly, distinctly.

ALBERT : And you gave him the beans you were supposed to use to buy a cow.

COOPER : No Albert, I gave him my ring.

ALBERT : Confining my conclusions to the planet Earth, the cocaine you found in James Hurley's gas tank was a match to what we found in Jaques car and Leo's house. You get the picture

COOPER : Even got the frame.

ALBERT : And he worked iwth Leo Johnson, currently appearing at Calhoun Memorial Hostpial as "Mr. Potatohead", the boots are a Circle Brand rare work boot. The ones we found haven't been worn or tampered with. The letter "B" from Ronette's finger was cut from a copy of FLESHWORLD. It's a perfect match. This particular edition features swinger's clubs for standard poodle enthusiasts. No comment.

James visits Cooper who tells the Hurley that he knows the cocaine was planted, but to stay out of trouble. In the reception area, Lucy's lunch date enters, Richard Trelaine, the head of the Horne's home furnishings department. "Capital," he smiles. "We'll go dutch."

Leland approaches Cooper at the stationhouse and tells him he knows who the man on the Wanted poster is. He relates to them the story of a summer house his family had on Pearl Lakes when he was a child whose next-door-neighbor was a man named Robertson who used to throw matches at him and say, "Want to play with fire, little boy?"

At the diner, Lucy tells Dick that she's pregnant and she thinks he is the father. In a nearby booth, James confesses to Maddie that he's concerned over Donna because she is acting so strangely when she enters and sees James and Maddie holding hands. She turns and runs out of the diner distraught to see the two of them affectionately touching.

Blackie makes a video of Audrey Horne, bound and drugged, which she will use as part of her ransom demands when she sends it to Ben Horne. "Ride the white tiger," Blackie says as Audrey as the drugs enter Audrey's system. "She won't ever want to come down, just like her daddy did to me."

The One-Armed Man returns to the Sheriff's office to sell Harry some shoes but when he sees the wanted poster of Bob, he becomes uneasy and excuses himself for a moment. In the conference room, Shelly is uncooperative under questioning from Cooper about Leo's involvement with the murder. Shelly refuses to say anything damaging against her husband. "I'm not going to say anything against him, I love him," Shelly says. Realizing that she is holding out on them, Cooper thanks her for coming by and shows her the door.

COOPER : Okay Shelly, that's fine. Thank's for coming iin. I think Shelly has thought long and hard about this and maybe some day with a little luck and some topflight medical attention she'll have Leo back. The same old Leo that you obviously still love. Maybe then he'll realize what a wonderful person he's married to.

SHELLY : What?

COOPER : Thanks again Shelly. Best of luck.

Shelly leaves.

TRUMAN : What's going on?

COOPER : Smells like insurance money.

In the bathroom, the One-Armed Man loses control of himself in one of the stalls and yells, "Bob, I know you're near. I'm after you now" as he injects himself with an unknown medication.

Jean Renault (Michael Parks), who has been recruited by Blackie to bring Ben Horne the ransom demands, gives Audrey another shot of heroin and Blackie shows him the video of Cooper. Renault tells Battis and Blackie that he wants Cooper to avenge his brothers deaths and adds ominously, "Of course, we can't let the girl leave now either, can we?"

Sheriff Truman tells Cooper that he wants the chance to talk to Josie before Cooper officially brings her in for questioning which he agrees too. Hawk tells them that he found out that the Pearl Lake lot is empty. Truman tells Cooper that Philip Gerard and come by and was upset when he saw the picture of Bob. "Harry, remember in my dream, the one armed man knew Bob," Cooper says. When they find the empty syringe on the bathroom floor, Cooper recalls the giant's admonition, "Without chemicals, he points."

In Nadine's hospital room, Dr. Hayward ties her down with restraints becuase of her super-strength and suggests that Ed sing to her. When he does, she breaks free and thinks she's gong to cheerleading tryouts the next day. "You're only 18 once," Nadine exclaims. In the next room, Cooper and Truman visit Dr. Jacoby who has agreed to be hypnotized to help him recall the night Jaques Renault was murdered. Cooper questions him and Jacoby tells them about tape ripping, a figure putting a pillow over his head. "I know him," Jacoby says.

At Laura's gravesite, Donna brings the flowers that Harold has given her and starts to talk to Laura. "We need to talk," she cries Maybe you already know about me and James, but anyway after you died we kind of got together, but you probably knew how we flet before we did. How can you be so smart about things like that...and so stupid about so much else. I'm mad at you. When it was you and me and James it kind of worked. Now you're gone and I love James and it's a mess. Your cousin Maddie's here and I think there's something going on between the two of them and I'm afraid I'm going to end up losing both of you. I wanted so much to be like you Laura. To have your strength, your courage and look what it did. Look what it did to you. As much as I love you Laura, most of the time we were trying to solve your problems and you know what, we still are. Not mine or James or Maddie's, yours. Your dead, but your problems keep hanging around — it's like they almost didn't bury you deep enough."

James visits the Palmer's looking for Donna when he finds Madeline instead. He tells her his mom is drunk again and Madeline takes a disturbed James in her arms when Donna enters. She runs out followed by James. Inside, Madeline begins to cry over the chaos she's caused. "People think I'm Laura," she says. "I'm nothing like Laura." Leland comforts her. "If it could only be like those summers up at Pearl Lakes," he says when Cooper and Harry enter and arrest Leland for the murder of Jaques Renault.

Donna runs into Harold Smith's apartment crying about James when she sees Laura's secret diary open on his nightstand.

EPISODE ELEVEN

Written By: Jerry Stahl and Mark Frost & Harley Petyon & Robert Engels Directed By: Todd Holland

Airdate: 10/20/90

As the camera zooms out from one of the holes in the interogation room's corkboard, Harry and Cooper question Leland about him killing Jaques Renault.

HARRY : On Friday morning, March 3rd did you go to Calhoun Memorial Hospital?

LELAND : Yes, I was looking for the man who killed my daughter.

Dr. Hayward tells Cooper afterwards that Leland should plead insanity after which Andy approaches the Doctor about his sperm. He gives Andy a vial which he can take back for a sperm test. On the way to the bathroom, Lucy runs into him where she sees him with a copy of FLESHWORLD and is disgusted. When Andy drops the vial and searches under the chairs in the recpetion area, Coper asks Andy where he got his boots. He tells them he bought the Cirlce Brand boots from the One-Armed Man. They're the same brand as Leo Johnson's and Cooper believes its yet another clue.

At the Great Northern, an employee tells Ben that M.T. Wentz, the food & hotel critic for the Seattle Times, is coming to town and Ben tells him to stay alert for any signs of his arrival. Jean Renault arrives at Ben's office with the videotape of Audrey. "I'm just a messenger," Renault says. "They request a large sum of money. I require something else entirely." What Renault wants is Cooper and a stake in One-Eyed Jacks.

Norma receives a call from Janet at the Great Northern at M.T. Wendt's arrival in Twin Peaks and she tells Hank who runs out for tableclothes and other accessories. He tells Norma to give Big Ed a call so he can suggest the Double R to every stranger who pulls into his gas station.

Donna arrives at Harold Smith's for lunch. He shows her Laura's secret diary. Harold reads from it and Donna suggests that he turn it over to the police, but Smith says he's read the entire diary through, "I read this from cover to cover," he says. "There are no solutions here. Besides she gave it to me."

Ben Horne shows Cooper the tape of Audrey and tells him that he didn't call the Sheriff since he feared her kidnappers would kill Audrey. They're asking for $125,000, Ben tells Cooper, and he wants him to deliver the ransom. Josie arrives home and Pete tells her about Catherine's death.

Back at One-Eyed Jacks, Emory Battis drags a drugged Audrey into Jean Reanult where Audrey tells Renault that Battis has physically abused her. "That was wrong," Renault says. "It will never happen agains as long as you're with me. I spoke to your father this morning, you're in no danger. Everything is going to be fine." He shoots Battis who collapses to the ground.

Later that day, after unsuccessfully attempting to arbitrate the continuing problems between Andy and Lucy, Cooper asks Truman for the assistance of one of the Bookhouse Boys. "It would be better if you don't know why," he says. "Okay, I'll set it up," Harry answers.

At the Double R, a obese, bearded man enters and gets the royal treatment since Norma and Hank think its M.T. Wendt, the food critic. When he is escorted to the bathroom, Hank picks his pocket and take his identification, Daryl Lodwick, special prosecutor. Maddie tries to assure Donna that there's nothing going on because her and James and Donna asks for her help in obtaining Laura's second, secret diary.

Truman arrives at the Blue Pine Inn and finds Josie ready in all new lingerie she's purchased in Seattle, but even Harry is dubious. "Josie, were you really in Seatttle?" he asks. "Why didn't you tell me you were go ing?" Josie is upset that Truman may suspect her of wrongdoing, but as they fall into a passioante embrace, an Oriental man stands outside the window as the thunderstorm intensifies.

Judge Sternwood (Royal Dano) arrives, with his beautiful assistant Sid, to arbitrate Leland's case while Dick Trelaine offers $650 to Lucy to pay for her abortion which enrages her and she refuses throwing the money back in his face. Sternwood speaks to Leland and agrees to wait until morning to set bail and starts off to the Great Northern. Cooper asks Harry if he has arranged for one of the Bookhouse Boys to meet him that evening. "He'll be there," Truman says.

Mr. Tajimora, a mysterious Oriental gentenam checks in at the Great Northern, immediatley arousing the suspicions of the clerk who thinks it could be M.T. Wentz, the food critic. Josie introduces Pete Martell to the Oriental Man who was peering in the window who she says is her brother, Jonathan. Once Pete leaves, Josie tells Jonathan, "There might be a problem with Hank." "I'll deal with him," Jonathan answers. "Are we suspected." "Certainly not," she answers as he expresses concern over the nature of her relationship with Sheriff Truman.

When Cooper arrives at the Roadhouse to meet up with one of the Bookhouse Boys he is surprised to find Truman waiting at a barstool in casual attire ready for his own undercover assignment. As Hank closes up the Diner for the evening, Jonathan arrives and incites Hank into attacking him. He easily evades Hank's thrusts and punches and levels him with several judo kicks. "Blood brother," Jonathan tells Hank. "Next time, I'll take your head off."

EPISODE TWELVE

Written By: Barry Pullman Directed By: Graeme Clifford

Airdate: 10/27/90

At 6:42 AM Cooper awakens and does a handstand in his hotel room at the Great Northern. In his inverted position he sees a note underneath the bed. Addressed to my special agent, Cooper opens it. "I've Gone North," the note reads. "Jack may have the answer. Love, Audrey."

In the Sheriff's Office, Hawk tells Truman that two old ladies live in the house on Pearl Lakes he was investigating. Cooper arrives and tells Truman he knows where Audrey is. At the hospital, Mr. Pinko (Squiggy from LAVERNE & SHIRLEY) is demonstrating disability equipment for Shelly and Bobby for their house which doesn't function very well.

In court, Leland pleads not guilty of murder at his arraignment. The prosecution urges that he be denied bail. Harry, who speaks in Leland's defense, is able to have Palmer released on his own recognizance.

Donna vows to Harold that she'll share her life with him if he let's her read Laura's secret diary. "I'll read it to you," he says, "but it cannot leave this room." Harold begins a notebook devoted to her exploits. Donna says she's going to take the diary for safekeeping and read it at home. When Harold follows her out, he shrivels up and collapses to the ground. Donna brings him back into the house.

Back at the courthouse, Sternwood refuses to try Leo because he is incapacitated and tells Cooper, "The woods are wondorous here, but strange." Nadine returns home to her house thinking she is still in high school. Ed tells Nadine that her parents are on vacation abroad when she pulls the door off the refrigirator.

Mr. Tajamora insists on seeing Ben Horne regarding Asian investments in the Ghostwood Estates project. Despite having already sealed a deal with the Icelanders, Ben is willing to reopen negotiations when he is presented with a $5,000,000 check from the mysterious businessman. As Tajamora leaves, Hank appears from behind a secret door and tells Ben, Cooper is on his way to the office. He arrives just as the call comes in from Jean Renault asking Ben to leave the ransom money at a headless merry-go-round by the Columbian Bar north of the Canadian boarder. When Cooper leaves with the money in serialized de nominations, Ben tells Hank to follow Cooper, bring back Audrey and the money. "What about Cooper?" Hank asks. "Cooper isn't coming back," Ben says.

Donna tells Maddie where Harold keeps the secret diary in his house and plots with her so that she can sneak it and steal it while she keeps Smith occupied. Jean Renault, preparing for the rendezvous with Cooper, attaches a knife to his arm.

Andy, who has replaced Lucy, while she's visiting her sister calls for the test results on his sperm count. He's told that "he's a whole damn town" and is quite pleased by the results. Hawk tells Cooper that the One-Armed man was spotted at the Robin's Nest Hotel on Route 9, but although he had disappeared they found the same drug as before. Deputy Brennan calls the number Lucy left for her sister and gets an Abortion

Clinic. He is horrorified.

Maddie enters the diner where she finds James having a cup of coffee. He is disturbed when she leaves abruptly pretending that she is bringing coffee to her Uncle Leland. At Harold's, Donna relates a story about a time she went skinnydipping with Laura and three older boys; Josh, Rick and Tim in the lake. Harold dutifully takes copious notes (SEE: DEAR DIARY)

Outside One-Eyed Jacks, Cooper and Harry stake out the area. As they approach the back entrance, Truman knocks out a guard (Mike Vendrell) and they sneak inside loooking for Audrey. They discover Jean Renault and Blackie talking.

Harold shows Donna his orchid's while Maddie waits patiently outside. When Harold excuses himself for a moment, Donna uses her flashlight to summon Maddie into the apartment. Meanwhile at One-Eyed Jacks, Cooper runs into Nancy, Blackie's sister and twists her arm and forces her to take him to Audrey. They enter the room where Audrey is being kept and Cooper reaches over her. Spotting Nancy unsheathing a knife in the dressing mirror, he grabs her wrist and knocks her out. Cooper puts Audrey over his shoulder and starts out.

Outside Blackie's office, Truman watches as Jean kills Blackie and when he prepares to fire at Renault, he is spotted and a gunfight ensues with the Canadian mobster vanishing in the firefight. Harry meets up with Cooper and Audrey as they begin their escape. A guard (Bob Apisa) stops them and draws a gun. Caught, just as they were about to escape they turn away in defeat when the guard collapses with a knife in his back. Hawk appears on the stairway. "It's a good thing you guys can't keep a secret," Hawk says as he retrieves his hunting knife. As they flee, Hank spots them leaving and notifies Ben via walkie talkie when he is captured by Jean Renault who pulls his identification from his pocket which says Daryl Lodwick, the same wallet Hank stole from the prosecutor in the diner.

As Maddie searches through the secret drawer, Harold hears a noise and spots her. Donna runs to him as Harold grabs a gardening tool and rushes out with the forked instrument in hand. The two girls shudder in the conrer as Harold raises it to his raise and then slices it across his face.

EPISODE THIRTEEN

Written By: Harley Peyton & Robert Engels Directed By: Lesli Linka Glatter

Airdate: 11/3/90

After leaving Harold's house, Donna meets with James and kisses his him, happy to be in his arms again.

At the Sheriff's office, Truman tells Cooper that it was Jean Renault he spotted who was obviously out for revenge against Cooper judging by the videotape he saw at One-Eyed Jacks of Cooper undercover in freeze frame. Cooper tells Harry about the heroin Audrey was injected with and realizes that Audrey was the bait for him and is remorseful. "You got her back," Truman tells him which is the important thing. "You're the best lawman I've ever known," he continues. "But sometimes Coop, you think too much."

Cooper returns the money to Ben Horne and tells him what happened suspicious of Ben and informs him about Jean Renault and that he escaped. Ben hugs Cooper and thanks him for his help. At Shelly's Bobby wheels in Leo while the insurance man in a loud plaid shirt gives him a check, a very small check for Leo's in-home care. "I had to quit my job for this," Shelly says in anguish.

Donna tells Truman about the secret diary that Harold has, but the sheriff is reluctant to believe her when Gordon Cole (David Lynch) arrives looking for Cooper. He has arrived with details of Albert's report when Hawk arrives with the One-Armed Man.

Ben finally speaks to Audrey and tells her how upset he was over her disappearance. She warns him that alot has come to her attention during her incarceration at One-Eyed Jacks. Horne discourages her from talking, but Audrey insists on having Cooper drive her home. "We can all go together," Ben offers.

Jonathan warns Josie that she must return to Hong Kong and that the mysterious Mr. Eckhert will make it worth her while. Josie says she'll return, but only once she has the insurance money that she has waited five years for.

James meets Maddie on a dock where they discuss their feelings for each other. Both realize it's wrong to get involved and Maddie fears that everyone believes it's just because they think she's Laura that they like her. "I'm going home tomorrow," she tells him. "So this is good-bye?" James asks. "I guess it is," she answers.

Josie arrives at Ben's office demanding the money she is owed and although he is reluctant to deliver on her demands until the land and money is in his hands, she warns him that she will reveal incriminating evidence about the illegal Horne dealings dangling the key to safety-deposit box in front of his nose. Ben gives her the check from Tokyo Mr. Tajamora gave him for five million dollars.

A comotose Leo is decorated with a party hat and given a cake to welcome him back home while Shelley and Bobby dance merrily around his inert body. Cooper, meanwhile, arrives at the sheriff's office and sees Gordon. "Albert thinks you're in over your head," Cole tells Cooper and hands him a cryptic letter he received which has a chess move, "2-4K" imprinted on it from Windom Earle.

Back at the Horne's, Ben says he will not take Leland back into his employ unless he is positive that Palmer is fully recovered. Leland rattles off several different options for maximizing the Horne's return on the Ghostwood project and Leland passes the test restored to Ben's good graces.

When Harry enters Josie's house, he finds Mr. Lee carrying her baggage out the door to the car. Josie tells Harry that Mr. Lee is her valet and says she has to leave. "Josie, I love you," Truman pleads as she walks out the door. Tajamora confronts Benjamin about the money he gave him for Ghostwood, "Why haven't I gotten anything from you?" he asks. "I gave you five milion dollars. You waste my time." Horne assures him that's not the case and says the fire has delayed the transaction. "I know all about fire," Tajamora answers coldy. "My parent's were at Nagasaki." In the middle of their conversation in the Timber Room, Leland starts singing excerpts from THE KING & I. When Ben tries to get him off the stage, he joins in the chorus hoping that it's just Leland trying to prove he was insane to get off the hook for the murder of Jaques Renault. Pete Martell tries to unsuccessfully strike up a conversation with Tajamora and offers him a saki.

Under interogation and deprieved of drugs, the One-Armed man, Philip Gerard, is transformed and the voice of the inhabiting spirit Mike resonates throughout the room. He tells those assembled that Bob was Mike's familar. "He is Bob, eager for fun," Mike warns. "He wears a smile. Everybody run...We were once partners...Few can see Bob's true face, the gifted and the damned!" Under further questioning Mike reveals that Bob is "in a large house made of wood surrounded by trees. The house is filled with many rooms, each alike, but occupied by different souls, night after night." A realization immediatley dawns on Agent Cooper, "The Great Northern Hotel."

EPISODE FOURTEEN

Written By: Mark Frost Directed By: David Lynch

Airdate: 11/17/90

As Gordon Cole prepares to depart for another assignment he wishes everyone the best as they drink coffee in the Sheriff's Office reception area. "On my way as soon as I finish my coffee," Cole says as he downs a cup of steaming black coffee. As he shares a final handshake with the assembled group he walks up to Gerard and says, "Take good care of Mike."

The deputies round up the occupants of the hotel and bring them to the One-Armed Man as Ben Horne stalks the corridors of the hotel. Gerard collapses and starts screaming as Horne enters and demands to know what's going on amid the chaos.

In Harold Smith's apartment, Hawk finds him hanging from the rafters where he finds Laura's secret diary, much of it shredded. At the Palmer House, Madline sits down with Leland and Sarah and tells them she is planning to return home to Missoula later that day. They are both supportive, but disappointed that she is leaving. "You'll come back and visit," Leland says to her.

"I'm a lonely soul," the note reads that Harold Smith left before hanging himself. "Poor guy," Truman says. "It's a good thing Andy didn't see this one." Back at the Johnson residence, Bobby realizes that the insurance money once applied to the bills of $1014 leaves $42 in cash for the two of them. "Bobby, you said you were going to take care of us," Shelly says and as Briggs tells her he needs to go home, Leo screams.

In Ben's office, Audrey confronts her father about One-Eyed Jacks. "You remember Prudence?" she asks as he looks up in shock confessing that he's owned the brothel for five years and that Laura only worked there for a brief time.

AUDREY : Did you sleep with her?

BENJAMIN : ...Yes.

AUDREY : Did you kill her?

BENJAMIN : I loved her.

Shelly tells Norma, reluctantly, that she has to quit the diner to take care of Leo and is tearful as she says farewell to her surrogate mother, Norma. Big Ed and Nadine enter, giddy as a schoolgirl. At the Johnson house, Bobby and, his best friend, Mike find a microcasette in the heel of one of Leo's workboots.

Cooper examines the diary and says that in it he has found repeated refrences to Bob and intimations about abuse and molestation. It says Bob is a friend of her father's. Audrey enters and tells Cooper that her father owns One-Eyed Jacks and was evasive when she asked whether he killed Laura.

"We need a warrant," Cooper tells Truman. "A warrant for the arrest of Benjamin Horne." In Ben's office Mr. Tajamora is meeting with Ben when Cooper, Truman, Andy and Hawk arrive to arrest him. "I happen to be in a meeting," Horne tells them as they barge in. "Can you be a little more specific."

TRUMAN : You're wanted for questioning in the murder of Laura Palmer. Is that specific enough for you?

BENJAMIN : I'm sure this is some sort of dreadful mistake.

TRUMAN : You can come quietly or we can drag you through your lobby in handcuffs.

BENJAMIN : Is this some sort of sick joke because if it is, I know people in high places

COOPER : You better do what he says.

BENJAMIN : Get of here, go on. I'm going to go out for a sandwich.

As Benjamin runs for a secret door, the deputies grab him.

BENJAMIN : You can't do this to me.

COOPER : It's already done.

Takiyama watches as Horne is hauled away in handcuffs to the police station and taken to a holding cell. When they arrive the Log Lady appears. "We don't know what will happen...or when," she says. "But there are owls in the Roadhouse."

Pete Martell is fixing himself a late night snack when Mr. Takiyama appears and kisses him. Repulsed, he staggers back until the man's deep, distorted voice becomes reassuringly feminine — it's Catherine, in disguise.

Sarah Palmer crawls down her living room steps and has a vision of a horse in the living room. She collapses as Leland oblivious to her predicatment casually adjusts his tie.

Cooper, Truman and the Log Lady arrive at the Roadhouse where Julee Crusie is singing with her band on stage. James and Donna, who have reconciled, are sitting at a booth in the corner. "His whole life was in that house and I violated it," Donna says of Harold Smith to James. "I think he was hurt in a way I couldn't figure out."

Enjoying the Julee Cruise show, and tapping along, Cooper is slowly transported to another world as the band onstage disappears replaced by the Giant onstage who warns, "It is happening again." Cooper is powerless to act as we see Leland at home looking in the mirror and seeing the frightening face of Bob reflected back. As Madeline comes down the stairs smelling something burning, scorched engine oil, the smell of Bob, Leland/Bob attacks her. "You're not going back to Missoula, Montana," he screams as he delivers several crushing blows and after dancing with her inert body smashes her head into a picture frame and than inserts the letter R underneath her fingernail. Cooper watches the giant as he vanishes and the elderly Great Northern room service attendant walks over to him and says "I'm so sorry."

Cooper looks up at the stage as Julee Cruise reappears and his head dissolves in front of the red drapes while Madeline's dead body lays in Leland's living room.

EPISODE FIFTEEN

Written By: Scott Frost Directed By: Caleb Deschanel

Airdate: 11/17/90

Donna and James arrive at the Palmer residence to say good-bye to Madeline who Leland tells them has already left as he putts hundreds of golf balls inside his house. "You can write her," he assures them. "I'm sure she'd be glad to hear from you." When they leave, Leland retrieves his golfing club bag from the closest where Madeline body is and places it in the trunk of his car.

Ben Horne, incarcerated for Laura's murder, is visited by his brother Jerry who is going to be serving as his attorney. "Did you kill her?" Jerry asks. They wax nostalgically about their childhood and recall Louise Dumbroski, a childhood girlfriend who used to dance with a flashlight when they were kids. In the recpetion area, Lucy returns with her sister Gwen who is introduced to the station personnel. "You must be that native person I've heard so much about," Gwen says to Hawk. "How you must hate us white people after all we've done to you." "Some of my best friends are white people," Hawk answers.

Visiting the Great Northern, Cooper and Truman find Leland dancing with a golfclub in hand and they inform him that Ben has been arrested for his daughter's murder. Leland, feigns anguish over the fact that his best friend has been taken into custody for Laura's murder, but when he is alone breaks out into a horrible laugh as we once again see Bob's face.

In the interrogation room, Cooper shows Ben Laura's secret diary where she says "One day I'm going to warn the world about Ben Horne." Cooper deducts that perhaps he felt she could threaten his business which arouses Ben to anger. Jerry asks for a moment to consult with Ben, "As your friend, your attorney and your brother Ben, I strongly suggest you get yourself another lawyer," he says.

Things go from bad to worse for Ben as Bobby listens to Leo's microcassette in which he recorded the conversation in which Ben told him to torch the Packard Saw Mill. Writing a note to Ben, unaware he has been incarcerated, Bobby prepares for a new career in business.

Norma's mother, Vivian, arrives at the Double R Diner with her new cousin, Ernie who says he's a financial anaylst but is actually caught by Norma betting on sporting events. Philip Gerard, still inhabited by Mike, escapes from the room he is being kept at the Great Northern in search of Bob.

In the Sheriff's Office, Peter comes to enlist Truman's help in finding Josie realizing that she has told them both different stories about the identity of the mysterious Mr. Lee. Their conversatin is interupted when Truman is notified that Gerard has escaped. Andy arriving at the station faints when he sees Lucy holding her sister's baby thinking its his own.

While Truman is out of the station, Pete sneaks down to the holding cell where he plays a cassette tape of the alive and well Catherine Martell who is the only one who can corroborate the fact that Ben was not with Laura the night of her murder, but, in fact, with her. She demands that Horne sign over Ghostwood Estates in exchange for her affadavit. Ben goes wild in his cell as Pete leaves laughing.

Leland almost drives Sheriff Truman and Cooper off the road while on his way to the golf course. Pursuing the reckless driver, not aware its Leland, Cooper and Truman are not totally taken aback to see that the driver of the automobile is indeed Leland Palmer. He promises to be more careful and asks Cooper if he'd like to play golf. Opening the trunk where Madeline's corpse is stored, Leland reaches for a golf club as Cooper approaches. Just as he's about to reach the trunk, Harry receives an urgent message that Gerard has escaped. As Cooper and Truman drive off, Leland looks in his rearview mirror only to see Bob's image reflected back.

Hawk returns Gerard to the stationhouse while Andy questions Lucy about the idenity of her baby's father. Cooper asks Mike if Ben Horne is the killer. "Bob has been close," he says. "But is not here now." "Who's Bob?" asks a befuddled Jerry Horne demanding that his client, Ben, either be released or charged. Cooper is reluctant to press charges suspecting that Ben is innocent, but Truman who is fed up with the supernatural "mumbo-jumbo" officially presses charges against Ben for the murder of Laura Palmer.

COOPER : I think we're saddling the horse before we're ready to ride

TRUMAN : I don't follow.

COOPER : I don't think Ben Horne killed Laura Palmer.

TRUMAN : What.

COOPER : We should release him.

TRUMAN : Cooper, I have backed you every step of the way but I have had enough of the mumbo jumbo. I have had enough of the dreams, the visions, the dwarves, the giants, Tibet, and the rest of the hocus pocus. We have hard evidence against Ben Horne, it's my job to lock him up.

Cooper agrees with Truman. "It's your backyard, sometimes I forget that."

Eating dinner at the Timber Room at the Great Northern, Hank meets Ernie, Norma's stepfather for the first time and realizes that it is Ernie "The Professor" Niles, a former prisonmate of his. Ernie who wants to put the past behind him can't as Hank plots to blackmail Ernie for his continued silence about Niles dubious past.

11:05 PM in Cooper's room, he tells Diane that on this dark, starless night the trail narrows. "The last few steps are always the darkest and most difficult," he recites into his taperecorder when Audrey comes in asking if they arrested her father. "All I ever really wanted was for him to love me, but he's ashamed of me," she says. "No, he's not," Cooper assures her. The phone rings with disturbing news and Cooper warns Audrey to return to her room...and lock the door. Joining up with Truman by the lake, they rush down to an embankment where Madeline Ferguson's corpse lies decomposing in the night.

EPISODE SIXTEEN

Written By: Mark Frost & Robert Engels & Harley Peyton Directed By: Tim Hunter

Airdate: 12/1/90

The screen dissolves from an image of Madeline Ferguson's corpse to that of Albert Rosenfield, Cooper, Truman and Deputy Hawk walking through the woods. Albert tells the others that under Madeline's fingernail he discovered the letter "O", "more fan mail" from the same killer who murdered Laura. Truman tells them he is going to alert the relatives when Cooper tells him, "Don't make any calls. I need 24 hours." "For what?" Truman asks. "To finish this," Cooper answers. Even the usually acerbic Albert is dour, "Just find this beast before he takes another bite," Rosenfield says.

At the Double R Diner James meets Donna. They hold hands as Donna says, "I could sing about last night." James slips a ring on her finger and tells her, "I just think we should be together all the time...if that's all right with you." "It's perfect," answers the lovestruck Donna.

By the counter, Norma's mother, Vivien complains about the omlettes while Deputy Andy Brennan recites the french phrase "I'm a lonely soul" over and over in the stool next to her. Donna overhears the deputies mutterings and approaches him. "It's French," Andy says. Donna tells him that Mrs. Tremond's mysterious grandson told her this before she left her apartment while delivering food for the Meals-On-Wheels program. Andy tells her that it was what Harold Smith wrote in his suicide note.

Donna takes Cooper to see the elderly Mrs. Tremond, but instead of finding a frail, old lady and her strange grandson, an obese, loudmouthed woman answers the bell (Mae Williams). "I'm Mrs. Tremond," she tells them. When Donna asks about her mother, the woman tells them that her mother died three years ago and that she has no children. When Cooper beckons Donna to leave, the woman realizes that she is Donna Hayward and gives her a letter she received from Harold Smith addressed to Donna's attention. She opens the letter and finds out it is one of the missing pages from Laura Palmer's secret diary.

"February 22nd," Donna reads to Agent Cooper. "I had the strangest dream. I was in a red room with a small man dressed in red and an old man sitting in a chair. I tried to talk to him and tell him who Bob is becasue I thought he could help me, but my words came out slow and odd. It was frustrating to try and talk. I got up and walked to the old man and than I leaned over and whispered the secret in his ear. Somebody has to stop Bob. Bob's only afraid of one man, he told me once — a man named Mike. I wonder if this was Mike in my dream. Even if it was only a dream, I hope he heard me. Nobody in the real world would believe me."

Donna continues, "Feburary 23rd. Tonight is the night that I die. I know I have to because it's the only way to keep Bob away from me, to tear him out from inside. I know he wants me, I can feel his fire. But if I die, he can't hurt me anymore." "Laura and I had the same dream," Cooper tells Donna and Deputy Brennan. "That's impossible," Andy says. "Yes it is," Cooper replies impassively.

In the room Gerard is being held at the Great Northern, Dr. Hayward warns Cooper that if he isn't given his medicine he may die, but Cooper is determined to get to the truth at whatever the cost. Still inhabited by Mike, the One-Armed Man, Gerard, tells Cooper "he's on the path." He reveals that the killing spree him and Bob once went on was the equality of appetite and satisfaction, a golden circle. Cooper realizes the analogy to his ring which was taken by the giant. "The giant, he is known to us here," answers Mike. "He can help you find Bob. You must ask him first. You have all the clues you need."

As Cooper leaves the room, he runs across the senile waiter who found him when he was shot. "I know about you," the waiter tells him once again. "That milk will cool down on you, but it's getting warmer now." Cooper realizes that he's on the right track and the old man somehow holds the answer to the bizarre riddles he is gradually unlocking.

Truman and his deputies are searching Ben Horne's office when they discover a phone call was made to the Palmer residence the night of Laura's murder. Albert shows Cooper the results of Ben Horne's blood test.

Lucy and Andy are arguing at the Sheriff's office over who is the father of her baby while a repairman installs new fire detectors in the stationhouse. Andy calls Richard "Dick" Trelaine and demands that he come down for a talk.

In his prison cell, Ben Horne receives a visit from the Japanese businessman Mr. Tajimora. (Richard Beymer continually proves to be one of the most compelling reasons to stay with the show, he's just been phenemonal throughout). "You are in prison," Tajimora says . "A momentary inconvenience, I assure you," Ben answers. Removing his shoe, Tajimora sticks his shapely foot into the cell and Ben realizes that Tajimora is actually Catherine in disguise. "Benjamin Horne," she says. "You're a slimy rat bastard and I intend to make whatever exists of your pathetic existence a living hell." In return for her promises of vouching for his whereabouts the night of Laura's murder, Ben signs over the Ghostwood Estates property to Catherine.

Donna stops at the Palmer House to give Leland a tape of the night Maddy and James and her recorded a song. Leland takes it and promises to send it to Maddy. Donna tells him the police found Laura's "secret diary" when Beth Ferguson, Madeline's mother calls and says that her daughter never arrived in Missoula. Leland assures her that he drove her to the bus station (NOTE: Only two episodes ago, Madeline said she was driving home and in the next episode Leland said he took her to the bus station).

"It's the strangest thing," Leland says to Donna when he hangs up the phone. "She never made it home." To cheer her up, Leland puts on a record and becomes more menacing as he begins his transformation into Bob (where's the smell of burning motor oil though?) and starts to dance with Donna when the doorbell rings. Truman tells him that there's been another murder and that they need Leland's help. He agrees to accompany the Sheriff.

Donna flees into the woods for a rendezvous with James, but when she tells James what happened and that she suspects Madeline is dead, James flees on his motorcylce. "Don't leave me," she cries out and he drives off.

As a thunderstorm (it only rains in TWIN PEAKS when something dramatic is about to happen, a real tip-off) rages over the town, Cooper assembles the prime suspects as the Roadhouse; Ben Horne, Leo Johnson, comotose in his wheelchair with Bobby Briggs and Leland Palmer (who never really seemed to be much of a suspect to Cooper, beats me as to what made him change his mind). "Hail, hail, the gangs all here," Horne jokes as lightning flashes ominously above while Rosenfield, Truman, Hawk and Big Ed look on.

"As a member of the Bureau, I spend most of my time seeking simple answers to difficult questions," Cooper tells the assembled group. "In the pursuit of Laura's killer I have employed Bureau guidelines, deductive technique, Tibetan method, instinct and luck, but now I find myself in need of something new which, for lack of a better word, we shall call magic."

"Would you like us to hum," Horne says dubiously. "A Tibetan chant perhaps?" "I think it's going terfically well, don't you?" Albert says in all seriousness to his nemesis Truman.

At that moment, Major Briggs enters with the old waiter from the Great Northern. He found him on the road and he tells them the man wanted to be driven to the Roadhouse ("the owls are in the Roadhouse"?). The Old Man takes out a piece of chewing gum and gives it to Cooper. "I know that gum, I used to chew it when I was a kid," Leland says to the Old Man. "That's my most favorite gum in the world." "That gum you like is going to come back in style," the Old Man answers as the mystery comes full-circle. The lightning illuminates all the suspects in much the way Cooper has gained illumination into the crime as he remembers his dream and Laura leans over to him, but this time he can hear what she says.

"My father killed me," she tells him. The giant appears and gives Cooper back his ring.

Now realizing its Leland inhabited by Bob, Cooper feigns arresting Ben to get Leland to the stationhouse. As they leave, he gives the Old Man a thumbs up who returns his gesture with a mock salute as a perfectly frame shot of the Major standing with Leo and Briggs looks on (one of the greatest single images in the show since Cooper, Truman and Hayward approached Jaques Renault's cabin in Glatter's fifth episode).

Entering the Sheriff's station and heading down to the cells, Leland asks if Ben is going to be charged. Cooper whispers to Truman and when they reach the cell they hurl Leland into it and lock the door. "Hawk, take Ben up and release him," Cooper says as Leland flies into a rage, screaming wildly.

TRUMAN : How did you know?

COOPER : Laura told me. In her dream.

TRUMAN : We're going to need a lot stronger evidence than this.

They cuff Leland who speaks out as Bob and confesses to having killed Laura...and Madeline. "I guess I kinda of sorta did," Bob/Leland says. "I had this thing for knives. JUST LIKE WHAT HAPPENED TO YOU IN PITTSBURGH THAT TIME, HUH COOPER?"

Upstairs, Lucy meets with Dick Trelaine and Andy and tells them she's going to keep her baby and until it's born they won't know who the cfather is. Dick puffs away on a cigarette and the smoke ascends towards the newly installed fire alarms.

Outside Leland's cell, Cooper reveals to Truman how he realized Palmer was responsbible for Laura's murder. He tells him that in his dream the little man danced which Leland did constantly after his daughter's death. He also tells them that they knew Bob, the killer, was a grey-haired man and that after Leland killed Jaques, his hair turned grey.

The letters under the fingernails were part of the name Robertson, who Leland had told them were his next door neighbors when he was a child up at Pearl Lakes, and Cooper says that Mike told them that Bob inhabited people he said were his children thus Robertson, son of Robert. "Bob was spelling his name, a singaure on a demonic self-potrait," Cooper tells them.

"This Bob can't really exist," Truman says. "Leland's just crazy, right?" At that very moment, Leland begins to recite the errie chant that Cooper had heard in his dream and Mike had recited under questioning ending with the chilling "Fire Walk With Me." As they start to leave, the fire sprinklers are set-off by Trelaine's cigarette and Bob flees Leland's body after ramming his head repeatedly into the solid steel prison door.

As Leland is dying, he realizes that he killed his daughter and is anguished over the realization. "Laura," he cries out. "I killed her. I killed my daughter." He explains how the parasitic demon Bob took control of him as well. "I was just a boy," Leland reveals. "I saw him in my dream. He asked me if I wanted to play. He offered me and I invited him in and hec ame inside of me. When he was inside I didn't know and when he was gone I couldn't remember. He made me do things, terrible things." He explains that Bob wanted to use Laura, but "she was strong, she fought them."

Leland's life begins to ebb away as Cooper holds his head in his lap as the sprinklers continue to stream into the cell soaking the assembled officers. MacLachlan recites a speech that sounds like it's straight out of DUNE. "Walk into the light," he tells Leland. "Know yourself and abide in that state. Look to the light. Into the light, Leland, into the light." As Leland dies, he sees Laura coming out of the light towards him.

Reflecting on the case, Truman, Cooper and Albert walking through the woods acome across Major Briggs (just out for a morning walk or a human host to the extraterrestrial beings who seem to have made TWIN PEAKS their new home. You be the judge).

"He was completely insane," Truman says. Even the usually down-to-earth Rosenfield finds it hard to accept psyhosis as the cause of Leland's affliction, he was no Norman Bates, he was more like Linda Blair. "People saw him in visions," Albert says.

"I've seen some strange things but this is way off the map," Truman says. "I'm having a hard time believing."

Cooper looks at him solemnly. "Harry, is it easier to believe a man would rape and murder his own daughter?"

The episode ends on a depressing note as Rosenfield speculates that Bob is " the evil that men do" which leads the investigative trio to question where Bob is now and if they have actually allowed him to escape. That evening, we see what presumably is Bob's spirit shooting through the woods and an owl ascending into the night sky.

The same week that TWIN PEAKS finally resolved the Laura Palmer arc in Tim Hunter's sixteenth episode, TV GUIDE printed a scathing attack on the show epitomizing every aspect of the anticipated PEAKS backlash that had been brewing ever since the murderer was revealed. Monica Collins condemmed the show's writers whom she said "ignored the basic tenets of drama. There must be an overriding sense to it all. There has to be a transcendent authority in telling the story." The fear of the show's writer's that people would think they were actually achieving a "cosmic laugh" at the expense of the viewer which was actually the furtherest thing from their minds was presented in virulent fashion by Collins. "Every time I watch Peaks, I hear an echo of laughter - from the show's writers. I imagine them stiting around a big table and screaming with delight as they heap one wild thing on another."

"We're not trying to goof on anyone," Co-Producer Robert Engels told me and Mark Frost even said at an ABC press conference once that he wouldn't waste over two years of his life for a "cosmic laugh". I have no doubt that this is true, but I also agree that Hunter's resolution to the TWIN PEAKS Laura Palmer storyline may very well be a dubious turning point for the show.

Collins says in her review that the season finale of TWIN PEAKS first season when Cooper was shot was "the pivotal moment when PEAKS peaked and started its donwhill slide" and I would have to vehemenly disagree. Although the season did start slowly by the time Glatter seized the reigns of the show's third second season episode, PEAKS was continuing to peak. Even as viewer discontent grew and the audience eroded it wasn't until the Palmer saga's final flourish that the show stumbled.

Despite the seemingly baffling revelation that Leand was the killer, viewers who had stayed with the program remained riveted regardless of their feelings about the identity of the murderer because so many questions remained unanswered and so much had still been left unexplained. They soon learned their faith was not misplaced as the following episode, directed in superb fashion by Caleb Deschanel, was a powerhouse follow-up to Lynch's crucial installment in the saga (I almost bought the whole Bob thing and Frank Silva scared the hell out of me). Unfortunately, Hunter's coda, Episode Sixteen, wrapped the mystery up in a tidy little fashion and most disturbingly the ambiguity which the series had struggled to achieve was lost. Even as we saw Leland kill Madeline there was always the possiblity that Bob was a twisted figment of the Palmer families collective imaginations, but Hunter's finale (and, this must be attributed to the writer's) strongly suggested that Bob was very, very real. The magic and the mumbo jumbo which helped make TWIN PEAKS proved to be the source of its undoing. With all of Hunter's great style in delivering the goods, the finale fell strongly on the side of the supernatural diseplling any doubts that perhaps all of the crazy Tibetan fantasies of Cooper were just part of an extremely overactive imagination. They gave him character, they even gave him clues, but to give him the answer after months and months of investigation was having too many pieces randomly falling into place rather conveniently in the end.

There's a certain intrinsic appeal to the spectacle of the gathering of suspects in a room which harkens back to the classic Agatha Christie mysteries, but to have the answer be as simple as Cooper recalling Laura whispering in his ear, "My father killed me" is a let-down. Yes, the spookiness of this this scene with Major Briggs showing up with the Old Man in the rain and Donna and Cooper discovering the old woman, Mrs. Tremond, has been dead for years are effective, but when the mystical is mistaken for an adequate way to answer a legtimate detective saga, it's a misstep. To have the formidable and funny Albert Rosenfield suddenly side with Cooper seems like a betrayal of the character. His concerns may be global, but they've never been otherworldly.

Perhaps, part of my dissatisfaction is because it's always disappointing when you read the final chapter of a book or put the last piece in a jigsaw puzzle. The fun is reading it or building it. When you've finished, there's little else to do but move on even though the show will feel the loss of Ray Wise who was nothing short in his role of Leland Palmer (let's hope that maybe the late Leland has a twin brother out there somewhere). Hopefully, now that TWIN PEAKS is moving on to its future mysteries, the show will remain equally engaging and boldly innovative so that even when the end of the road isn't quite satisfing, the trip is well worth making.

APPENDIX

A TWIN PEAKS FREAKS FILMOGRAPHY

Or What To Watch The Other Six Nights

A Very Subjective List By The Author

BLUE VELVET David Lynch's "prequel" to TWIN PEAKS starring Kyle MacLachlan and Dennis Hopper.

CHARADE Has nothing to do with TWIN PEAKS. I just personally think it's one of the greatest suspense/thrillers ever made. So there. Starring Cary Grant and Audrey Heprburn.

DOUBLE INDEMNITY If you think the double-dealing and chicanery in TWIN PEAKS is compelling, it's worth taking a look at the film from which it all came from. A noir classic whose tone is echoed in the darker reaches of TWIN PEAKS.

DUNE Worth another look if only to see the similarities to David Lynch's work on TWIN PEAKS.

ERASERHEAD PEAKS veterans abound in the first, commercial release from director David Lynch.

KISS OF THE BEAST/FULL MOON JUNCTION For Fenn fans only. Two dreadful films starring Sherilyn Fenn in which she spends more time naked than she does clothed. DEMON is slightly more interesting as it was made by Charles Band, the former mini-mogul whose indpendent film studio thrived on 50 cents schlock films like this. A modern day Roger Corman whose films always offer a lot of t & b (tits and blood).

LAURA Otto Preminger's classic film about dual identies with an incredible cast and an absolutely compelling story which paved the way for TWIN PEAKS.

PSYCHO It has a town called Fairville in it and the late Simon Oakland as a loquacious physciatrist who would be played by PEAKS Warren Frost in the Showtime prequel, PSYCHO IV. Those are pretty slim reasons, but you never need a reason to watch PSYCHO, do you?

RIVER'S EDGE Directed by TWIN PEAKS' director Tim Hunter, this chilling film about suburban youth being deadened to violence in everyday life is a brilliantly written film about a teenager who kills his girlfriend and the reaction (or lack thereof) of his friends to his henious crime.

ROBOCOP Miguel Ferrer in the role that brought him to the attention of David Lynch. Lots of violence and lots of fun.

SUNSET BOULEVARD Another film noir classic which bears less of a resemblance to TWIN PEAKS, only offering the original Gordon Cole in one of the greatest films about the film industry ever made.

THE BELIEVERS Mark Frost written film about voodoo cults in Manhattan. And you wonder why he's working in television again?

THE HIDDEN Kyle MacLachlan's first foray as an extraterrestrial FBI agent. No owls here, but plenty of action. Directed by NIGHTMARE ON ELM STREET II's Jack Shoulder, a sleeper hit co-starring Micahel Nouri.

THE LAST EMPEROR A chance to see that Joan Chen can really act after all in one of the greatest films of the 80's. One of the first films in a long time that actually deserved to win Best Picture.

THE PRESTON STURGES COLLECTION Only now first receiving the recognition this director so richly deserves this filmmaker is worshiped by the entire TWIN PEAKS writing staff and any of his classics are well worth renting; THE PALM BEACH STORY, THE LADY EVE, THE GREAT McGINTY, SULLVIAN'S TRAVELS. Take your pick!

TOUGH GUYS DON'T DANCE Directed by Norman Mailer and scored by Angelo Badalamenti, this is one of the best "awful" movies ever made. Featuring the same morbid, off-the-wall humor that makes TWIN PEAKS so endearing and feature outrageously bonkers performances from Ryan O'Neil, Lawrence Tierney, Isabella Rosellini and Wings Hauser. Oh man, Oh God..Oh man, Oh God... Oh Man.......

VERTIGO Another Madeline who is killed in a haunting love story from the master of suspense, Alfred Hitchock.

WEST SIDE STORY Beymer and Tamblyn together for the first time. Great Leonard Bernstein music, great dancing, great songs. Great fun!

WILD AT HEART See what TWIN PEAKS would be like if ABC didn't have a Standards & Practices Department. Well worth watching. Sometimes brilliant, other times indulgent.

ZELLY AND ME Tina Rathborne directs David Lynch and Isabella Rossellini in one of the least seen movies in history. Most families Super 8 movies have gotten more exposure. A curiousity piece for Lynch's legions to see the director in front of the camera.

GLOSSARY

A Reference Guide To Everyone & Everywhere In TWIN PEAKS

1400 RIVER ROAD
The home of Margaret, the log lady

AB NEGATIVE
Jaques Renault's blood type

BANKS, TERESA
the first murder victim who was killed a year prior to Laura Palmer

BARNEY & FRED
The aliases used by Agent Cooper and Big Ed Hurley while undercover at One Eyed Jacks. They pretend to be two high rolling oral surgeons from the Twin Cities

EASTER PARK
Town park near the lake where Dr. Jacoby tracks Madeline down to when he receives a recording in which she pretends to be Laura Palmer. Jacoby is attacked by Leland.

BATTIS, EMORY
The manager of Horne's department store who is also a recruiting officer for One Eyed Jacks.

BIG ED'S GAS FARM
The gasoline and service station owned by Big Ed Hurley in Twin Peaks.

BIG JAKE MORRISSEY
Properitor of the Bookhouse, a local hangout for Twin Peaks residents.

BLACK ROSE
The nickname for Blackie O'Reilly, the manager of One Eyed Jacks

BLUE PINE LODGE
The home of Josie and the late Andrew Packard and also the residence of Catherine and Pete Martell.

BOB
The evil entity which possessed Leland Palmer and killed Laura Palmer and Madeline Ferguson.

BOOKHOUSE BOYS
a historic secret society, now led by Sheriff Truman, assembled to fight the evil in the woods. Other present members include: Ed Hurley, Joey Paulson and James Hurley.

BRADY, ALICE
Bank guard at who removes Laura Palmer's safe deposit box for Agent Cooper's inspection (Reference: The Brady Bunch/played by Ann B. Davis)

BRENNAN, ANDY DEPUTY
Twin Peaks Sheriff's Department Deputy. Prone to crying fits when faced with violent crime and boyfriend to receptionist Lucy Moran.

BRIGGS, BETTY
mother of Bobby Briggs and wife of Major Briggs.

BRIGGS, BOBBY
Boyfriend of Laura Palmer. Bobby is a member of the high school football team and carries on a secret affair with Leo Johnson's wife, Shelly.

BRIGGS, GARLAND MAJOR
An army major whose secret work for the government is classified although we are told it involves the search for intelligent life in the galaxy and the reception of extraterrestrial radio messages. Father to Bobby Briggs.

BROKEN CIRCLE STABLES
Twin Peaks stables where Laura Palmer housed her horse Troy.

CALHOUN MEMORIAL HOSPITAL
Main hospital facility in Twin Peaks

CASH & CARRY
Supermarket in Twin Peaks features a wide array of food and beverage products. Features the world's second largest meat and produce department (the first is in Waltham, MA).

CHET
Character on the television soap "Invitation To Love"

COLE, GORDON
FBI Bureau Chief and Agent Dale Cooper's superior. Cole suffers a significant hearing loss and is played by series co-creator David Lynch (Reference: Sunset Boulevard/head of Paramount Pictures)

COLUMBIAN BAR
Bar in Canada situated near abandon amusement park where the ransom money for Audrey Horne was to be dropped off

COOPER, DALE
Federal Bureau of Investigation Special Agent charged with investigating the murder of Laura Palmer and attack on Ronette Pulaski (Reference/D.B. Cooper).

DAHLI LAMA
Consulted with the Beatles in their post-mop top phase. Inspiration to FBI Special Agent Dale Cooper whose secret dream is to return the Dahli Lama to his rightful place as ruler of Tibet.

DIAMOND COUNTY
The County in which Twin Peaks is situated in Northern Washington.

DIANE
Recipient of Special Agent Cooper's audio recordings relating to his investigation in Twin Peaks.

DOUBLE R DINER
Popular diner in Twin Peaks owned by Norma Jennings.

DR. STANICEK
Doctor to Lucy Moran who determined she was pregnant.

EARLE, WINDOM
Former partner of Agent Dale Cooper in Pittsburgh.

ECKHERT, MR.
Mysterious Hong Kong businessman who has control over Josie Packard and employs Johnny Lee.

EMERALD/JADE
Split-personality character on the soap opera "Invitation To Love".

ERNIE "THE PROFESSOR" NILES
Husband of Vivian Jennings, mother of Norma Jennings. Served a prison term with Norma's husband, Hank.

FAIRVILLE
Neighboring town to Twin Peaks (Reference: Psycho)

FATHER CLARENCE
Priest who taught Laura Palmer Sunday school and delivered the eulogy at her funeral.

FERGUSON, MADELINE
Deceist cousin of Laura Palmer from Missoula, Montana bearing an unnatural resemblance to Laura.

FIELDING, JOE
Fairville doctor who performed post-mortem on Laura Palmer before the arrival of Albert Rosenfield (Reference: Fairville is a neighboring town to the Bates Motel in PSYCHO).

FLESHWORLD
popular adult monthly in which Laura and Ronette submitted erotic photos of themselves to.

FRANKLIN, TERRY
Student in Laura Palmer's high school home room class.

GERARD, MICHAEL PHILLIP
The One Armed man possessed by the spirit of Mike. Searches for Bob (Reference: THE FUGITIVE)

GHOSTWOOD COUNTRY CLUB & ESTATES
Proposed development to be built on the former sight of the Packard Sawmill by Twin Peaks real estate magnate Ben Horne

GREAT NORTHERN HOTEL
Popular 200 room resort located above a waterfall in Twin Peaks. Owned by Ben Horne. The hotel did not appear in the most recent AAA listing.

GRIMES, MARTHA
Student in Laura Palmer's high school home room class.

GWEN MORAN
Sister to Lucy Moran who recently gave birth to a baby daughter.

HARTMAN, MAX
Football Coach at the Twin Peaks High School.

HAYWARD, DONNA
Daughter of Doctor William Hayward and best friend of Laura Palmer. Currently seeing James Hurley.

HAYWARD, EILEEN
Wife of Dr. William Hayward confined to a wheelchair. Played by Mary Jo Deschanel, wife of TWIN PEAKS director Caleb Deschanel

HAYWARD, GERSTEN
Youngest daughter of Dr. William Hayward. Played by Alicia Witt, Atredies younger sister in DUNE.

HAYWARD, HARRIET
13 year old daughter of Dr. William Hayward

HAYWARD, WILL DR.
Foremost doctor in Twin Peaks and father of Donna Hayward. Played by Warren Frost, father of TWIN PEAKS co-creator Mark Frost.

HEIDI
hefty German girl who works at the Double R Diner.

HEMINGWAYS
Another name for the Roadhouse which in addition to providing a variety of alcholic beverages is well stocked in literary offerings as well.

HILL, "HAWK" TOMMY DEPUTY
Twin Peaks' Sheriff's Department Deputy of Indian descent.

HILL, BERNIE
The original name for Hawk's character

HOGAN, JANICE
Next door neighbor of the Palmer family.

HONEYCUTT, MARGARET
Laura Palmer's senior class home room teacher.

HORNE, AUDREY
Daughter of Benjamin Horne. Can tie a cherry stem with her tounge.

HORNE, BENJAMIN
Twin Peaks businessman, father of Audrey and Johnny Horne and owner of the Great Northern Hotel and the brothel, One Eyed Jacks.

HORNE, JERRY
Younger brother of Benjamin Horne.

HORNE, JOHNNY
Retarded son of Benjamin Horne prone to dressing up like an Indian. Was babysat by Laura Palmer before her death.

HORNE, SYLVIA
Wife of Benjamin Horne and apparently oblivious to everything going on in Twin Peaks.

HURLEY, ED
Owner of Big Ed's Gas Farm and husband to Nadine Hurley. Carrying on secret affair with Norma Jennings.

HURLEY, JAMES
Biker, member of the Bookhouse Boys and former lover of Laura Palmer. Has an alcoholic mother who he rarely sees. Presently seeing Donna Hayward.

HURLEY, NADINE
Crazy, drape obsessed wife of Ed Hurley. Had an eye shot out by her husband while on their honeymoon. Currently thinks she's 18 and trying out for cheerleading squad after coming out of a coma induced by a suicide attempt.

INVITATION TO LOVE
Popular soap opera on television in the town of Twin Peaks.

JAOBY, LAWRENCE DR.
Town psychiatrist with a penchant for Hawaiin customs. Counseled Laura Palmer.

JARED
Featured player on "Invitation To Love".

JENNINGS,"HANK" O.HENRY
Recently paroled husband of Norma Jennings imprisoned for vehicular manslaughter.

JENNINGS, NORMA
Wife of Hank Jennings and owner of the Double R Diner.

JENNY
Featured player on "Invitation To Love".

JERRY LANCASTER
Featured player on "Invitation To Love".

JOHNSON, LEO
Vicious trucker and husband of Shelly Johnson. Currently in a coma, Leo was responsible for several crimes before being shot by Hank Jennings including arson, wife abuse and the murder of a mynah bird.

JOHNSON, SHELLEY
Wife of the sadistic Leo Johnson. Currently having an affair with Bobby Briggs.

JONES, MIDGE
High school sweetheart of Pete Martell

JORGENSON, SVAN
Norwegians businessman who visited Twin Peaks with the interest of investing in the Ghostwood Estates. Left town after the murder of Laura Palmer.

JUPITER
Laura Palmer's cat killed by a hit and run driver.

LAMPLIGHTER INN
Popular eatery at Highway 2 near Lewis Fork boasting an exceptional cherry pie and clean and comfortable rest room facilities.

LE SPARKWOOD CAFE
Restaurant located in Twin Peaks, competes wtih Double R Diner. Not reviewed by us.

LODWICK, DARYL
Diamond County prosecutor who prosecuted the state's case against both Leland Palmer for the murder of Jaques Renault and Leo Johnson for the alleged murder of Laura Palmer.

LOG LADY
the strange occupant of 1400 River Road. Carries around a log which she says gives her wisdom. Husband was killed in a fire the day after they were married.

LOOMER, MIDGE
Secretary at the office of vetenarian Bob Lydecker. LOST DUDE RANCH
Featured in the book "The Scarlet Letter" and a reference Audrey Horne gives to obtain employment at One Eyed Jacks.

LOUISE DOMBROWSKI
Pre
teen love interest of Ben and Jerry Horne, best remembered for dancing in their room with a flashlight in the dark.

LOWTOWN
Adjoining town to Twin Peaks where during a run to obtain cocaine, Bobby Briggs shot a gang member after they began chasing him and Laura down.

LYDECKER, BOB
Twin Peaks vetenarian and friend of Philip Gerard.

MARTELL, CATHERINE
Wife of Pete Martell and manager of the Packard sawmill. Presumed killed in the mill fire, but reappeared as mysterious Japanese businessman.

MARTELL, PETE
Husband of Catherine Martell. Discovered body of Laura Palmer.

MAX
Deputy guarding Philip Gerard in the Great Northern when he is put under protection by Cooper.

MEADOWLARK
Variety of bird seen in Twin Peaks.

MILFORD, DWAYNE
86 year old mayor of Twin Peaks currently serving his 23rd consecutive term in office.

MONTANA
Featured player on "Invitation To Love".

MOONEY, WILSON
Hank Jennings attorney

MORAN, LUCY
Receptionist at Twin Peaks Sheriff's Office.

MORISSEY, JAKE
Owner and manager of the Roadhouse. Also called: Big Jake.

MRS. JACKSON
Secretary to principal of Twin Peaks high school.

MYNAH BIRD
Native of Southeast Asia, Idonesia. Feeds on fruit

NEFF, WALTER
Insurance salesman who sold Josie Packard and Ben Horne life insurance policy on Catherine Martell (Reference: DOUBLE INDEMNITY/played by Fred McMurray)

NELSON, MIKE
Best friend of Bobby Briggs and former boyfriend of Donna Hayward.

O'REILLY, BLACKIE
Madame of One
Eyed Jacks.

O'REILLY, NANCY
Sister of Blackie and lover to Jean Renault.

ONE EYED JACKS
Brothel and casino located north of the Canadian border owned by Ben Horne

PACKARD, JOSIE
Oriental wife of the late Andrew Packard and former owner of the Packard sawmill. Lover to Sheriff Truman.

PACKARD SAWMILL
The foremost employer in Twin Peaks burned down in a fire set by Leo Johnson at the behest of Ben Horne. Owned by wife of founder Andrew Packard, Josie until sold to Benjamin Horne.

PACKARD, ANDREW
Late wife of Josie Packard and brother of Catherine. Killed in mysterious boating accident, possibly murdered by Hank Jennings.

PACKARD, GIOVANNA PASQUALINI
Original character name for Josie Packard.

PALMER, LAURA
Homecoming queen and founder of Twin Peaks meals on wheels program. Daughter of Leland and Sarah Palmer murdered by Bob.

PALMER, LELAND
Possessed dad of Laura Palmer. Murderer of Laura Palmer and Madeline Ferguson. Favorite song: Come On, Get Happy.

PALMER, SARAH
Wife of Leland Palmer and gifted with psychic ability.

PAULSON, JOEY
Member of the Bookhouse Boys.

PRUDENCE
alias used by Audrey Horne while working at One Eyed Jacks.

PRYNNE, HESTER
alias used by Audrey Horne to obtain employment at One Eyed Jacks.

PULASKI, JANEK
Employee at Packard Sawmill and father of Ronette Pulaski.

PULASKI, MARIA
Original name of Janek Pulaski's wife in pilot script.

PULASKI, RONETTE
Friend of Laura Palmer's who barely escapes the train car in which Laura is murdered. Found nearly comotose, Ronette lapses into a coma which she awakens from a week later. Previously employment: Perfume Counter at Horne's Department Store, One Eyed Jacks Hospitality Girl.

PULASKI, SHARON
In pilot script, original name for Ronette.

PULAKSI, SUBARIS
Mother of Ronette Pulaski.

RENAULT, BERNARD
janitor at Roadhouse and brother of Jaques and Jean Renault.

RENAULT, JAQUES
Overweight bartender at the roadhouse and dealer at One Eyed Jacks. Was at the cabin the night of Laura's death. Murdered by Leland Palmer.

RENAULT, JEAN
Brother of Jaques and Bernard who engineers the ransom of Audrey Horne and plots to kill Agent Cooper. Murderer of Blackie O'Reilly.

RIDGELY, THEODORA MRS.
buys "Invitation to Love" scent at perfume counter in Horne's Department store.

ROBIN'S NEST MOTEL
Hotel where the One Armed Man was staying upon his return to Twin Peaks.

ROSENFIELD, ALBERT
Federal Bureau of Investiagion Forensics Expert sent to Twin Peaks to perform a through autopsy on Laura Palmer.

SHAPIRO, DENISE
Former girlfriend of Deputy Hawk and Ph'd in Sociology at Brandeis Univeristy.

SHELVY, DR.
Doctor at Calhoun Memorial Hospital in charge of the Ronette Pulaski case.

SHORTY
owner of pool hall adjoining the Roadhouse.

SID
Shapely female assistant to travelling Judge Sternwood.

SMITH, HARROLD
Agoraphobic meals on wheels shut in. Possesed Laura Palmer's secret diary. Committed suicide by hanging himself.

SPARKWOOD MOUNTAIN ROAD
Main road leading out of town through the woods and into the mountains outside of Twin Peaks.

STEADMAN, DAN SHERIFF
In pilot, original name for Sheriff Harry S. Truman.

STERNWOOD, JUDGE
Circuit Court judge for Twin Peaks

THE GRANGE
Ben Horne's house adjoining the Great Northern hotel.

THORSDOTTI, HEBBA
Attractive member of the Norwegian delegation and, according to Jerry Horne, "the future ex Mrs. Horne"

THORSON, EINAR
head of the Norwegians delegation sent to Twin Peaks to explore the possiblity of investing in Ghostwood Country Club and Estates.

TIBET
Country north of India once ruled by the spiritual Buddhist leader, the Dahli Lamma.

TIMBER FALLS MOTEL
Hotel in which Catherine Martell and Benjamin are having a liasion while Agent Cooper and Sheriff Truman burst in on the One Armed Man.

TIMBER ROOM
Dining area in the Great Northern Hotel.

TOJAMURA
Japanese businessman who is actually Catherine Martell in disguise. Role credited to fictitious actor Fumio Yamaguchi.

TREMAINE, RICHARD
Former lover of Lucy Moran's and manager of the home furnishings section at Horne's Department Store.

TREMOND, MRS.
Meals on wheel recepient who lives next door to Harold Smith.

TRI-CITIES
County in which Twin Peaks is located.

TROY
  Horse given to Laura Palmer on her 12th birthday by her father which was actually a gift from Ben Horne.

TRUAX, FRED
  Mill worker fired by Catherine Martell after Josie closes the mill for the day Laura Palmer is killed.

TRUDY
  Waitress at the Great Northern played by Jill Rogosheskie, wife of Exeuctive Story Editor, Robert Engels.

TRUMAN, HARRY S.
  Sheriff and head of the Twin Peaks police deparment named after the former president of the United States.

VIVIAN NILES
  Mother of Norma Jennings.

WALDO
  A mynah bird, "Gracula Religiosa", commonly known as Hill mynah. Killed by Leo Johnson and witness to the murder of Laura Palmer. Capable of reproducing human speech patterns (Reference: the Otto Preminger motion picture LAURA).

WENTZ, M.T.
  food critic for the Seattle Times who travels icognito.

WHITE, GILMAN
  Bobby Briggs' attorney.

WOLCHEZK, GEORGE
  principal of Twin Peaks high school.

YOLANNI
  Dr. Jacoby's Hawiian wife.

DARK SHADOWS

- 1966: ABC premieres *Dark Shadows* on its afternoon schedule. The gothic romance soap barely makes an impact, and six months later is threatened with cancellation.

- 1967: Producer Dan Curtis decides to go for broke by adding a true element of horror to the proceedings: a vampire. Actor Jonathan Frid is cast as the vampire with a heart, Barnabas Collins.

- 1967-1969: *Dark Shadows* becomes the highest rated show on ABC's daytime schedule, and launches an unprecedented soap opera phenomenon, turning Jonathan Frid into a superstar.

- 1970: The ratings start to decline and ABC decides to cancel the series. MGM releases the motion picture *House of Dark Shadows*, featuring the entire television cast.

- 1971: MGM releases the second feature film, *Night of Dark Shadows*. Plans for a third are scrapped, when Curtis decides to put the whole thing behind him.

- 1971-1982: The show is syndicated, slowly at first. Fandom grows.

- 1982-present: *Dark Shadows* conventions are held throughout the country, new merchandise is constantly being produced.

- 1989: MPI Home Video begins releasing the episodes on video cassette. Sales are phenomenal.

- 1990: NBC begins production on a new prime time version of *Dark Shadows* to begin airing in the fall. An entirely new cast fills out the old roles, with Dan Curtis (*The Winds of War, War and Remembrance*) producing, directing and co-writing. Also, Pioneer publishes *The Dark Shadows Tribute Book*

The Dark Shadows Tribute Book
Written by Edward Gross and James Van Hise
DARK SHADOWS was the only supernatural soap opera, running daily. Beginning as a Gothic soap, producer/creator Dan Curtis (THE WINDS OF WAR, WAR AND REMEMBRANCE) recognized that something was mixing. He added actor Jonathan Frid as vampire Barnabas Collins to the mix, and history was made.
THE DARK SHADOWS TRIBUTE BOOK is the ultimate guide to the series, providing interviews with the cast and crew (including Jonathan Frid) who detail the inner workings of the show; a look at the phenomenon the series inspired, a DARK SHADOWS history and a guide to the first 600 episods following Barnabas' initial appearance and complete names and addresses of fan clubs and magazines. This volume is unlike any that has been published on the show before.
$14.95............164 pages
Color Cover, Black and White Interior Photos
ISBN#1-55698-234-8

KING HITS BIG, BIGGER, BIGGEST

'"After selling US harcover and paperback rights to Viking/NAL for 4 books and for a sum placed between $30 and $40 million, Stephen King has sold book club rights of the work to the Book-of-the-Month Club for another large figure, this time around $5 million.

"With the various foreign rights sales, the 4 works—DARK HALF, a collection due in 1990; and 2 novels, NEEDFUL THINGS and DOLORES CLAIBORNE, set for 1991 and '92—have so far earned King some $50 million.

"The Book-of-the-Month Club has also licensed rights to an additional 18 King books and is creating a 20-title Stephen King Library."

—Science Fiction Chronicle, May 1989

The Unofficial Tale Of Beauty And The Beast
Revised 2nd Edition. Written by Edward Gross
Not since STAR TREK has a television series appealed so strongly to the imagination of the television audience.

THE UNOFFICIAL TALE OF BEAUTY AND THE BEAST is the ultimate "bible" to the series, providing in-depth interviews with story editor-producer Howard Gordon, directors Paul Lynch, Alan Cooke and Richard Franklin; a look at the creation of the series and an incredibly detailed episode guide. This revised 2nd edition adds an interview with Ron Perlman, who has captured the hearts of millions via his portrayal of the noble lion-man, Vincent and an interview with actor Tony Jay, best known as Underworld villain, Paracelsus.

$14.95.......164 pages
Color Cover
ISBN#1-55698-261-5
Also Available in Hardcover: Contains only First Season -Rare Collecter's Item $60.00

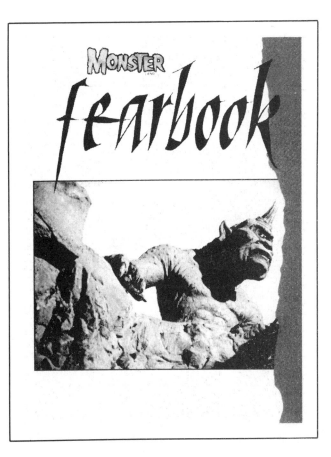

MONSTERLAND FEAR BOOK
Edited by James Van Hise and Forrest J Ackerman

Devoted to horrors past and present, the MONSTERLAND FEARBOOK presents profiles of classic films of terror, and interviews with those people who have brought them to the screen. The macabre ingredients of this volume indepth examinations of *20 Million Miles to Earth, The Beast From 20,000 Fathoms, Freaks, The Seventh Voyage of Sinbad, Halloween* and *Curse of the Demon*. In addition, it features an interview with Stephen King and a guide to creating your own monster masks. *The* perfect gift for for your favorite monster! $14.95

The Unofficial Story of The Making of a

WISEGUY

BY EDWARD GROSS

Secret File: The Unofficial Making Of A Wiseguy Written by Edward Gross
Innovative. Intelligent. Unpredictable.
These words come to mind when discussing WISEGUY, the show currently revolutionizing the television medium while gathering one of the strongest cult followings to greet a network series in many years.
SECRET FILE: THE UNOFFICIAL MAKING OF A WISEGUY goes behind the scenes of this explosive series, profiling star Ken Wahl, presenting conversations with co-stars Jonathan Banks and Jim Byrnes, and interviewing the producers, writers, directors and guest stars. Also including an in-depth episode guide to the first two seasons and profiles of every villain that has come up against Organized Crime Bureau agent Vincent Terranova.
$14.95.............140 pages
Color Cover, Black and White Interior Photos
ISBN#1-55698-256-9

Couch Potato Inc.   5715 N. Balsam   Las Vegas, NV 89130   (702)658-2090

Boring, But Necessary Ordering Information!

Payment:

All orders must be prepaid by check or money order. Do not send cash. All payments must be made in US funds only.

Shipping:

We offer several methods of shipment for our product. Sometimes a book can be delayed if we are temporarily out of stock. You should note on your order whether you prefer us to ship the book as soon as available or send you a merchandise credit good for other goodies or send you your money back immediately.

Postage is as follows:

Normal Post Office: For books priced under $10.00—for the first book add $2.50. For each additional book under $10.00 add $1.00. (This is per indidivual book priced under $10.00. Not the order total.)
For books priced over $10.00—for the first book add $3.25. For each additional book over $10.00 add $2.00.(This is per individual book priced over $10.00, not the order total.)
These orders are filled as quickly as possible. Shipments normally take 2 or 3 weeks, but allow up to 12 weeks for delivery.
Special UPS 2 Day Blue Label Rush Service or Priority Mail(Our Choice). Special service is available for desperate Couch Potatoes. These books are shipped within 24 hours of when we receive the order and should normally take 2 to 3 days to get from us to you.
For the first RUSH SERVICE book under $10.00 add $5.00. For each additional 1 book under $10.00 add $1.75. (This is per individual book priced under $10.00, not the order total.)
For the first RUSH SERVICE book over $10.00 add $7.00 For each additional book over $10.00 add $4.00 per book.(This is per individual book priced over $10.00, not the order total.)

Canadian shipping rates add 20% to the postage total.
Foreign shipping rates add 50% to the postage total.
All Canadian and foreign orders are shipped either book or printed matter.
Rush Service is not available.

DISCOUNTS!DISCOUNTS!

Because your orders keep us in business we offer a discount to people that buy a lot of our books as our way of saying thanks. On orders over $25,00 we give a 5% discount. On orders over $50.00 we give a 10% discount. On orders over $100.00 we give a 15% discount. On orders over over $150.00 we giver a 20 % discount.

Please list alternates when possible.

Please state if you wish a refund or for us to backorder an item if it is not in stock.

100% satisfaction guaranteed.

We value your support. You will receive a full refund as long as the copy of the book you are not happy with is received back by us in reasonable condition. No questions asked, except we would like to know how we failed you. Refunds and credits are given as soon as we receive back the item you do not want.

Please have mercy on Phyllis and carefully fill out this form in the neatest way you can. Remember, she has to read a lot of them every day and she wants to get it right and keep you happy! You may use a duplicate of this order blank as long as it is clear. Please don't forget to include payment! And remember, we love repeat friends.

COUPON PAGE

_____Secret File: The Unofficial Making Of A Wiseguy $14.95 ISBN # 1-55698-256-9

_____Number Six: The Prisoner Book $14.95   ISBN# 1-55698-158-9

_____Gerry Anderson: Supermarionation $14.95

_____Calling Tracy $14.95 ISBN# 1-55698-241-0

_____How To Draw Art For Comicbooks: Lessons From The Masters

ISBN# 1-55698-254-2

_____The 25th Anniversary Odd Couple Companion $12.95   ISBN# 1-55698-224-0

_____Growing up in The Sixties: The wonder Years $14.95   ISBN #1-55698-258-5

_____Batmania $14.95   ISBN# 1-55698-252-6

_____The Year Of The Bat $14.95

_____The King Comic Heroes $14.95

_____Its A Bird, Its A Plane $14.95   ISBN# 1-55698-201-1

_____The Green Hornet Book $14.95

_____The Green Hornet Book $16.95 Edition

_____The Unofficial Tale Of Beauty And The Beast $14.95   ISBN# 1-55698-261-5

_____Monsterland Fear Book $14.95

_____Nightmare On Elm Street: The Freddy Krueger Story $14.95

_____Robocop $16.95

_____The Aliens Story $14.95

_____The Dark Shadows Tribute Book $14.95   ISBN#1-55698-234-8

_____Stephen King & Clive Barker: An Illustrated Guide $14.95 ISBN#1-55698-253-4

_____Drug Wars: America fights Back $9.95 ISBN#1-55698-259-3

_____The Films Of Elvis: The Magic Lives On $14.95   ISBN#1-55698-223-2

_____Paul McCartney: 20 Years On His Own $9.95   ISBN#1-55698-263-1

_____Fists Of Fury: The Films Of Bruce Lee $14.95   ISBN# 1-55698-233-X

_____The Secret Of Michael F Fox $14.95   ISBN# 1-55698-232-1

_____The Films Of Eddie Murphy $14.95   ISBN# 1-55698-230-5

_____The Lost In Space Tribute Book $14.95   ISBN# 1-55698-226-7

_____The Lost In Space Technical Manual $14.95

_____Doctor Who: The Pertwee Years $19.95   ISBN#1-55698-212-7

_____Doctor Who: The Baker Years $19.95   ISBN# 1-55698-147-3

_____The Doctor Who Encyclopedia: The Baker Years $19.95   ISBN# 1-55698-160-0

_____The Doctor And The Enterprise $9.95   ISBN# 1-55698-218-6

_____The Phantom Serials $16.95

_____Batman Serials $16.95

MORE COUPON PAGE

_____Batman And Robin Serials $16.95

_____The Complete Batman And Robin Serials $19.95

_____The Green Hornet Serials $16.95

_____The Flash Gordon Serials Part 1 $16.95

_____The Flash Gordon Serials Part 2 $16.95

_____The Shadow Serials $16.95

_____Blackhawk Serials $16.95

_____Serial Adventures $14.95   ISBN#1-55698-236-4

_____Trek: The Lost Years $12.95   ISBN#1-55698-220-8

_____The Trek Encyclopedia $19.95   ISBN#1-55698-205-4

_____The Trek Crew Book $9.95   ISBN#1-55698-257-7

_____The Making Of The Next Generation $14.95   ISBN# 1-55698-219-4

_____The Complete Guide To The Next Generation $19.95

_____The Best Of Enterprise Incidents: The Magazine For Star Trek Fans $9.95
                                                    ISBN# 1-55698-231-3

_____The Gunsmoke Years $14.95   ISBN# 1-55698-221-6

_____The Wild Wild West Book $14.95   ISBN# 1-55698-162-7

_____Who Was That Masked Man $14.95   ISBN#1-55698-227-5

NAME:_____

STREET:_____

CITY:_____

STATE:_____

ZIP:_____

TOTAL:_____ SHIPPING_____

SEND TO: Couch Potato, Inc. 5715 N. Balsam Rd., Las Vegas, NV 89130

·COMING ATTRACTIONS·

_____Top Gun : The Films Of Tom Cruise $14.95

_____Encyclopedia Of Cartoon Superstars $14.95

_____The Films Of Harrison Ford $14.95

_____Sinatrivia $9.95

_____How To Build Models $14.95

_____The Fab Films Of The Beatles $14.95

_____New Kids On The Block $9.95

_____Swashbucklers $14.95

_____Happy Days Companion $14.95

_____Trek Fans Handbook $9.95

_____The Green Hornet Book: Revised And Updated $14.95

_____Rocky And The Films Of Sylvester Stallone $14.95

_____Santa Cat $9.95

NAME:_____

STREET:_____

CITY:_____

STATE:_____

ZIP:_____

TOTAL:_____ SHIPPING_____

SEND TO: Couch Potato, Inc. 5715 N. Balsam Rd., Las Vegas, NV 89130